Replacing Home

Replacing Home

FROM PRIMORDIAL HUT
TO DIGITAL NETWORK
IN CONTEMPORARY ART

Jennifer Johung

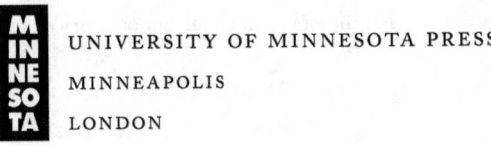

UNIVERSITY OF MINNESOTA PRESS

MINNEAPOLIS

LONDON

Published by the University of Minnesota Press
111 Third Avenue South, Suite 290
Minneapolis, MN 55401-2520
http://www.upress.umn.edu

Library of Congress Cataloging-in-Publication Data

Johung, Jennifer.
    Replacing home : from primordial hut to digital network in contemporary art / Jennifer Johung.
        p.   cm.
    Includes bibliographical references and index.
    ISBN 978-0-8166-7287-5 (hardcover : alk. paper)
    ISBN 978-0-8166-7288-2 (pbk. : alk. paper)
    1. Place (Philosophy) in art.   2. Site-specific installations (Art).
3. Art, Modern—20th century—Themes, motives.   4. Art, Modern—
21st century—Themes, motives.   I. Title.   II. Title: From primordial
hut to digital network in contemporary art.
    N8236.P46J64 2012
    709.05—dc22

                                                          2011016768

The University of Minnesota is an equal-opportunity educator and employer.

For John and Loretta

Contents

REPLACING HOME

On a rooftop in Manhattan, the partial reflection of one body is caught in a curving surface of mirrored glass, just as another body passes along the other side, both held together for a moment at the end of the afternoon sun, against the urban sprawl of New York City below. A box of property deeds passes from hand to hand; the corresponding plots are rediscovered again after thirty years, which provokes one woman to don bright yellow clogs and lead a group to and from some of those forgotten, hidden slivers of city property, her soles trailing light footprints of chalk that mark new temporary lines of access. A man sits alone, atop a small white fiberglass island that rocks gently above the surface of a lake. A shipping container, transformed into a fully functional living unit, docks into a vertical framework along a city's shore just as another docks out, about to board a cargo ship for another destination. Across Rwanda, Japan, Turkey, and India, makeshift homes are constructed within hours using paper tubes. A woman puts on a reflective bodysuit, zipping it completely over her head. Another takes off her dress and transforms it into a dining table. Hours after logging on to a Web site and designing a dome of light, a young boy in Mexico City looks up to see a bright canopy of searchlights above the Zócalo, blocks from his home, where just days before a riot had broken out in front of the Court of Justice.

What do all of these moments have in common? Each attests to the desire to be in place and to belong at home; each is also attuned to the ways in which we currently experience spatial situation as dispersed throughout our globalized world. Drawn from contemporary art and architecture, these events—actualized and imagined by Dan Graham, Gordon Matta-Clark and a group of new *Odd Lots* artists, Andrea Zittel, Lot-ek, Shigeru Ban, Lucy Orta, Hussein Chalayan, and Rafael Lozano-Hemmer—challenge present-day narratives of drift and dislocation, and respond to our ever-present impulse to find home. *Replacing Home: From Primordial Hut to Digital Network in Contemporary Art* examines a wide range of contemporary site-specific installation art in relation to nomadic, portable architecture, focusing on the methods and systems of being in place that coalesce once these practices are put into dialogue.

Many of us are rarely in one place for very long these days, much less in place at all. We are able to move great distances over actual land and through virtual space, whether by choice, in response to natural catastrophe, or under duress of political crisis. Yet we cannot deny that we still care about being in place, that we need to be housed, and that we want to belong somewhere. The changing definition and experience of place has interested theorists, historians, and dwellers across the centuries, particularly during times of spatial expansion and its accompanied social transitions. According to Michel de Certeau, place acknowledges an ordering system realized through spatial practices that locate "the inscription of the body" in that very order.[1] Places are thus embodied by specific human passages and pauses through space. Likewise, for art historian David Summers, real space can be defined neither outside of human social experience nor apart from human orientation, cardinality, and making, although these kinds of embodied spatial experiences are increasingly under threat by modern Western globalization.[2] Such an expansive conception of space offers modern dwellers endless pathways that relentlessly disperse all reliable and sustainable placeholders. As we give in to, or are pushed into, a transitory way of life, whether over land or Internet, in which our movements across an unbounded multitude of places are increasingly possible, our experiences of spatial boundaries are extraordinarily challenged by numerous kinds of border crossings.

Indeed, founding and feeding the very questions posed by this book, nomadism has for a while now become the material and conceptual operation through which all kinds of spatial, social, and discursive sites are unmoored from their fixity. As conceptualized by Gilles Deleuze and Félix Guattari in their collaborative *A Thousand Plateaus*, nomadology entered critical American discourse with its translation into English in the mid-1980s. For Deleuze and Guattari, "nomad space" is smooth, open-ended, deterritorialized, heterogeneous, and shifting, as opposed to the sedentary, undifferentiated "striated space" confined to fixed points between preset paths and determined by the Cartesian grid. As "a space of contact, of small tactile or manual actions of contact, rather than a visual space," nomad space articulates a human trajectory rather than an abstract relation between moving bodies and changing sites.[3]

For Deleuze and Guattari's nomad, "every point is a relay and exists only as a relay. A path is only between two points, but the in-between has taken on all the consistency and enjoys both an autonomy and a direction of its own."[4] The nomad's mode of dwelling is thus determined by these ongoing passages. Unlike the migrant who is defined by his directed motion from beginning to end points, Deleuze and Guattari's nomad does not transition from one site to another but, rather, takes deterritorialization as, paradoxically, a spatial territory. Identifying this phenomenally multidirectional movement toward and away from ever-defining spatial sites, as well as an autonomous and in-between stasis, nomadism is "a stationary process, station as process."[5] According to Deleuze and Guattari, then, this deterritorialized territory of the nomad is localized and yet not delimited or, in other words, specifically sited again and again over time, and so not fixed. The nomadic site, in effect, can be conceptualized not only through but as the operation of spatial situation.

The underlying assumption here is that nomadic deterritorialization can be chosen or is at least the favorable way of thinking past boundary restrictions. In the early 1990s, however, postcolonial and feminist critiques of Deleuze and Guattari's concept of nomadism instead brought attention to the material realities of other kinds of nomads forced from their homes, invisibly outcast and socially illegitimate, thus challenging the uninhibited, borderless mobility conceptualized as intellectually radical yet ultimately only experienced by a select few. While nomadism conceptually reimagines spatial specification, releasing all kinds of fixed sites from their limiting frameworks, a return to material specificity was at the heart of the cultural critiques raised. What became unavoidable was the lack of racial, gendered, and economic details in Deleuze and Guattari's mystified, generalized, and conceptual notions of the deterritorialized nomad.[6]

For Gayatri Spivak, this construction of the exoticized other in service of those with underexamined cultural superiority negates the conditions for resistance that much of the world must still struggle to obtain.[7] In denaturalizing bodies in the name of a radical intellectual agenda, those fighting for subjecthood are stripped of their embodied specificities without ever having the chance to assume them. As cultural geographer Caren Kaplan asks, "who dares let go of their respective representations and systems of meaning, their identity politics and theoretical homes, when it is, as Kafka rightly noted, a matter of life and death here."[8] Challenging the liberating effects of dispersion that are romanticized as freer, purer, or simpler, Kaplan cautions against critical practices that bracket the larger material contexts for diaspora. Instead, she claims that deterritorialization can never escape colonialist discourse, that it is "always re-territorialization, an increase of territory, an imperialization" that seeks to become like or assume the peripheral territory that those with power have established.[9]

In the late 1990s, however, cultural revisions of nomadism began to emphasize the relational implications of nomadic thinking where fluidity and fixity, movement and stasis, globalization and locality, metaphor and materiality could be intricately interrelated—one affording the other. Rosi Braidotti has suggested a revised dialogue with Deleuze and Guattari's nomadism, arguing that it does not stand for homelessness or displacement as an end goal and as such "is not fluidity without borders but rather is an acute awareness of the nonfixity of boundaries. It is the intense desire to go on trespassing, transgressing."[10] Yet while a nomadic model may honor the changeable and multiple boundaries of both social and spatial definition, Irene Gedalof still concedes that nomadism's model of deterritorialization can only be useful if it is able to redefine situated location. Writing in 2000 and echoing earlier critiques, Gedalof is cautious to celebrate Braidotti's theorization of nomadic subject formation that still nonetheless simplifies nomadism as "joyful, purely voluntary 'lines of flight.'"[11] Gedalof urges that "nomadic trajectories cannot simply sidestep location and take to the road. . . . What should be important then, even within the terms of a Deleuzian project is *not* 'the going,' but a different kind of relationship with the space one inhabits, that resists the striations of binary logic."[12] Gedalof thus rethinks nomadism through locality, and so less in terms of "the going" and more in terms of newly particularized spatial relationships within localized spatial sites. Such a rethinking, which is taken up by this book, implies that nomadism should be conceptualized through the moments of grounding that intersperse motion.

Yet we must also be wary of championing the local as a means of transgressing the homogenization of the global. A "politics of location" had already emerged in the 1980s as a celebration of difference, yet Caren Kaplan warns that such thinking in turn "prepares the ground for appropriation, nativism, and exclusions."[13] Kaplan understands the global and the local as two intertwined spatial articulations of modernity. Indeed, while Ronald Bogue apologizes for Deleuze and Guattari's misinformed anthropological categorizations, he too makes clear that their critical objective was nevertheless "to articulate two tendencies—the nomadic and the sedentary—that have inner coherences and manifest themselves in mixed forms."[14] The implicit challenge launched by this book is, then, to understand the mechanisms of the nomadic relationship between fixity and fluidity in order to consider the ever-problematic relation between its theoretical and material operations. John Noyes, writing in 2004 at the same time as Bogue, urges us to also think of two nomadisms in terms of their "interrelatedness, their mutual exclusivities."[15] One concept defines the subject by mobility and a technically induced compression of space and time. The other recognizes the socially and politically outcast subject. How, asks Noyes, are we to take "a conceptual model of a lifestyle, a socio-economic regime, a mode of production as a model for critical thought?"[16] And, as this book will urge, how are we to find a means to incorporate that critical method into a material practice, if nomadism must be revalued not only through metaphor but materialism? "There is a great difference," Edward Said reminds us, "between the optimistic mobility, the intellectual liveliness and the logic of daring . . . and the massive dislocations, waste, misery, and horrors endured in our century's migrations."[17] At the core of nomadism's contemporary critical potential, then, is the specification of a material practice that responds, on the one hand, to the intellectual project that resists material confinements and, on the other, to the exchange and loss of material objects, structures, and situations.

So without fully celebrating our nomadic release from territorial borders or longing nostalgically for a return to tightly localized communities, this book asks: what does it mean, now in light of our multiple movements and temporary situations, to draw a spatial boundary? Who gets to choose to be spatially situated, for however long, and who has that situation chosen for them? If we take on this worry, and I do believe that even the most hardy and well-traveled of us can acknowledge a desire to be in place, we must admit that we continue to care about spatial situation and belonging, even as some of us might relish our physical ability to move past boundaries, while others of us may foreground our intellectual capacity to blur fixed frameworks of knowledge and experience. But how might we be in one place, whether voluntarily or involuntarily, where we could find ourselves lingering with others? And how does this one place become a home? If to be in one place is to be still, perhaps to belong and to find home however momentarily or accidentally, then how can we situate ourselves while also on the move, both toward and away from each other?

In the five chapters that follow, I argue that contemporary art and architectural practices of being in place can be conceptualized in terms of an ongoing process of replacing home. In order to be and belong in one place over time, we have to incompletely and partially replace the ways in which we were just situated, by renewing and reusing material constructions, and by reforming and resituating connections with others. As a method and system of being and belonging, replacement identifies an infinitely extendable act of being in the place of something or someone again, without fully taking that site's or that body's place, and thus not subsuming, destroying, or erasing what was there. According to such a paradigm, to be in place is to always be in the process of resituation, where spatial substitutions offer moments of social reattachment and engagement.

I make these proposals with a deep allegiance to performance theory and practice, as both have intervened into the disciplines of contemporary art and architecture. Beyond its initial attachment to the theatrical event and defined most broadly as the study of embodied experiences in specific spaces and over time, a performance-based methodology attends to both temporal and object-based frameworks of knowledge and experience.[18] As such, performance acknowledges and can negotiate between the structures and processes of being in place. As Elin Diamond writes in her introduction to *Performance and Cultural Politics*, "performance is always a doing and a thing done. On the one hand, performance describes certain embodied acts (and/or the watching self). On the other hand, it is the thing done, the completed event framed in time and space and remembered, misremembered, interpreted, and passionately revised across a pre-existing discursive field."[19] Performance theory pays close attention to the unfolding of cultural activities, and it also pauses to consider moments of stillness among and within those actions. It is a way of radically destabilizing our conception of fixed forms while simultaneously attesting to the necessity of the form itself, however variable over time. Diamond goes on to argue: "Common sense insists on a temporal separation between a doing and a thing done, but in usage and in theory, performance, even its dazzling physical immediacy, drifts between present and past, presence and absence, consciousness and memory."[20] A performance lens therefore recognizes when and how certain bodies and sites overlap in order for meaningful experiences to be both initialized and reinstated in time.

For Peggy Phelan, performance also "honors the idea that a limited number of people in a specific time/place frame can have an experience of value which leaves no visible trace afterward."[21] If we consider spatial situation along these lines, we can acknowledge how sites and places are continuously determined through the ephemeral, variable experiences of viewing, rather than remaining tied to the formal spatial parameters defined by the sited object or structure. Art and performance theorist Nick Kaye associates this experience of spatial situation with the "incursion" of performance into the visual arts in the mid-1960s.[22] In particular, Kaye suggests that performance defines site specificity, not only as a mode of art making but also as a way of locating specific sites over time. Although site-specific artwork initially determined an indivisible relation between the artwork and the spatial registers of its making and receiving, as spatial situations are constantly displaced, the site of art practice has also transformed from locationally bound to nomadically unbound. Nonetheless, across such a transformation, the viewer's engagement with the art object situated within a specific location continues to incorporate a phenomenological understanding of place, however dispersed, into the aesthetic domain of art. Site-specific artwork engages with the viewer, making her aware of her own body existing within the site, so that as well as instating the presence of the site, the work also calls for the bodily presence of the viewer—a spectatorship that unfolds in real time and space.

Early explorations of site specificity in fact challenged Michael Fried's infamous indictment of this new "theatricality" of the art object, as posed in his 1967 essay "Art and Objecthood"—an indictment Fried launched against the valorization of the position, time, space, and experience of the viewer.[23] Subsequent site-specific explorations have turned critical attention to the particular kind of viewing experience that takes place within the art institution. As the fixity of spatial specificity itself was interrogated, the site therefore radically diverged from the physical conditions of the work's location. No longer primarily tied to a studio practice, many artists now work on call, invited by art institutions to configure works in a number of locations. In response to this common process of dismantling and reinstalling contemporary art, the site of the work now circulates, unattached spatially.

For art historian James Meyer, this mobile site may or may not incorporate a physical location, and it certainly does not privilege this place.[24] Instead, site specificity is now a process occurring between sites and a mapping of the bodies that move between them. In refusing to resist the mobilization of sites, artists are determining spatial situations by way of "a nomadic narrative," to use Miwon Kwon's phrase, paved by the multiple passages of the artist in relation to a dispersed set of viewers.[25] Indeed, in charting the experiences of being and belonging in one site as proposed by site-specific art installations since the 1970s, Kwon confesses that we are currently "out of place all too often."[26] She goes on to suggest that "we are culturally and economically rewarded for enduring the 'wrong' place"—where a wrong place can be defined most generally as a place that cannot be called home.[27] Those who are forced by war, famine, environmental catastrophe, or political crisis to seek refuge elsewhere will surely not agree that they are rewarded for leaving their homes; yet as site-specific art practices confirm, both our chosen and forced spatial situations do seem to resist sustained experiences of belonging.

In the face of our nomadic narratives, then, can we activate a network of belonging that is extended through a variety of places and over a course of time? The art world has turned its attention to the unfolding of embodied experiences, increasingly offering modes of participatory practices that bring people together. As open events, situations, encounters, and procedures consistently take the place of formalized objects, contemporary art calls on its viewers not only to witness the unfolding of actions on site but also to engage with the proposed conditions through which such actions occur. Within these art practices, embodied interactions between viewers are central, thereby enacting the equally celebrated and maligned leap that persists in art today, from receptive contemplation to active undertaking. Whether named as "relational aesthetics" by the French art critic Nicolas Bourriaud, or "social aesthetics" by the Danish curator Lars Bang Larsen, these participatory forms of contemporary art offer situations for social exchange that seem to be increasingly lacking in our world.[28] Allotting for this trend, art historian Hal Foster suggests that "discursivity and sociability are in the foreground of art today because they are scarce elsewhere."[29] Jacques Rancière also recognizes that a "loss of the 'social bond,' and the duty incumbent on artists to work to repair it, are the words on the agenda."[30] So it is not only that we are out of place, but that we are out of place with each other. However, Foster warns against any easy inscription of a democratic politics into this art's sociability, for an open frame with an undecided material outcome does not necessarily make for a participating community free of contradiction and conflict. "Sometimes politics are ascribed to such art on the basis of a shaky analogy between an open work and an inclusive society," he argues, "as if a desultory form might evoke a democratic community, or a non-hierarchical installation predict an egalitarian world."[31] Instead, free and open accessibility along with full participation are often impossible, and thus the confirmation of conventional social hierarchies seems more likely.

Foster's argument against what he calls Bourriaud's "happy interactivity" can also be productively considered in relation to new forms of public art practice that focus on community participation. In public art's newest genre, named by Arlene Raven as "art in the public interest," the artist intervenes directly into a specific community in order to engage with its social, economic, and political concerns.[32] Suzanne Lacy also identifies this new public art as being produced from within a relational, collaborative network involving the individual artist and a group of community participants.[33] Implicit is the artist's desire to embed herself in the larger social agenda, where intervention may lead to community transformation. Taking on this spatially specific social function, Grant Kester has celebrated the dialogical exchanges that arise between community participants, as cultural identities are both solidified and transformed.[34] Yet parallel to Hal Foster's critique of socially relational art, W. J. T. Mitchell has named this socially conscious public art utopic because of its impulse to construct an ideal, imaginary landscape of free public access. For Mitchell, this public art represses the violence required to dissipate conflict, instead "veiling it with the stasis of monumentalized and pacified spaces."[35] Mitchell opposes the "utopian" with the "critical" production of art that disrupts the image of such pacified spaces and interactions, instead making visible the contradictions and violence that public space and collectivity encode.

As performance theorist Shannon Jackson notes, "in the past few decades, both art-making and social inquiry have been induced to avow their heteronomy, the degree to which their making and their thinking were 'governed by external rules,' that is, contingent and interdependent with a world that they could not pretend to transcend."[36] Enmeshed within the very unegalitarian material realities of this world, spatially specific and relational art practices, as well as public art situated in specific communities, rely on a performance-based orientation toward open-ended processes that are, in turn, driven by various levels of social participation. But as artists are increasingly called on to repair disappearing social bonds, we must consider how those social conditions are made accessible within specific sites, and how they are not. We must acknowledge the means by which social reattachments and engagements are rendered legitimate, and when they are not. And we must qualify participation by specifying the construction of public collectives and communities.

These are the contexts that have impelled architectural theory and practice toward performance-oriented vocabularies, design concepts, and methods of construction. As a 2003 symposium on performative architecture attested, a comparable shift has recently been articulated in architectural theory so that buildings are no longer only conceived as objects but, rather, are designed and constructed according to what they do, or how they interact with their environmental sites while also anticipating their inhabitants' changing needs. As David Leatherbarrow notes, architects and theorists must now ask, "In what ways does the building act?"[37] Because a building's function varies according to each user or inhabitant, thus remaining inconsistent over time, Leatherbarrow argues for an expanded concept of architecture that is defined according to each building's capacity to perform a specific task in relation to a specific inhabitant's aesthetic or operative desires, and in response to both spatial and phenomenal flux over time.

Although contemporaneously termed, *performative architecture* arguably has roots in much earlier conceptualizations of a building's responsive relationship to its users, dwellers, and landscape. I take great inspiration from architectural historian Vincent Scully's mode of analysis, in which he consistently links formal attributes of building to the changing experiences of moving through the architectonic complex, inclusive of both structure and site.[38] By focusing attention on the mutually constitutive relationship between a formal structure and its variable use, Scully activates the static building, conceiving of it instead as an embodied, living form. This activation depends on human dwellers and users, and their desires, motivations, demands on, and movements through the total architectonic complex. These participants act as mediators who continually construct and reconstruct the links between the natural site and the built form, while also revising their understanding of their spatial situation within the larger world. While Scully's particular focus is on sacred structures and ritualized relationships between building and body, what remains at stake for architecture, in approaching a performance framework for design and use, is an understanding of building as both a spatial structure and a temporal process of ongoing situation.

As building practices respond to the increasing flow of people, goods, structures, and capital, architecture encompasses both spatial situation and flux, and thus, argues Stephen Cairns, "comes to be imbricated with the effects of a particular kind of movement that carries ongoing, multiple, intermittent and intensified investments in place."[39] Domestic structures have long been at the heart of efforts to reinvest in these changing experiences of place. In fact, from antiquity to modernity, the impulse to return to familiar structures and idealized modes of domestic dwelling has assuaged anxieties associated with nomadically expanding spatial and social frameworks that result from industrial and technological developments, ranging from advances in iron and steel production, transportation, and telecommunications. In response to such developments, architecture has developed a narrative of origin that returns to and revises so-called "primitive" domestic dwellings in order to reconstitute an intimate relationship between bodies and their changing spatial environment.

As the opening chapter will explore in more detail, such close connections are imaginatively possible in an idealized past but are threatened at present in reality.

Nonetheless, this book proposes that spatial situation can be achieved by returning to past formations of home and approximating ways to replace them in the present. The introduction of processes of replacement within the impulse to return to original forms of building challenges conventional linear historiography, so that home is activated as an ongoing event that loops forward and backward over time, and across various analogous structures. Architectural forms and systems of home are framed by the comings and goings, departures and landings, of specific bodies in momentary contact over a variety of specific places. Within these ongoing passages and intersections, replacement attends to the moments and sites of grounding, where bodies linger temporarily in spaces with each other, and where the conditions for spatial situation are conceived through specific material negotiations between mobility and stasis.

Providing the impetus for a series of ongoing spatial and social replacements, a performance methodology encourages us, as artists, architects, and dwellers, to address both the architectural formations of home and the systems of homecoming and homemaking. In launching a dialogue between art and architecture over questions of being and belonging in place from a performance platform, I find a wealth of possibility in the unfinished, contested, renewable processes that afford home. Again I turn to Elin Diamond, who notes that the refusal of completed forms

> creates the terminology of "re" in discussions of performance, as in *re*embody, *re*inscribe, *re*configure, *re*signify. "Re" acknowledges the pre-existing discursive field, the repetition—and the desire to repeat—within the performative present, while "embody," "configure," "inscribe," "signify" assert the possibility of materializing something that exceeds our knowledge, that alters the shape of sites and imagines other as yet unsuspected modes of being.[40]

This potential to radically alter the given landscape of beings and things around us occurs through a practice that performance theorist Peggy Phelan articulates as "representation without reproduction."[41] Repetition thus opens onto revision, resituation onto replacement.

As structures are partially repeated and renewed, and as bodies come upon them and each other again, the performance of replacing home can also be described as a partial haunting made materially real. While imbued with memory, longing, and nostalgia, spatial replacements nonetheless emphasize rematerialized specificities through surrogate lines of connection between past and present structures and dwellers. Performance theorist and theater historian Joseph Roach identifies surrogation and substitution as key players in the re-creation of cultural activities, specifically necessary for the ongoing life of communities that are dispersed across space and time. As departures and losses leave social roles within diasporic communities empty, alternates are put into place so that social networks can continue to function, while collective memory "selectively, imaginatively, and often perversely" attempts to forge continuity in the face of discontinuity.[42] Although Roach's particular focus is on the circum-Atlantic intercultural exchange of bodies, rituals, and customs between Europe, Africa, and the Americas beginning in the eighteenth century, his articulation of "the three-sided relationship of memory, performance, and substitution" transfers well onto contemporary processes of finding, structuring, coming, and going toward home.

While Roach identifies an ongoing series of embodied substitutions through which communities survive, I am concerned with the unfolding and renewing of structural surrogacies that initialize and reinstate, repeat and revise embodied interactions in place. Gaston Bachelard has associated home with an oneiric concept of "poetic space" that primarily attests to the dream-state conflation of past memories and images; but how can these be actualized?[43] As past and present, present and absent, conscious and remembered forms of home coalesce, how are these returns, revisions, and replacements materialized? Replacing home responds to the longing for a return to intimately familiar spaces by proposing substitutes in the form of renewable artifactual analogies that are capable of expanding belonging across ever-new sites. As remembered experiences of home are constantly revised within and across surrogate structures, tenuous dependencies begin to form between those bodies temporarily held in place. Replacing home therefore affirms precarious moments and sites of material reconnection between bodies and the various spatial environments in which they are momentarily enmeshed.

We want to be able to move through spatial borders, and yet we also want to linger and belong in some of those places. *Replacing Home: From Primordial Hut to Digital Network in Contemporary Art* begins by recognizing a pattern of return and renewal within modes of spatial situation, a pattern that is viable because of structural reusability and phenomenal revisitation. Functioning through modular components, reusable structures either seek to escape from or are embedded within current experiences of nomadism and must alternately support isolation or collective social engagement. From individual to shared rematerializations of home, from private to public arenas of interaction, this book considers the social ramifications of situating temporary communities in which public visibility and legibility are key, in which the politics of public participation are unveiled, and in which spatial and social dependencies are reimagined, in order to ultimately propose a socially engaged program of replacing home.

The book first revisits architecture's ideal form of situated dwelling—the so-called "primitive" hut—through the vantage point of contemporary art practice. Builders and theorists have consistently returned to the hut during times of social and spatial transition and uncertainty. But while a return to the hut has historically acted as an attempt to renew an intimate, immutable connection between human beings and their world—as enacted within ancient Egyptian, Greek, Roman, Jewish, and Japanese rites, and narratives from Vitruvius, Laugier, and Le Corbusier, among others—such a model must now be revised so as to address narratives of nomadic dislocation. The first chapter, "Returning to the Hut," considers how the hut can be rendered as a contemporary model for being and belonging in increasingly limitless modern space. I analyze contemporary artist Dan Graham's mirror and glass pavilion sculptures, which are both installed artworks and usable shelters, focusing on his 1991 *Two-Way Mirror Cylinder Inside Cube*, which Graham likens to the engraving of a hut central to Marc-Antoine Laugier's eighteenth-century *An Essay on Architecture*.[44] Instead of reinvoking the hut's stable situation as Laugier and many before him did, Graham's construction offers momentary and fragile instances for viewers to meet and cross paths.

As bodies come together and apart, meeting and crossing over time, space is determined and affected by human interaction and thus no longer remains abstractly fixed. In order to challenge our experiences of owning fixed space, the artist Gordon Matta-Clark purchased and proposed an artistic use for commercially unusable, inaccessible slivers of New York City in the early 1970s. Suggesting an experience of belonging that is unattached to ownership, the second chapter, "Reusable Sites," examines Matta-Clark's *Fake Estates* property project, never finished in his lifetime, in relation to its 2005 reexhibition as *Odd Lots*. The reexhibition included new artists—including Francis Alys, Mark Dion, Dennis Oppenheim, and Mierle Laderman Ukeles—who returned to and reused Matta-Clark's original sites. The renewal of specifically embodied interactions with Matta-Clark's unfinished *Fake Estates* project was not only initiated through the participation of each new artist; their individual pathways of return to Matta-Clark's work also instigated a collective replacement of conventional modes of ownership and belonging. Indeed, the group nature of the *Odd Lots* reexhibition proposes a permeable determination of space, as activated through the presence and movements of various bodies. These multiple and overlapping pathways of revisitation suggest that reuse and replacement together identify a network of spatial ownership that is determined through the passages and pauses of dwellers rather than situated within the owned site.

How, then, do specific spatial structures activate this process of passages and pauses? The third chapter, "In and Out of Place," turns to contemporary modular and mobile architectural constructions that attend to the movements of their inhabitants across the globe. Andrea Zittel, for example, constructs compact living units that can fold in and out like sides of a box for spatial variation and transportation. Lot-ek reforms a shipping container into a *Mobile Dwelling Unit* but also imagines it capable of docking in and out of preestablished harbors located around the world. As bodies come together and apart, across a series of sites and over a course of time, so too do the component parts of these kinds of nomadic habitations. Easy to transport and quick to assemble, modular structures must, however, address both chosen and forced dislocation, responding not only to those who are continuously on the move, but also to those who are seeking temporary refuge. With that in mind, the chapter turns to Japanese architect Shigeru Ban's modular paper tube architecture that provides immediate emergency relief to victims of natural disasters and political upheaval.

Cast aside from any stable infrastructure for being and belonging in place, and oftentimes socially invisible, those rendered homeless must rely on what can be carried on their own backs. The fourth chapter, "Visibly Skinned," looks at body encasements that skim the wearer's surface or reproduce the skin, and that take inspiration from the architectural collective Archigram's 1960s experimentations with dematerialized structures. Beginning in the early 1990s, the artist and activist Lucy Orta developed individual and then multiply linked *Refuge Wear* in response to the first Gulf War, the following economic recession, and the increasingly ignored problem of homelessness. Individual, expandable, remarkably colorful, and reflective, Orta's body architecture seeks to make visible the forced mobility of those without homes, calling attention to the socially outcast categorization of its wearers. For British fashion design label Vexed Generation, transformable and protective garment-shelters become urban armor that masks specific bodily features. Evicted from public sites, or not legally allowed to gather in force, wearers are afforded an anonymity that in turn offers the potential for publically visible gatherings. In a similar negotiation of visibility and invisibility, fashion designer Hussein Chalayan has created garments that cover and move with the body, then secretly transform into furniture and coalesce into rooms, protecting and transporting the structures of home. Addressing the dispersal of individuals forced to flee, Chalayan offers the potential for social cohesion both in and out of the public eye. Launched across the practices of art, architecture, and fashion design, these contemporary second skins offer immediate, transportable shelter, while also proposing new systems for public housing that visibly situate wearers within a legitimate social framework.

Proposing participatory modes of engaging collectively, though not equally, in the experience of public space, the last chapter, "Networked Dependencies," focuses on two interactive Internet and site-based projects. Developed by new media artist Rafael Lozano-Hemmer and named "relational architecture," *Vectorial Elevation* and *Under Scan* were large-scale urban installations and responsive environments commissioned by local culture councils to engage passersby in civic areas. With online participants and on-the-ground viewers coming upon one another in temporarily transformed real and continually transformable virtual spaces, Lozano-Hemmer's relational architecture provides the conditions for networked events that happen in both real and digital space, and that oftentimes determine unpredictable social connections. Architecture conceived as a fluid, expansive, and inclusive spatial network has a history that reaches back well before the digital age. Yet recently, participatory networks of situation and belonging have begun to acknowledge existing forces of social, economic, and political agency and legitimacy that ultimately allow some and not others to choose their spatial situation. In Lozano-Hemmer's relational architecture, ongoing interactions between real and virtual sites and structures, as well as their past, present, and future contexts of building, using, owning, and dwelling, together determine the uneven ways in which participants gain or lose access to spaces of belonging. Revealing the dependencies that exist within this network of bodies and spaces encourages us to imagine how we collectively, and thus with the help of others, come to be in place again and again.

One

RETURNING TO THE HUT DAN GRAHAM'S *TWO-WAY MIRROR CYLINDER INSIDE CUBE*

Atop 548 West Twenty-second Street in Manhattan, visitors to the Dia Center for the Arts could climb a short staircase and enter a raised wooden platform walled in regularly aligned glass panels and left open above. In the center of the platform, a two-way-mirrored glass cylinder projected convex, semitransparent images of visitors looking at themselves or at each other. Once inside, they could see through the glass, out toward the horizon, or down toward the grid of city streets below. They could also watch themselves or others float above that landscape, distorted differently in the concave interior surface of the cylinder. As clouds cleared, the glass walls became slightly more reflective, and as clouds built or light dimmed, the walls seemed more transparent. Every fluctuation in weather and sun, temperature and time, could vary the degree to which visitors were able to see and navigate around each other and, by extension, to understand and experience their spatial surroundings of angled glass, curved mirror, urban panorama, and limitless sky. Within each instance of viewing and moving through this structure, the material mediations and distortions that situate bodies in space and in relation to each other rendered visibility and spatial legibility vulnerable, and not to be assumed (Figure 1.1).

Opened to the public in September 1991 and accessible until January 2004 when the Dia Center closed its Twenty-second Street location, the artist Dan Graham's *Two-Way Mirror Cylinder Inside Cube* was both a usable architectural structure and an installed artwork. In his initial proposal

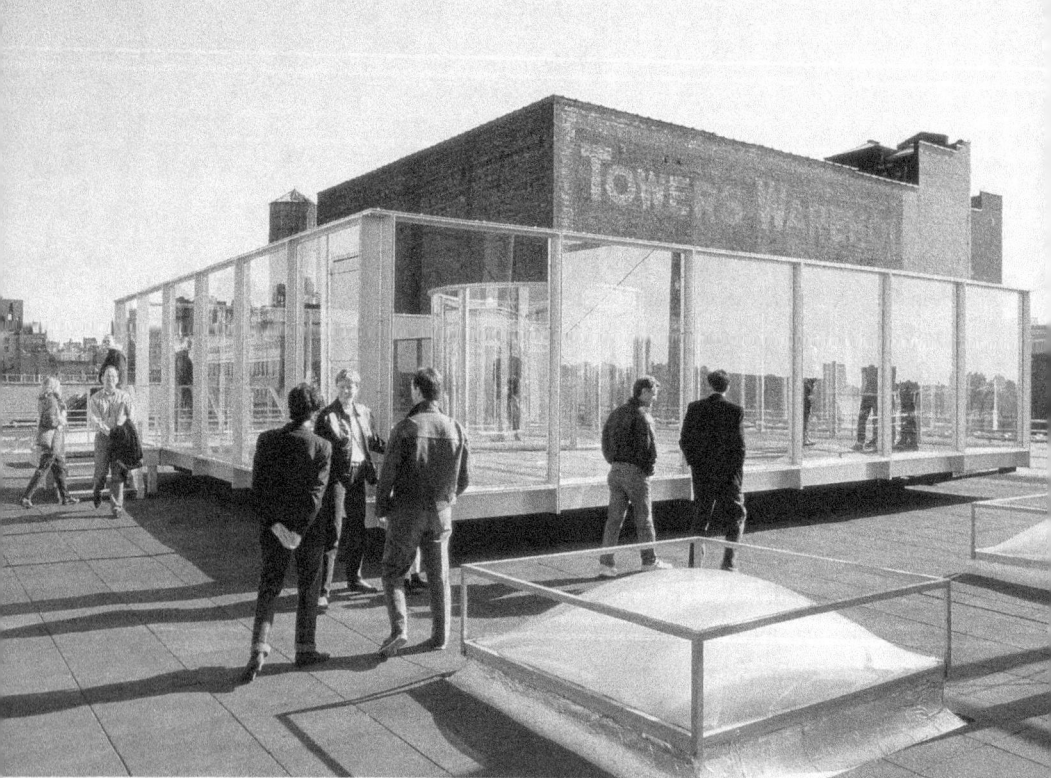

FIGURE 1.1. Dan Graham, *Two-Way Mirror Cylinder Inside Cube and a Video Salon: Rooftop Urban Park Project for Dia Center for the Arts, New York,* 1981/91. Two-way mirror, glass, stainless steel, wood, rubber. Installation at Dia Center for the Arts, New York, 1991. Courtesy of the artist and Marian Goodman Gallery, New York.

submitted to Dia, Graham notes that his self-categorized pavilion sculpture "evokes the notion of a rustic hut."[1] Conceptually revisiting and structurally revising one of the earliest forms of human building to which numerous architectural theorists have returned over the centuries, Graham participates in the history of architectural origins through the lens of contemporary arts practice. Commissioned and constructed specifically for its site, the pavilion sculpture was conceived in relation to the primordial hut's signature embedment into its surrounding landscape. The hut's site specificity, however, assured a situated form of dwelling, while Graham's work provided a museum with a multiuse glass-and-mirror space within which visitors could temporarily pause among often dizzying views and reflections. By positioning such a pavilion sculpture alongside the hut, Graham questions the contemporary viability of architecture's ideal model of spatial situation, while nonetheless reinvoking an ever-present longing to be secured in place and at home (Figure 1.2).

So how can the hut, as a historical motif and a material construction representing an intimate, permeable, and responsive relationship between humans and their world, function now in full recognition and acceptance of our limitless and disorienting expansions into space? Returning to one of the first human dwellings in an attempt to create continuity even in the face of discontinuous spatial experiences, *Two-Way Mirror Cylinder Inside Cube* engages with architecture's repetitive impulse to situate its ever-changing material advancements in the context of past constructions and spatial environments. Yet in acknowledging this impulse, Graham's structure also challenges the integration of prehistoric legacies and narratives of spatial situation into both modern methods of building and contemporary experiences of global displacement.

Rather than returning to the primordial hut in order to assure an abstract and nostalgic form of situated dwelling often materially impossible in the present moment of its invocation, I argue that Graham's structure instead proposes ongoing patterns of return, renewal, revision, and replacement that define current modes of spatial situation. The concept of spatial situation, and with it the possibility of being and belonging at home, can therefore be

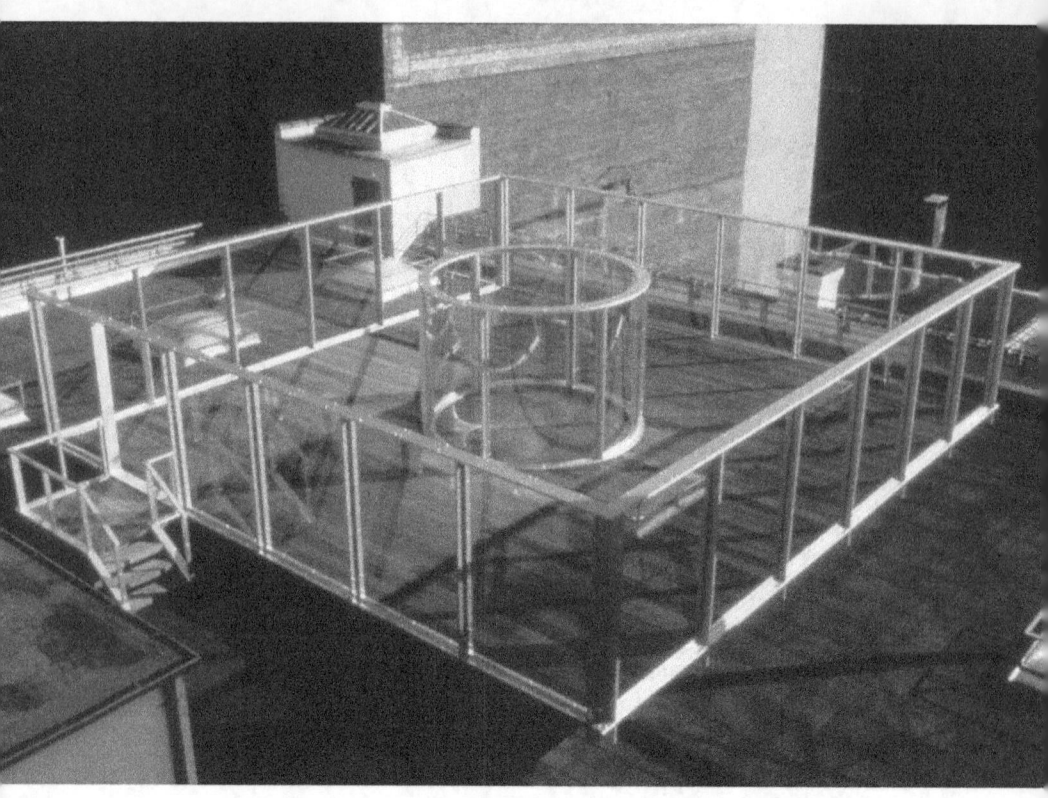

FIGURE 1.2. Dan Graham, *Two-Way Mirror Cylinder Inside Cube and a Video Salon: Rooftop Urban Park Project for Dia Center for the Arts, New York,* 1981/91. Courtesy of the artist and Marian Goodman Gallery, New York.

unmoored from its ties to the spatial structure as object. By bringing together the formal attributes of Graham's pavilion with the historical narratives of architectural origins, the material culture of early hut building, and the material complexities of modern architecture, my focus is not on what the hut returns to but, rather, the processes by which the return occurs and what those processes offer, both conceptually as well as materially, to present and future dwellers. I address the ways in which various patterns of return to the primordial hut are initiated and how they continue to operate through conceptual renewal and material revision, while also acknowledging the specific moments and sites in which these patterns are engaged by historians, theorists, builders, and dwellers.

Although Graham evokes the hut by materially confronting its conceptual enveloping in modern building practices, the hut's present and future ability to situate bodies in dispersed space remains possible. Indeed, I propose that Graham's structure unveils the uneasy contemporary context of the hut's potential usefulness in relating bodies to each other and to their spatial environment. On the one hand, Graham's *Two-Way Mirror Cylinder Inside Cube* is formally structured like a hut. Remodeled with modern materials, its four glass walls mimic an eighteenth-century revision of the hut's simple structure, while its inner cylinder echoes the round base of other prehistoric huts, as I will soon explicate. But on the other hand, its alternately transparent, semitransparent, and reflexive surfaces, as well as its engulfing of one hut form inside another, complicate construction and design, in turn expanding use. Again, on the one hand, Graham's pavilion sculpture operates like a hut; it collects bodies in one place, providing the conditions for their social interaction and for their spatial situation within the urban landscape. Yet on the other, viewers see themselves and others as mirror images, hovering high above the city, while their embodied contact is predicated on their movement through and variable use of the interior viewing spaces, as well as the adjacent video salon and café.

Through conceptual renewal and material revisions, Graham's pavilion sculpture ultimately activates a process of replacement, in which the function of the hut is no longer to return to a past model of spatially situated dwelling but, rather, to continuously resituate an event of homecoming, occurring in the present and projected into the future. Instead of reconstructing conditions for a real spatial situation, Graham's return to the hut affords embodied pathways and meeting points that constantly revise sites of momentary grounding and belonging in place. Replacement in fact indicates this ability to be in place again and again, however temporarily or incompletely. Influenced by visual recognition and phenomenal coordination, Graham's model of spatial replacement relies on the intersection of perceiving bodies that may individually or collectively use the surfaces and interior spaces in any number of ways. Viewers looking in the curved mirror define themselves as perceiving subjects in relation to other bodies. Viewers who see others through the glass, against the vast urban spread of the city, relate those bodies to the ever-increasing built environment and to the fluctuations in the surrounding landscape, as influenced by changing overhead light, cloud coverage, and weather conditions. Spatial replacement is thus activated through both planned and unplanned encounters between bodies viewing and using the space, and through their resulting temporary social interactions as contextualized within a visually unstable environment.

In approaching Graham's structure as a challenge to the prevailing conception of the hut, I argue that the presumed renewal of access to sites and modes of dwelling is not possible without a recognition of the precarious ways in which we may be either connected or disconnected to the built and natural world, and to our social formations, at any given moment. Nonetheless, Graham's revision of the hut as an ideal model for spatial situation, by way of a material reappropriation of modern architecture, reintroduces the possibility of connecting viewers and users to their spatial environment and to other bodies when all may seem out of place. Rather than establishing a construction of place, Graham's pavilion sculpture instead suggests modes of being tentatively held in place, as we pause and linger with each other. Participating in the ongoing search for sustained intimacies between bodies and spaces while also revealing the specific material contexts behind modernity's proposed solutions, Graham's conceptual renewal and material replacement of the hut continuously readjust the determination of accessible surfaces, boundaries, and sites within which bodies come together and come apart. *Two-Way Mirror Cylinder Inside Cube* thus offers variable conditions for bodies to meet and cross paths, so that being situated in the world and belonging in place can still be experienced, although more likely by accident or contingency, and within momentary and fragile instances.

RETURN AND RENEW

In his Dia Center catalogue entry for *Two-Way Mirror Cylinder Inside Cube,* presented in the form of a video, Graham specifies his reference to the "rustic hut" by showing the image that appeared as the frontispiece to French architectural theorist Marc-Antoine Laugier's 1753 *Essai sur l'architecture* (Figure 1.3). Providing the eighteenth century's most widely read revisitation of architectural origins, Laugier located the hut as the earliest human building. Laugier's version of prehistoric man is initially seen to be "enjoying the gift of nature; he lacks nothing, he does not wish for anything."[2] The forest gives shade while a cave provides protection against rain. Only when the darkness and stale air of the cave begin to aggravate him does man resolve to assemble a self-standing shelter. With the simplest of forest branches fallen within reach, Laugier's paradigmatic builder, with no apparent association to any kind of social community, constructs a four-columned structure with a pitched roof. Early man's fundamental relationship to nature was thus easeful and complicit, as first caves then branches were readily available for use when deemed necessary.

But even more significant for Laugier, and what provided the impulse for his narrative rewriting, was the notion that this exemplary hut revealed the essential formal order of architecture that he believed architects should reinvoke in their own times. For according to Laugier,

> all the splendors of architecture ever conceived have been modeled on the little rustic hut I have just described. It is by approaching the simplicity of this first model that fundamental mistakes are avoided and true perfection is achieved. The pieces of wood set upright have given the idea of the column, the pieces placed horizontally on top of them the idea of the entablature, the inclining pieces forming the roof the idea of the pediment.[3]

By emphasizing the architectural object, this account of the original hut also offered the possibility of that object's representative function. But what is it about the perfect original structure that every future iteration of the hut represents? Implicit in Laugier's suggestion that the hut represents an ideal architectural order is the potential for the hut's reinstantiation over time, and thus embedded in the hut's conceptual function is a cycle of return and replication. Yet what exactly does it return to and aim to replicate?

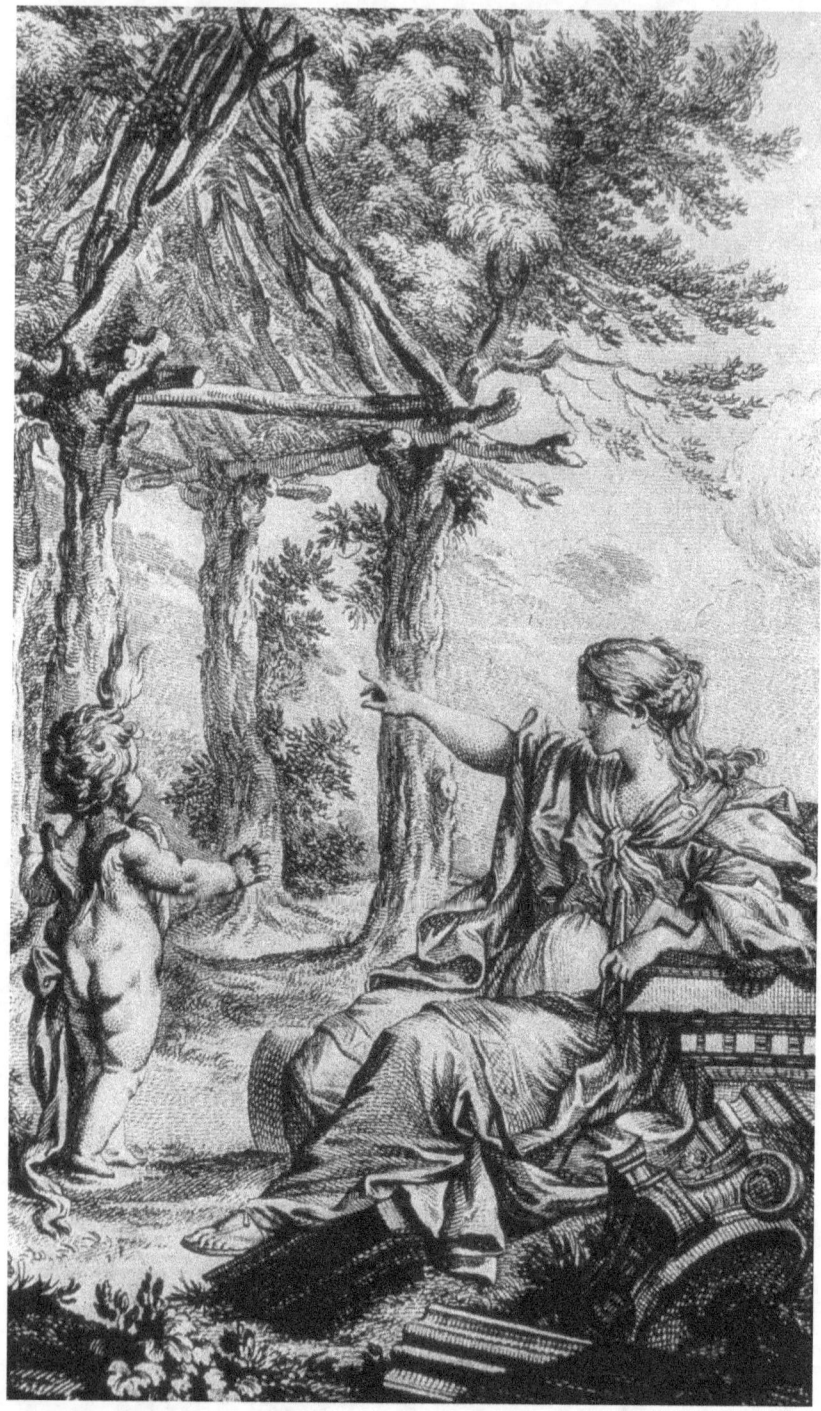

FIGURE 1.3. Frontispiece for Marc-Antoine Laugier, *Essai sur l'architecture*. Courtesy of Rotch Visual Collections, Massachusetts Institute of Technology.

Although Laugier explicitly focuses on the material form of the hut as object, his narrative of return and replication finds its weight in the hut's conceptual signification. It is this notion that a return to familiar material forms can provide access to more abstract understandings of spatial situation, regardless of whether such understandings are experientially viable, that serves as a provocative point for Dan Graham to explore. As the philosopher Karsten Harries clarifies, with reference to Laugier's narrative: "Works of architecture represent buildings. Representing buildings, they denote a building type."[4] For Laugier, architecture should represent the original hut structure built by man alone, so that without unnecessary ornament, modern builders and dwellers could continue to navigate nature's given schema in their own time, prevailing over "the rough sketch which nature offers us," to use Laugier's words. Such a rough sketch would allow man's rational ingenuity to "embellish, smooth, and polish the work without touching the substance of the plan."[5] Thus Laugier's return to the hut aimed not only to provide architecture with an essential set of formal attributes, but it also rationalized human capacity to reasonably respond to changes as well as to right faults in the natural environment at any given time and circumstance. By extension, then, the act of revisiting and reconstructing the hut endows upon architecture the possibility of mediating human connections to the natural landscape. This architectural mediation operates by returning to and attempting to reconstitute the easeful conditions of an idealized past. As Harries affirms: "We are still not done with his primitive hut. We are still not done with the idea that architecture, too, is an art of representation."[6] As representations that negotiate a conceptual return to the original hut structure, all future building could, theoretically, continue to engage our faith in the ability to perpetually situate places in response to our variable surroundings over time.

At stake in each revisitation of architectural origins is, therefore, a renewal of the connection between humans and their world—a relationship that is revived by building practices particularly at times of spatial transformation and social development. In his essay "The Hut and the Altar: Architectural Origins and the Public Sphere in Eighteenth-Century France," architectural

historian Richard Wittman contrasts Laugier's account of the original primitive hut with Jean-Louis Viel de Saint-Maux's notion that the first building
was a sacred altar and not a sheltering hut. While Laugier emphasized human
rationale as the primary force in architecture's mediation with nature, Viel instead suggested that building practices arose from an ancient relation between
the earth and the heavens, and thus from a quest to relate earthly structures
to sacred beings at a time when such allegorical intimacies were possible. So
architecture's enduring role was to relate buildings to either earthly or heavenly
landscapes. Wittman frames Laugier's and Viel's incommensurable narratives as differing responses to a similar anxiety over the increased dispersion
of localized community formations and to the transformation of the public
sphere expanded through a developing print culture. Key to this transformation, Wittman proposes, is "the demolition of space from its primordial role
as the principal ground for social existence."[7] As a sense of French national
culture replaced specific, embodied experiences of space with a disembodied
and homogeneous concept of spatial unity, and as individuals formed social
networks in the abstract through printed discourse, architecture's capacity to
situate specific sites of belonging came under threat. In either case, the specific materiality of the hut or the altar is less significant than what each relays
about the context surrounding their resurrections. In both cases, these returns
to early building practices reinvoked certain primary conditions of dwelling
that were based on the real time and space of a specific encounter between a
body and its environment. Both narratives attempted to bring those ideal past
conditions into contact with a modern, elastic experience of space unmoored
from specific sites and deferred over time.

Yet neither narrative's account of architecture's original purpose is a
stable point of reference, since a return to the hut has consistently been the
premise of architectural treatises that theorize the original relation between
buildings, bodies, and the spatial environment, from antiquity to modernity.
Architectural historian Joseph Rykwert has undertaken the task of compiling
these numerous returns to the hut in his book *On Adam's House in Paradise:*

The Idea of the Primitive Hut in Architectural History. Rykwert's use of *primitive* gestures toward the mythical notions of early human building widely sustained throughout the modern exoticizations and racializations of non-Western cultures that are consistently present in narrativized returns to the past. Instead, I will use the term *prehistoric* to specify these narratives by introducing the largely ignored material culture of early human structures and settlements. I will also use the term *primordial* to retain a sense of the idealized past, reinvoked most strongly during the massive historical and cultural discontinuities occurring during transitions from premodern architectural construction to the burgeoning modernity of the eighteenth-century period of Enlightenment, through nineteenth-century industrialization, to twentieth-century modernism.

Across these ruptures Rykwert positions the hut as "a paradigm of building: as a standard by which other buildings must in some way be judged, since it is from such flimsy beginnings that they spring."[8] In fact, Laugier's eighteenth-century account of the hut returned to and reimagined even earlier understandings of human building, which in turn theorized architecture's role in the development of situated communities. Writing during the first decade of the reign of Augustus, circa 30–20 B.C., after decades of civil war, the Roman architect Vitruvius linked the appearance of the first hut-like human shelters to man's ability to intervene in the natural environment, using its given materials in order to form places of meeting and communication. Vitruvius began his own narrative with the invention of fire, which inspired early man to start congregating in a specific site and to acquire a common language. Describing the evolution of human building, which unlike Laugier involved social engagement, Vitruvius detailed the following:

> When many people came into a single place, having, beyond all other animals, this gift of nature: that they walked, not prone, but upright, they therefore could look upon the magnificence of the universe and the stars. For the same reason they were able to manipulate whatever object they wished, using their hands and other limbs. Some in the group began to make coverings of leaves, others to dig caves under the mountains. Many imitated the nest

building of swallows and created places of mud and twigs where they might take cover.[9]

Recognizing the larger cosmic order and the need to make their place within it, early humans created shelters while also forming social networks that allowed them to observe and learn from each other. Again, architecture's role is one of relation and connection, this time between people as well as between people and a changing spatial environment. Eventually, as Vitruvius recounts, early imitations of animal nests were transformed into houses with brick walls, stone foundations, and tiled roofs. Vitruvius's widely influential narrative of discovery, manipulation, participation, and cooperation in early human building thus advanced a consistently responsive negotiation between social formation and spatial situation—a negotiation that many architects and theorists have since revisited over the centuries.

Going back even further in time to consider ancient Greek, Roman, Jewish, Egyptian, and Japanese sacred rites, and again suggesting that architecture's role in connecting bodies and landscapes extended at times to heavenly beings and spaces, Rykwert notes that the earliest versions of the primitive hut were either built or alluded to during ritual practices in order to perform a community's embodied identification with the spatial environment and the sacred beings housed there. Rykwert focuses on ritual practices that involved a reconstruction of the buildings inhabited by early ancestors, both to conceptually return to an original condition of spatial intimacy with land and earthly and sacred bodies, and also to resituate those conditions in the present through material reenactments and structural surrogates. As Rykwert contends, ancient ritual practices that continue to the present day are "rites of urbanized, or at any rate semi-urbanized peoples, implying a more permanent, more elaborate form of building against which the primitive hut provides a memento of origins."[10] The origins at stake are therefore relational, providing a primary analogy between "hut, land and world on the one hand, and hut and body on the other."[11] The hut, then, along with its narrative of origin, develops in response to the changing natural environment as humans socially participate in defining their place in the world and among others.

Theorists, builders, and dwellers alike return to the hut because social, economic, and cultural factors affecting our expanding or disorienting spatial experiences collectively urge us to revisit building practices that have and may yet still offer situated modes of dwelling. In fact, since the hut represents a renewed connection with the natural landscape, it has also served as an imagined refuge outside of modern urban expansion. For Gaston Bachelard, the primordial hut acts as a dream image that releases dwellers from modernity's overcrowded house and city, linking them instead to an ideal, serene, and unchanging past. Bachelard's image of the hut as refuge remains easily accessible in the imagination, so that even someone who is sitting in his family room can "listen to the stove roaring in the evening stillness, while an icy wind blows against the house, to know that at the house's center, in the circle of light shed by the lamp, he is living in the round house, the primitive hut, of prehistoric man."[12] Emphasizing the psychological force of the hut as a visual motif, Bachelard suggests:

> Primal images, simple engravings are but so many invitations to start imagining again. They give us back areas of being, houses in which the human being's certainty of being is concentrated, and we have the impression that, by living in such images as these, in images that are as stabilizing as these are, we could start a new life, a life that would be our own, that would belong to us in our very depths.[13]

As an image of stability framed in stark contrast with the chaos of modern life, the hut offers a way to release dwellers and travelers from dislocated spatial experiences, grounding them instead in an imagined intimacy with a world that no longer exists.

In ancient to modern narratives, and whether through reason, myth, ritual, or nostalgia, the desire to return to the material formation of the hut is an attempt to reinvent as well as to renew lines of connection between building, land, and bodies just as social and spatial transitions may force distance between them. In fact, although Joseph Rykwert retraces his way back through the centuries in order to chart a historical continuity centered on the paradisal prehistoric hut, his theme of return finds its ultimate goal in the ongoing renewal of architecture's central role in spatial experience and, by extension, world understanding:

> In the present rethinking of why we build and what we build for, the primitive hut will, I suggest, retain its validity as a reminder of the original and therefore essential meaning of all building for people: that is, architecture. It remains the underlying statement, the irreducible, intentional core, which I have attempted to show transformed through the tensions between various historical forces.[14]

Yet while Rykwert focuses his argument for the inevitable renewal of prehistoric dwelling on a mythical return to original and essential modes of situated architecture, a position that ultimately seems unviable in our contemporary moment fraught with both chosen and forced global diasporas, I do find critical potential in his ultimate claim that "the desire for renewal is perennial and inescapable. The very continued existence of social and intellectual tensions guarantees its recurrence."[15]

But how do these patterns of return lead to renewal? How is architecture, in both its conceptual role and its material functionality, renewed? My contention is that the multiple and ongoing returns to the hut ultimately provoke the renewal of situated or still modes of spatial experience, but that these renewals are not enduring and so the patterns of return must operate through material revisions as well. For the hut not only acknowledges that architecture represents a stable understanding of our place in the world, but it also continuously and variously acts as guide to connect dwellers with their spatial environment, particularly during times of flux. As seen through its multiple narrative reiterations, the hut, as guide, is not fixed but, rather, is ever changing, acting as both a stable and flexible motif.

In architectural theory, the impulse to return has conventionally signaled a renewal of situated, habitable structures, often in relation to sacred sites and monuments. Yet, in spite of our contemporary fragmentation and distrust of origins, and with it the unraveling of the racialized myth of the primitive, a broader concept of incomplete return and continual revision can, even now, provide a theoretical framework for our contemporary experiences of being spatially situated. While we may no longer be concerned with a return to or an imitation of the original human construction, we can still be drawn to the means by which buildings allow us to return home, affording us the opportunity to resituate and even replace our experiences of belonging.

RETURN AND REVISE

Dan Graham's material evocation of the hut reactivates an ongoing desire to be in place, even in the face of dislocation. However, his pavilion sculpture returns to the hut in order to demonstrate its unfeasibility as a contemporary model for situated dwelling, or at best, the need for a completely new narrative that instead makes apparent both the desire for and impossibility of such a return. Graham locates Laugier's model as a typological precedent for his pavilions in order to call attention to the ever-growing distance between humans across space. He explains: "The rustic hut was supposed to be a reduction to man's and architecture's original nature, to its self-sufficiency, when there was no oppression of man by man: Architecture and Man were closest to Nature."[16] As Graham's statement makes clear, this supposedly unchallenged and consistently reinvoked claim represents the hut as the primordial architectural symbol for an easy, blissful, responsive, and permeable relationship between humans as well as between humans and their spatial environment. The hut represents connection between buildings, bodies, and landscapes at an idealized time in which humans need not worry about protecting or separating themselves from each other. In Laugier's narrative, early man existed without either social or spatial conflict and in close relation to his natural landscape; Laugier's eighteenth-century return to the hut, and the return of those before and after him, aimed to conceptually reconstitute those conditions in the present. Graham's pavilion sculpture, instead, refuses to conflate past and present spatial contexts and building practices. Graham reinvokes Laugier's hut not in order to revive a connection to the spatial environment but, rather, to reveal the invisible ways in which modern architecture continues to uphold an illusion of transparent intimacies between buildings and bodies. For although there may be formal similarities between the two, Dan Graham's alignment of his own contemporary structure with Laugier's reconception of the primordial hut draws explicit attention to the break in situated spatial experiences, countering the longing for return with an unveiling of the hut's repeatedly uncritical resuscitation at particular moments of cultural transition.

In addition to describing his pavilion sculptures as "primitive shelter and landscape," Graham further qualifies the Dia Center's mirror-and-glass structure as "both an optical device and an architectural modification of a previously unused rooftop."[17] In doing so, he materially realigns and revises the primordial hut with the material properties of modern architecture. As we have seen, the historical impulse to return to and to renarrativize the origins of building characterizes an attempt to recontextualize vastly different material developments as not so very different after all. Modern architecture also falls prey. In fact, in charting the new architectural possibilities of open-plan transparency, modern architect Le Corbusier also invoked a hut narrative. In his seminal 1926 text, *Vers un architecture*, Le Corbusier argued that a return to prehistoric hut building proposed a model for navigating the technical developments of nineteenth-century industrialization in relation to modern building and spatial experience. "Primitive man has halted his chariot; he has decided that here shall be his home ground," Le Corbusier narrated. "He chooses a clearing and cuts down the trees that crowd it in; he levels the ground about it; he makes a path to the stream. . . . This path is as straight as his tools, his hands and his time will let him make it. . . . The door of the hut opens on the axis of the enclosure—and the door of the enclosure faces exactly the door of the hut."[18] This idealized builder fulfilled two essential conditions of architecture: he built according to units derived from the human body and according to rationally measured geometry. These two aspects determined early man's coordinated connection to his natural landscape and defined architecture as capable of achieving its ultimate goal of housing the human body in relation to nature. Like others before him, Le Corbusier's modern architecture aimed to universally systematize embodied connections to the built environment, and so his alignment of modern building materials with the prehistoric hut served to rationalize material advancements in architectural practice by integrating those developments into an intimate relation between body and landscape.

Graham takes on modern architecture's materials and methods while refusing to idealize the conflation of the hut's modern and prehistoric narratives of spatial situation, instead unveiling the complexities of both and denying the resolution of their differences. The transparent, open-plan design of Graham's pavilion, and its placement on the rooftop of the Dia Center, revisits characteristic attributes of modern architecture, mimicking its flexibly usable interiors and returning to an area that Le Corbusier had consistently converted into usable terrace space, in such well-known structures as his Villa Savoye, built between 1928 and 1930 in Poissy, France (Figure 1.4).[19] Graham also reappropriates, along with his pavilion sculpture's rooftop location, one of modern architecture's key building materials: transparent and mirrored glass. In fact, in addition to referencing the hut structure, the Dia Center's *Two-Way Mirror Cylinder Inside Cube* also alludes to the modern office building with its two-way mirror and glass facades. As Graham explains:

> The 1980s corporate office building's two-way mirror glass facades are one-way reflective on the outside (reflecting the sky and other building facades) and do not allow visual penetration by the spectator of the interior, but give the interior viewer a transparent view of the exterior. My pavilions subject this one-way relation to a serious transformation, being equally transparent and reflective both inside and outside.[20]

While affording flexibly useful interior spaces that are responsive to the external environment and to a variety of users, Graham's structure confuses visual transparency between and across those boundaries and surfaces so as to challenge the reductive idealism of modern architecture as well as any easily afforded relation between bodies and urban landscape.

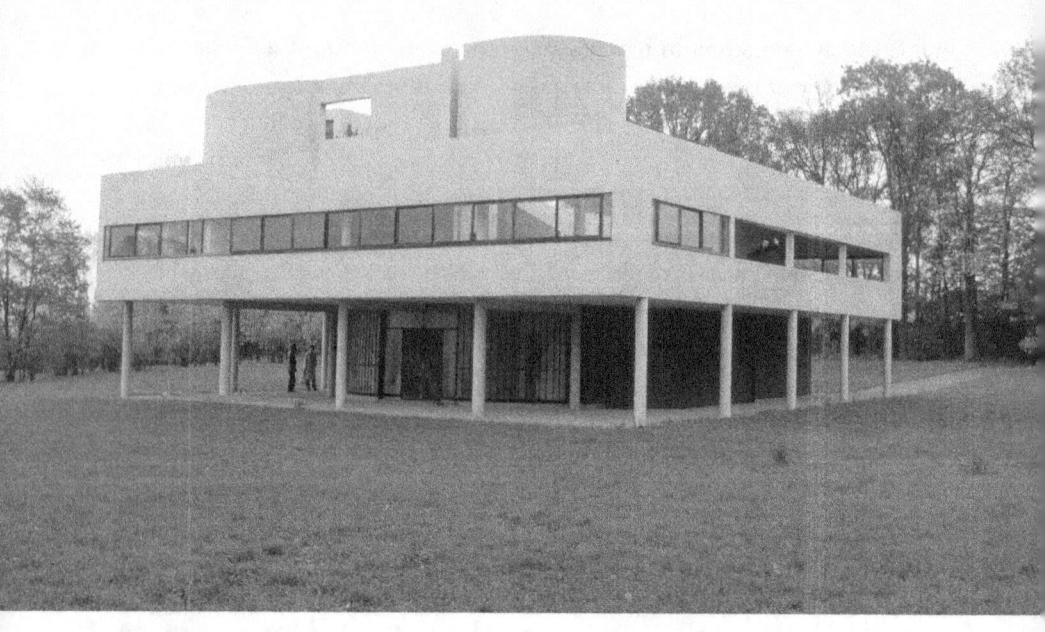

FIGURE 1.4. Le Corbusier, Villa Savoye. Photograph by Donald Corner and Jenny Young.

As a material, glass gives the illusion of transparency, of seeing exactly what is to be seen. But Graham contends: "At the same time that glass reveals, it conceals. If one looks into a glass showcase, one can have the illusion that the container is neutral, without apparent interest in the content of what it displays; or conversely, the appearance of what is contained can be seen as a function of the qualities of the container itself."[21] As evident in the use of glass, the conflation of material form and function was in fact a central aspect of modern functionalist architecture. With new building materials and engineering methods incorporating glass as well as iron and reinforced concrete, the theoretical definition of architecture began to shift toward a new determination of universal functionality, as newly available methods began to respond to newly imaginable demands. The resulting architecture was determined by its contained function, configuring an economically efficient plan for spatial use that was supposedly accessible to the widest possible public.[22] Writing about modern functionalist architecture, Graham emphasizes its "moral dimension; 'efficient' connotes a melioristic, scientific approach seemingly uncontaminated by ideology, which, pragmatically, has (capitalistic) use value."[23] For Graham, then, glass walls conceal corporate activities in the name of neutral transparency and universal access and appeal, so that modern social hierarchies of control can continue to be invisibly housed. In attempting to eliminate the disparity between the modern building's external public facade and its internal private operations, glass thus upholds the pretense not only of material but also of ideological transparency. Graham sees this pretense "justifying the use of technology or bureaucracy by large corporations or government agencies to impart their particular version of order on society."[24] In defiance of the material spatialization of capitalist interests, Graham builds his jointly artistic and architectural pavilion sculptures that reuse the very materials that supposedly uphold the tenets of social and spatial order. In Graham's hands, those same materials instead inhibit order.

Graham's focus on the material and ideological complexities of modern architecture also in turn encourages a reconsideration of the materiality of the hut, whose return in architectural narratives remains for the most part conceptual. Indeed, besides invoking a mythically original practice of building in order to restore architecture's essential features in the present moment, the material culture of prehistoric building engaged with social-spatial tensions in its own time in a way that can shed light on its enduring role as a repetitive historical motif. By attending to the early hut's material specificities, we can consider the specific attributes that continue to inform the numerous conceptual returns to a form of dwelling that is arguably best attuned to the variable spatial situations and cultural developments of its inhabitants over time. I suggest that alongside the narrative rearticulations of the hut, and in tandem with Graham's own critical attention to the materiality of modern architecture, we also must acknowledge the material details from prehistoric hut building and early habitation practices in the context of wider changes in the social and spatial environments.

The presumably first *Homo erectus* hut structure can be traced back to a seasonal camp called Terra Amata, dating from 400,000 B.C. and located near the shore of the Mediterranean, within what is now Nice. Excavated by the French archaeologist Henri de Lumley in the late 1960s and early 1970s, the major artifact of Terra Amata was a large ovoid-shaped hut made of upright sticks bent inward, presumably tied overhead to form a roof. Reconstructed from archaeological discoveries, we can imagine that the hut's interior consisted of large centrally aligned posts supporting a ridgepole that in turn supported the inwardly angled walls. In the center was a hearth or fire pit bounded by a line of stones. Following de Lumley's artifacts, we can also imagine that prehistoric humans assembled a number of these structures every year, forming a temporary community probably during fishing season, when a situated mode of existence was necessary to gather food over an extended period of time, and when social engagement consisted of collaborative hunting, preparing, preserving, and storing of food. The structures were quickly and easily built, perhaps even with assistance from others within the makeshift community, and then quickly and easily dismantled when the season ended and all parties moved on in their separate ways. Because the remains of Terra Amata seem unchanged over time, we can presume that settlers rebuilt in the same way, coming together in the same location from year to year.

For art historian Donald Preziosi, the alternately situated and nomadic camp of Terra Amata provides evidence that sociocultural developments, and not the development of biological capacities, initially influenced the building and sustaining of human communities—the visual representations of which appeared in portable and iconic imagery a quarter of a million years later. I turn to Preziosi's account of Terra Amata because his larger project of rethinking art history in terms of the embodied network of images, objects, structures, and makers, viewers, and participants engages with historical narratives as "a performance or actualization on the part of the users" and thus, I believe, foregrounds the kinds of phenomenal relations that allow the hut to function as both a repetitive motif and material construction.[25] Although operating within a nomadic framework, Terra Amata was nonetheless "a highly complex, regular, systematic object—systematic in the simple sense that it is composed of parts designed to interact in a fully integrated way, each serving differential functions: support, cohesion, bounding, separation."[26] Offered in Preziosi's account of the Terra Amata site is an emphasis on the function of the early hut structure, not only as paradigmatic in rethinking art history in terms of user participation, as is his argument, but also, I believe, paradigmatic in negotiating specific and changing material relationships between bodies and their social-spatial environment. The material culture of Terra Amata, as simultaneously a systematic configuration and a participatory framework for a roving social network, mediates between order and openness, structure and fluidity, localized and dispersed communities. It also materially affords the possibility of social and spatial continuity in spite of, and also because of, discontinuity.

That building practices should evolve through and because of an anxiety over social and spatial discontinuity should come as no surprise if we look to the arrival of the first situated Neolithic *domus,* which archaeologist Ian Hodder defines more expansively as the nexus of attributes, activities, and contexts associated with the experience of home. As social groups begin to expand and become more sedentary, the *domus* became the focal point for "the transformation of the wild into cultural."[27] In his study of the domestication of Europe in the Neolithic age, Hodder contends that "the social will to sedentism and intensification which ultimately led to economic domestications was created through drama, in the sense that emotions, feelings, and fears were aroused in the interplay of concepts surrounding the domus."[28] Homes thus became structures and sites of protection from the landscape, creating and activating separations between dwellers as well as demarcating specific spaces for certain uses and thus introducing social order into forms of spatial organization.

Analyzing the early Neolithic settlement of Lepenski Vir, situated on the Yugoslavian and Romanian border, and dating from around 12,000 B.C., Hodder notes the four different kinds of carefully delineated spaces. At the village level, there was a consistent spatial order, while the larger village plan appeared more varied in house shape and size, though there did not appear to be marked social ranking in these variations. Social order was spatially constructed and performed through each individual home structure, as relayed by the kinds of tasks undertaken within them. We can imagine how sustained domestic situation was encouraged through the large, central areas for food preparation, and also how this sense of the *domus* as a nurturing and protective site was furthered, as well as gendered, by the placement of female figurines and the burial of women and children directly under or around the structure. Thus the *domus* both signified a conceptual understanding and activated a practical upholding of home in terms of a situated community network, which was in exclusion and domination of the *agrios* or wild outside.

While early Neolithic settlements focused on separating the wild from the domestic, centralizing social operations within the *domus,* in the later Neolithic period the concept of the *domus* was extended to incorporate more of the outside environment. As animals aided agricultural production through the plowing of fields and as social competition led to warring and the development of necessary modes of defense, the relationships among individual built structures, communities, and the spatial environment were again transformed. Here we can imagine early humans developing farmland in order to harvest resources over time, and herding and controlling wild animals in order to demarcate, defend, and own a fixed portion of the landscape. Social engagement under these terms meant that settlers banded together in defense of their communities while also potentially considering how to extend their spatial reach into the communities of others. While Hodder's study sees hut construction as a situated, protective, and defensive rather than a nomadic building practice, as was evident in its earliest appearance at Terra Amata, his reading of the changing role of the Neolithic *domus* suggests that during times in which community formations began to vulnerably expand into undefined spatial parameters, the relationship between the structured, situated *domus* and the unknown, variable *agrios* was revisited and revised with new urgency.

By considering the material specificity and spatial-social contexts of early building practices, we can begin to understand why the hut became a powerful motif and why future iterations are deemed so necessary at particular moments throughout the centuries. In other words, as the material specificities of hut building are transformed over time into idealized narratives, we can clarify the hut's representative function. The material resurrection of the hut, as later reinvoked through its narrative returns, creates a historical continuity that negotiates transitions in the spatial environment. But an attention to the material culture of early hut building also clarifies the drastic differences and discontinuities that this historical continuity itself attempts to assuage and even erase.

Bridging early building practices with modernity's conceptual returns to the hut, Dan Graham's *Two-Way Mirror Cylinder Inside Cube* acts as a hinge between the prehistoric material culture of the hut, consisting of both nomadic and situated spatial experiences within a variable landscape, and modern architecture's glass-and-mirror buildings that attempt to universally situate its users within urban environments. Yet Graham's return to the hut does not attempt to resolve the differences between early and modern anxieties of being in and out of place. Rather, such differences—between past and present, concept and material, form and function—are kept both in play and in tension.

RETURN AND REPLACE

Conceptually returning to, renewing, and materially revising the hut, Graham's pavilion sculpture replaces spatial stability with experiences of spatial permeability and visual disorientation—experiences that can be linked to the transformations in modern Western spatial organization and its effects on globally expanded social experiences. Indeed, the question of whether or not sustained spatial situation is now possible drives Graham's reconsideration and revisitation of the hut. As art historian David Summers has argued in *Real Spaces: World Art History and the Rise of Western Modernism,* the centered, place-bound, and aligned "real spaces" of premodern spatial experience have been transformed by the globalization of Western modernity into centerless, limitless, and metaoptical space.[29] Indicative of a performance-oriented methodology, though not explicitly stated as such, Summers's concept of "real spaces" is centered on the observer, thus conjoining the act of viewing with the placement of the viewer's body in a social and spatial situation, as she behaves in a certain way through habit or expectation in front of or within the space of the object. Engaged by users, real spaces, such as those invoked by a return to the hut, retain a commitment to centered and situated sites, the lines of connection formed between those sites and the bodies inhabiting them, and the context of their continued use.

In light of modern Western spatial organizations that depart from real spaces, Graham frames the precariousness of contemporary spatial situation through the visual dependencies that link and unlink, orient and disorient, situate and resituate one body with and against another. One of the ways in which this connection between visuality and spatial situation can be understood is through the changing relationship between image making and reception across the history of art. In order to determine how a modern relation to real spaces can still be possible, Summers charts a world-historical narrative of image making and reception. His narrative tracks a continuum beginning with planar presentation—perfected in ancient Egypt in its passage toward linear perspective and the virtual presentation of space—as developed in fifteenth-century Italy—and ending with the modern Western conception of metaoptical space and by extension, its globally disorienting economic and political remappings. A discussion of Summers's wide-spanning spatial genealogy is applicable to my analysis of Graham because the reciprocity between spatial and visual experience ties image making and receiving to the changing contexts of the image's spatial location. And for Graham, the possibility of being in place is linked to the changing potential for bodies to visually align themselves in correspondence with their surroundings.

Throughout his detailed account of art making and situation from the earliest of stone tools found at Olduvai Gorge, in what is now known as Tanzania, to his implicit end in our contemporary digitally virtualized world, Summers consistently attends to the specificity of places and centers, the direction of paths leading to them, and the contexts of "facture," by which he means the conditions that existed for the object to have been made and for its making to be repeated.[30] Flat, frontal-facing, planar images present spatial dimensions independently from viewer completion within real spatial situations, while virtual images are dependent on a specific viewer location for completion in virtual space. Yet although imagistic premodern planarity does not map out a particular standpoint for the observer, Summers argues that the real architectonic configurations of such planar image making and receiving are conjoined, as the observer traverses the entire architectural complex. Thus the built environment, in its engagement with users, affects the connection between premodern planarity and modern virtuality. Within an architectonic understanding of planarity, the observer stops, starts, and completes the image's virtual volumetric space in her own real spatial situation. While emergent within these architectonics of planarity, virtuality, in contrast, clearly demarcates the spatial positioning and visual perspective of the observer in relation to the imagistic spatial representation and its modes of presentation, releasing the observer from an experience of real space. For Summers, though, real spaces are connected to virtual space, since the formats and locations of image presentation, even virtual, are always culturally specific, ready at hand, and shaped by larger social activities and purposes. The experience of real spatial situations—an experience renewed by the architectural revisitation of the hut—therefore remains for Summers viable even as our understanding and experience of space move toward the virtual.

However, in a seeming departure from both planar and virtual spatial situations, the modern Western experience of what Summers calls "meta-opticality" defines space as universally metric, homogenous, and measurable along coordinate axes and thus infinitely divisible and expandable. This conceptual understanding and practical inhabiting of space must be conceived of as culturally specific to a modern Western construction of the earth's surface as a metrical grid of interchangeable points that frame the spatial concept of a globalized world. Both natural and social orders are bound to this experience of centerless, ever-expanding space in which places are marked out for their economic viability as capitalist hubs of commerce, transportation, or defense. Indeed, as Graham's pavilion sculpture intends to make visible in its appropriation of materials and methods of modern architecture, and with it the ideology of global capitalism, metaoptical space is not merely a passive framework for the marking of social relations but also channels and controls natural and human resources.

Nonetheless, even though modern metaopticality seems to negate the possibility of real spatial situation, Summers believes that metaopticality is historically continuous with planar and virtual spatial understanding and therefore can be linked, however discontinuously or vulnerably, to spatial configurations present in both Western and non-Western prehistoric and premodern traditions. It is impossible to release ourselves from metaopticality, and indeed Summers's aim is not to propose spatial alternatives to metaoptical spatialization, for indeed metaopticality is the way, the only way, that our modern and contemporary bodies exist in space. Yet perhaps metaoptical space can in fact carry the possibility of yielding either intentional or unintentional real spaces. While modernity's relationship to real space, and to prehistoric and premodern spatial experiences, may be discontinuous, fractured, and temporary, if, as Summers argues, metaopticality is immanently and mutually constitutive within those earlier visual definitions and spatial determinations, then, in fact, spatial situation may still be possible.

Graham's pavilion sculpture puts Summers's theoretical proposal into practice, attempting to structure, temporarily inhabit, and potentially belong in limitless space, and seeking to find potential moments of real space within boundless metaopticality. Within Graham's structure, the possibility of real spatial situations is opened up through the momentary meeting points enacted as viewers move toward, across, and past each other. Centers, boundaries, alignments, and places associated with real spaces, though no longer specifically and spatially situated, can therefore be in the process of revision, to be redefined through paths and sites passed over, visited, or paused within, momentarily returned to and temporarily replaced.

Implicit in an understanding of contemporary spatial situation, then, is an experience of temporality, however disjunctive, as bodies use and revisit a variety of spatial sites. This alludes to the temporal dimension of my concept of spatial replacements—a process that continually reinvokes, revises, and renews sites of spatial situation. As art historian Whitney Davis argues in his review of *Real Spaces,* while Summers may have initiated "a long-overdue Kantian riposte to Heideggerean pretensions in the history and criticism of visual and spatial arts," pretensions that privilege temporality over spatialization in the analysis of human existence, there is nonetheless "a congruity between Summers' 'real space' and Martin Heidegger's 'original time.'"[31] Temporality must be a significant partner in any trajectory of human spatialization, for as Davis argues, "it is the temporality—the absolute historical time and cultural timing—of the differential, if mutually constitutive, immanences and emergences" that serves as the "essential schematisms of making."[32] An attention to temporality marks two kinds of complicit spatial understanding that are both key to processes of replacing. While real spaces, such as those offered by the hut, are actually real—meaning that they are manifested in space at particular historical and cultural moments—nonetheless their continuous return is notional, emerging instead through their conceptual and material replacements. The intertwinement of temporal and spatial experiences thus challenges us, as Davis argues, to "encounter complex historical-sequential orders, and we must recognize phenomena of memory, tradition, replication, anachronism, or prolepsis."[33] The development of real space and the ongoing variations in spatial situation proceed in a manner that is not linear or continuous but, rather, loops backward and forward, repeating, renewing, and replacing sites of being and belonging through human passages and pauses. When aligned with this kind of embodied mode of spatial temporality, the model of return so familiar in architecture's search for the real spaces of original dwelling can also be reconceived as discontinuous and incomplete.

While the transitional shift from prehistoric and premodern real spatial situations to modern dislocations has indeed elicited various conceptual returns to the hut in order to lessen anxieties among builders and inhabitants, Graham's contemporaneous replacement of the hut instead conversely invokes the newly disorienting ways in which we must navigate and situate ourselves within our ever-changing present spatial environments. In fact, Graham returns to the ideal situation of the primordial hut to renew our desire and to revise our material frameworks for being in place, but also most significantly to propose connections between visual dependencies and spatial replacements that are activated through embodied presence and movement.

In an exchange with the curator of his architectural works at the Camden Arts Centre in London, Graham discusses the operations of feedback and splitting that relate viewing, perceiving, and using bodies in his sculptural practice. Feedback is materially translated into the reflective surfaces of his pavilions, while conceptually it refers to the self-conscious reciprocity between viewers. Splitting acknowledges Graham's work between the genres of art and architecture, as well as video and performance, and includes his ongoing interest in multiple and simultaneous visual perceptions.[34] Both feedback and splitting visually situate bodies in relation to others even if visual access is distorted or fractured. Also implicit in the capacity of feedback and splitting to bring bodies into visual correspondence are the conditions of the pavilion's spatial environment, crowded or emptied of viewers, cloudy or clear skied, as well as the expanse of cityscape around and below. Reciprocal and multiple lines of visual contact in turn allow viewers to rest for a moment in place, determining spatial boundaries upheld by walls and surfaces as well as finding openings for proximate, embodied contact afforded by spatial enclosures. Real spatial situations may therefore become contingently available as viewers resituate themselves in line or in contrast with the presence and movement of others, a relation that is visually dispersed along the pavilion's surfaces and spatially disjointed within and around its boundaries.

By challenging lines of perspectival access and by resisting the optical resolution of object, body, and visual field, Graham's replacement of the hut with a sculptural pavilion not intended for dwelling therefore resituates the hut's material structure and use in critique of modern architecture's universal functionalism, and also in critique of architecture's functional relation to the ideal hut. Graham's pavilion structure makes visible the uneasy phenomenal negotiations that enable building to afford momentary situation by revising, visually complicating, and replacing modern mirror-and-glass constructions. In doing so, *Two-Way Mirror Cylinder Inside Cube* materially challenges the conceptual impulse to return to the primordial hut by refusing to guarantee that building practices lead to spatially situated or socially integrated dwelling. The patterns of return, renewal, revision, and replacement proposed by Graham disrupt, rather than complete, the search for an ideal spatially situated home as represented by the hut. Instead, these patterns activate the ongoing process of finding home, a process that is nonetheless punctuated with moments and sites of being at home.

For phenomenological philosopher Martin Heidegger, whose conception of temporality's grand narrative within human experience runs both counter to and yet also complicit with an understanding of spatiality, the body in motion within and between places, and thus in relation to built structures, inaugurates the unfolding of space and the potential for place-bound dwelling. Heidegger contends that the demarcation of spatial boundaries, and thus the essence and experience of space, only occurs upon the making or building of place. Although its place-making function allows for the space to unfold from specific locales, building only affords dwelling if these spatial markers create relations between human beings. In "Building, Dwelling, Thinking," a lecture presented to the Darmstadt Symposium in August 1951, Heidegger proposes that humans are "in dwelling" because

> they persist through spaces by virtue of their stay among things and locales. And only because mortals pervade, persist through spaces, by their very essence are they able to go through spaces. But in going through spaces we do not give up our standing in them. Rather, we always go through spaces in such a way that we already sustain them by staying constantly with near and remote locales and things.[35]

As Graham would agree, the act of building therefore cannot be assumed to always, or easily, lead to dwelling. But if building is the founding and joining of spaces through human relations, then it is capable of bringing forth what

Heidegger calls a "distinctive letting-dwell."[36] This concept of "letting-dwell" centralizes the human being's precarious, finite role as dweller. It also emphasizes the continual process of making, or the "bringing-forth" of locales from space. The essence of building is, then, to let us dwell, or to be, at home in the world. As we build, we must always be in search of what it means to dwell, in our own time, in our own places, in our own bodies—all of which, by definition, vary continuously. So we must, Heidegger says, "ever learn to dwell."[37]

To learn to dwell is, among other things, to learn to differentiate dwelling from a broader notion of architectural functionality, even if a building is used as a shelter. When Dan Graham built his hut-like structure as usable, traversable museum space but not as a home, he was making this very distinction; but he was also importantly asking us to rethink and replace our understanding of both dwelling and home. To dwell, the philosopher Karsten Harries specifies, "is to feel at home. Building allows for dwelling by granting a sense of place."[38] To feel at home, and by extension to be in the world, is thus aligned with the kinds of place-holders—like orientation, situation, repeated context of use—that Summers together defines as attributes of "real space." Heidegger himself may have felt at home because his farmhouse rested on a hillside in the Black Forest, opened onto a large grazing area for the farm animals, and faced outward toward the valley where his rituals of everyday living occurred. In effect, with its specific spatial situation and embedment within the landscape, Heidegger's farmhouse is one more version of the primordial hut and is itself another unrecoverable moment occurring in time past, impossible to completely replicate in our contemporary present.

But even if we recognize this conceptualization of dwelling as yet another narrative return to the hut, can Heidegger's notions of building and dwelling conceptually, as well as materially, apply to our contemporary lives? Is it even still possible to attain the kind of being in the world envisioned here? It may be that Heidegger's notion of dwelling already implicitly involves a constant and destabilizing movement toward and away from spatial situation. As architect Mark Rakatansky, contends, "one does not have to introduce drifting into dwelling (it is already there)."[39] In order to emphasize that dwelling is never arrived at but is a continual process of situating ourselves in our world, Harries turns to Heidegger's final claim, that we must "ever learn to dwell." "Genuine dwelling," Harries argues, "means not so much being at home but at most a continuous journeying home, a continuous homecoming, haunted by changing dreams of home."[40] Thus dwelling, activated as an ongoing event, is simultaneously a material structure and a process of making and remaking a home. In partnership with homecoming, I would add homemaking, which implies not only that there is a concept and structure of home that we are returning to and moving toward, but also that we are actively responsible for the finding, making, and situating of home over time.

If, following Heidegger, we cannot and should not ignore our ongoing paths toward dwelling and our continuous efforts at homemaking, then, as Harries suggests, architecture's role in shaping our spaces of being and belonging should take the form of "building tasks."[41] A building task is a significant replacement for a built structure, because a task is an act that celebrates a lack of fixity, authority, and that instead emphasizes the events and processes of its making and remaking. Dan Graham's pavilion sculpture enacts one such task, activating the ways in which space is framed by a changeable viewing and using public, and by extension, the ways in which real spatial situations may become contingently and temporarily available. His pavilion sculpture, as an art object and a museum extension, does not guarantee the possibility for spatial situation, much less dwelling. By providing the structural framework for an unavoidably disorienting connection to the environment through curving surfaces of two-way mirror and glass, Graham renders the hut contemporaneously unable to easily and transparently integrate bodies into their spatial environment, or to provide sustained dwelling. Instead, *Two-Way Mirror Cylinder Instead Cube* makes spaces for proximate and indirect, as well as artistic and commercial, encounters while engaging prehistoric, premodern, and modern frameworks for dwelling within both built and natural landscapes. The experience of lingering in one of these places or with one of these uses occurs as bodies visualize, move past, and resituate each other within the immediate surrounding environment of the pavilion, and out toward the larger urban landscape.

Visitors traversing Graham's pavilion are unlikely to say that they are at home in the structure. Indeed, Graham's return to the hut explicitly refuses to assure any sense of home, as the hut had evoked in all of its previous reiterations and revivals. Instead, Graham's own impulse to return to this ideal form of dwelling proposes ongoing yet disjunctive patterns of revision and renewal that ultimately replace both the conceptual and material processes of finding home over time. Finding, remaking, and resituating home are all offered as possibilities once our grip on spatial stability and location becomes loosened, our understanding and experience of spatial situation become more flexible, and our dependence on each other becomes both visually and spatially apparent. Vacillating between disorientation and reorientation, visitors are not aligned to the fixed site but, if anything, are tenuously drawn to each other. These moments of temporary meetings and crossings, as inspired by Graham's structure, can in fact initiate, resuscitate, and extend spatial resituation. We may then activate replacing home as a mode of tentatively returning to and being held in place by way of conceptual renewal and material revision—a process that integrates phenomenal pathways and pauses, historical resonances and present-day reenactments, and that sets in motion the prospect of belonging in place with others.

Two

REUSABLE SITES GORDON MATTA-CLARK'S *FAKE ESTATES* AND THE *ODD LOTS* EXHIBITION

On October 14, 1973, the real estate section of the *New York Times* presented a report on the city's auctioning of tiny property plots. Appearing over time, between and inside of larger lots drawn up by architects and city planners, these unusable gutter-spaces, small in size and odd in dimension, could be purchased at bargain prices by anyone interested in owning a piece of New York City. One such interested party was the artist Gordon Matta-Clark. At the time of the newspaper interview, Matta-Clark had just come away with a sliver measuring one foot by ninety-five feet, another one without any pedestrian access, and had bid furiously on but lost yet another lot measuring four by five feet. Speaking to the *Times* reporter, Matta-Clark explained that he planned on using his purchases as new works of art. "The artworks," he proposed, "will consist of three parts: a written documentation of the piece of land, including exact dimensions and location and perhaps a list of weeds growing there; a full-scale photograph of the property, and the property itself. The first two parts will be displayed in a gallery, and buyers of the art will purchase the deed to the land as well."[1] Nothing of the kind, however, was unveiled during Matta-Clark's short lifetime.

Until a few years ago, what anyone knew about the initial development of this real estate project was ambiguous, contradictory at best. But in 2003, *Cabinet* magazine's editorial team undertook this task, dedicating an issue to a fervent, much-needed search for information on the location of the original lots, Matta-Clark's process of acquiring them, and the development of his intended art project. Interviewing those in close contact with the artist, editors Jeffrey Kastner, Sina Najafi, and Frances Richard began to piece together a narrative. They discovered two batches of deeds pertaining to a total of fifteen small parcels of land, fourteen in Queens and one on Staten Island, bought by Matta-Clark on October 5, 1973, and by his assistant, Manfred Hecht, on January 11, 1974. They learned that it was his friend Alanna Heiss who first introduced Matta-Clark to the city's auctions. Heiss, founder of the Institute for Art and Urban Resources, a small organization that uncovered abandoned sites around the city in order to open temporary exhibition spaces, recalled that Matta-Clark had accompanied her to an auction at the Roosevelt Hotel. While Heiss pined over the larger lots that were well beyond her means, Matta-Clark instead became interested in the slivers of property up for sale, all listed in the price range of twenty-five to seventy-five dollars. The next time the two friends went to an auction, Matta-Clark made his first purchase.[2]

Retracing the artist's steps was not, however, the ultimate goal of *Cabinet*'s interaction with Matta-Clark's unfinished work. In fact, the magazine also initiated a cycle of return, reuse, and replacement by launching a project of their own that reactivated and extended Matta-Clark's initial work-in-progress. Along with their detailed research, which was published in the Spring 2003 issue, *Cabinet* also presented three new proposals by contemporary artists Jimbo Blachly, Matthew Northridge, and Clara Williams, who were each commissioned by the magazine to create work related to one of Matta-Clark's property plots of their choice. Each commission was informed by the material dimensions of the original site, and in turn informing Matta-Clark's exploration of spatial ownership and belonging. All three commissions, very much like Matta-Clark's initial involvement with his property plots, remained notional proposals on paper.

A couple of years later in 2005, *Cabinet* again revisited *Fake Estates*. The magazine applied to repurchase the ten remaining lots since repossessed by the city due to delinquent tax bills. Even though the city was no longer auctioning off gutter-spaces, the editors were able to acquire annually renewable property licenses for some of the original sites. The magazine then partnered with the Queens Museum of Art and the White Columns gallery in Manhattan—an outgrowth of the 112 Greene Street exhibition space that counted Gordon Matta-Clark as a founder. *Fake Estates* was then renamed *Odd Lots* and reborn into two new and interconnected exhibitions. At the Queens Museum of Art, Matta-Clark's gutter-space slivers were marked out on a panoramic map of New York, accompanied by multimedia documentation detailing the city's layers of urban planning that led to the creation of these odd lots over time. The White Columns gallery in turn hosted a series of artworks commissioned by a group of contemporary artists who responded both individually and as a group to Matta-Clark's initial project.

Like the proposals by Blachly, Northridge, and Williams, which were also exhibited in their printed form at White Columns, the group show returned to the actual sites and revisited key issues proposed by *Fake Estates* in its earlier incarnations. Individually, each artist renewed and broadened a dialogue with Matta-Clark's critique of spatial ownership. As a group, the *Odd Lots* artists also interjected new ways of challenging the demarcation of property and its ties to phenomenal experiences of being in place by raising issues that forced potential owners to confront the violence of fixing and protecting spatial sites, as well as the social transactions and environmental flux that occur when space is determined to be useful. The renewal of specifically embodied interactions with Gordon Matta-Clark's unfinished plans for his *Fake Estates* project therefore instigated a collective replacement of conventional modes of ownership and belonging. Indeed, the group nature of the *Odd Lots* exhibition activates ownership as an ongoing process by which a site's use-value is redetermined over time through the presence and passages of multiple bodies, rather than situated in the owned object or built structure. Responding to Matta-Clark's initial concerns with the obsessive nature of owning and exchanging parcels of space in order to ultimately be in place and at home, the *Odd Lots* group show specifies a networked construction of property that collectively, though not equally or consistently, informs an experience of belonging that can be traced through the meeting points between bodies within the various changing spatial sites. In other words, once released from conventions of containing space, ownership can be translated into a process that connects bodies within spaces and in turn proposes modes of belonging that can be unattached from the demarcation, valuing, and protection of spatial sites and structures.

The revisitation of *Fake Estates* thus initiated multiple avenues of return, in each of which a specific site was reused and a specific material past of Matta-Clark's project was resurrected in the temporal present, while together forming extended lines of material and phenomenal alliances through which spatial situation and ownership continue to be recalibrated. Expanding on the first chapter's focus on patterns of incomplete return and partial renewal within modes of spatial situation, this chapter suggests that these patterns are enacted through material reaccessibility, structural reusability, and embodied revisitation that together render conventional notions of property unviable. Reuse and revisitation therefore determine a permeable rather than fixed ownership of space through which experiences of reowning, replacing, and ultimately belonging both in and across spaces are opened up as possibilities. By extension, the determination of home shifts away from its structural fixity and toward a homebound experience of belonging temporarily with others across materially analogous but also changeable sites.

Matta-Clark and the *Odd Lots* artists continuously replaced connections between sites, buildings, and those who pass through, pause within, use, and reuse them. Supporting rather than resisting these changing relations between spaces and bodies, this network of artists, builders, locations, objects, viewers, participants, and inhabitants was spatially specific while unfolding over time that was discontinuous. Passing through and around these sites on paper, in galleries, and in actuality, artists and viewers alike permeated both past and present lines marking out spatial situations, continually rendering them porous and vulnerable to transformation. By moving from one spatial location, its form, and time of representation to another, viewers not only repossessed Matta-Clark's resistant means of inhabiting space, but they also replaced the fixed sites of ownership as lines of temporal and spatial linkage. The delineation of property sites was, therefore, retraced by specific passages, alternately accessible and inaccessible at various times to different bodies. These passages of revisitation, much like the reexhibition, suggest that reuse rather than disuse, and replacement rather than displacement, together identify a mode of spatial ownership through which a new kind of being in place can be offered. For according to Gordon Matta-Clark and all of the *Odd Lots* artists, we may indeed belong to sites that we pass over and in spaces that we do not individually or equally own.

REUSE AND REVISIT

Accompanying Gordon Matta-Clark on a visit to several of his newly owned plots in 1975, the artist Jaime Davidovich brought along his video camera and recorded as his friend measured several of the plots' dimensions, drew their property lines on the ground in white chalk, and took his own photos.[3] The video is the only documentation of Matta-Clark's contact with his small properties. Davidovich recalls: "We would go to some of the places, and people would get upset; people would yell at me . . . and he would go with the measuring tape, and try to find as many places as possible."[4] As Matta-Clark's friend Betsy Sussler, also along for the visit, explains: "He understood quite well the psychological and political factors involved in walking onto a person's property to inform them that his piece of forgotten land he'd bought was in fact part of their driveway."[5] Such comments, and the video footage that supports them, underline the conceptual foundation of Matta-Clark's envisaged art project, in which property and its mode of economic and social exchange determine the demarcation of space through ownership and protection.

Indeed, Matta-Clark's very act of purchasing slivers of unusable and oftentimes inaccessible land intervened in the workings of the real estate market by questioning the determination of property, rendering the seemingly useless possibly useful, and challenging the fixed boundaries and ownership of space. In buying commercially unusable land that bordered on, cut through, or was situated between other larger lots, Matta-Clark reinvested these gutter-spaces with another imagined artistic use, attempting to reverse their useless-ness by reengaging them as ownable properties. Turning to *Fake Estates* in her formidable study of Matta-Clark's artistic career, art historian Pamela Lee notes that "the absurdity of real estate is laid bare as a bad pun."[6] When unusable sites are also up for sale, to be bought and revalued, the real estate market's division of space into economically valuable units is then hyper-extended infinitely.

Rearticulating Hegel's views on property in relation to Matta-Clark's project, Lee goes on to suggest: "If Hegel argues that property's 'essence' con-sists in its use and 'vanishing,' Matta-Clark parodizes this idea through literal-izing it. For him, property's essence consists equally in its *attrition*; it is ac-corded value as property only when it passes into a state of uselessness or ruin."[7] According to Hegel, the using up of property thus defines the fullest enact-ment of a subject's ownership and the simultaneous negation of her owned property.[8] However, the inaccessibility of many of Matta-Clark's gutter-space properties renders the vanishing of property as always already in process with-out necessitating a particular owner's negation of it. "When I bought those properties at the New York City Auction, the description of them that always excited me most was 'inaccessible,'" Matta-Clark says in an interview with art journalist Lisa Bear: "What I basically wanted to do was to designate spaces that wouldn't be seen and certainly not occupied. Buying them was my own take on the strangeness of existing property demarcation lines. Property is so all-pervasive. Everyone's notion of ownership is determined by the use factor."[9]

Indeed, Matta-Clark's inaccessible property sites were already useless without offering the opportunity to use them up.

But what happens if ownership is no longer tied to the spatial framing of useful structures and locations? Through Matta-Clark's imagined project, unusable sites are not primarily revalued in terms of their ability to offer new spatial openings but, rather, in terms of their redefinition as spaces of social intervention—spaces that bring artists, viewers, neighbors, buyers, owners, and city planners in contact with each other—in order to make visible the ways in which space is carved up by the presence and movements of bodies. In fact, the passages of bodies together, apart, and across both useful and seemingly useless sites activate different processes of spatial definition, capable of unmooring property lines as well as social formations, as ever ready to be revisited and realigned. Ownership understood through these kinds of circumstances is a permeable process, in which usable sites and using bodies circulate in a responsive manner. This continuous redrafting of space renders the experience of belonging on site, in built structures, and with others as no longer attached to spatial ownership. Instead, the presence and movement of bodies initiate a continuous process of renewed legitimization of sites both past and present—sites that oscillate between usefulness and uselessness. Through these interactions between shifting sites and moving bodies, Matta-Clark's experimentation with property engages with spatial ownership as a temporal network in which spatial belonging, however precarious or temporary, can be replaced over and over again.

The process of specifying spatial parameters through the presence and movement of bodies has been the defining feature of site-specific art practice, to which Matta-Clark's jointly architectural and artistic work is most closely tied. Such practices attend to the intertwining of bodies and sites, where the body in motion held momentarily in a particular space renders that site temporarily visible, socially legible, and specifically useful. But although bodies and sites come together and apart, their interaction is not always reciprocal or co-legitimating, for as Gordon Matta-Clark's engagement with property reminds us, sites and built structures can also be subsumed and rendered illegible by urban expansion, redevelopment, and multiple economic exchanges. The impulse to renew the usability of a site in the face of decay or abandonment finds its drive in the very bodies that use and disuse, pause within and pass over, leave and return to that specific space.

In recognition of Matta-Clark's attention to the embodied practices through which specific sites are opened up, framed, and collapsed, Donald Wall categorizes Matta-Clark's work by its commitment to process-based performance, or to use Wall's terms, a "performance constancy," as opposed to a conventional art or architectural-based materialization of an "object constancy."[10] Wall's concept of "performance constancy" signals an inherent tension in Matta-Clark's practice that exists between a work's temporal unfolding and its specific spatial situation, or between duration and stasis. In an interview with Wall, Matta-Clark qualifies his practice as "an ongoing act for the passer-by" that "provides a stage for the busy pedestrian in transit."[11] The site acts on the passing bodies as they in turn act on the site. Such performance-based terminologies of act and stage articulate a link between a potential action manifested and endured in time, on the one hand, and the spatial parameters in which that action occurs, on the other. If performance is constant, it must go on endlessly—meaning that the embodied encounters can occur again and again as those sites and acts are revisited and reused. Yet for Matta-Clark, this endless process must also be spatially sited, so that actions and encounters afford certain moments of pausing in place and within specific spaces before resuming again.

Following a performance orientation that understands spatial situation over time, we must also acknowledge that these ongoing processes of material revisitation and spatial redefinition are punctuated with particular instances and sites of reappearance, since moments and materializations that have already occurred in the past are not completely gone but may return and can be reused. "While my preoccupations involve creating deep metaphoric incisions into space/place, I do not want to create a totally new supportive field of vision, of cognition," Matta-Clark postulates in his interview with Wall. "I want to reuse the old one, the existing framework of thought and sight."[12]

Reuse—of materials, experiences, encounters, concepts, and paradigms—is significantly antithetical to both spatial fixity and temporal closure, instead operating through material and temporal replacements.

Writing about his friend's legacy, the artist Dan Graham celebrates Matta-Clark's process of revisiting inaccessible, indeterminable, or forgotten spaces in order to continuously renew phenomenal accessibility and by extension to replace social legibility attached to those who inhabit or move through the sites. This impulse to revisit and reuse challenges the modern ideology of progress that discards the old and moves quickly on to the new. In order to expose what Graham names "the containment of the environment according to capitalist interests," as exemplified by the carving up and selling off of all kinds of spaces as property, Graham understands Matta-Clark's practice as "an attack on the cycle of production and consumption at the experience of the remembered history of the city."[13] Though Graham gestures specifically to his colleague's more famous building cuts, Matta-Clark's act of purchasing gutter-spaces to reuse in future artwork can also "reveal the just-past," as Graham describes, and in fact may propose the means by which such a revelation can occur.[14] While the splits, fissures, voids, and holes that Matta-Clark effected in properties that were outmoded or ready for demolition literally revealed the material past just below the surface of the new—in works such as *Splitting*—his imagined *Fake Estates* project and its subsequent renewal by *Cabinet* magazine together centralize the living practices and paths of spatial users and dwellers, whose movements and pauses reuse material residues and resuscitate embodied connections from the past within the structures and encounters of the present moment.

Graham's evocation of the "just-past" references the social critique of cultural theorist Walter Benjamin, whose challenge to modern historical progress finds resonance in Matta-Clark's own art practice. In fact, material cycles of reuse and phenomenal pathways of revisitation invoked by Matta-Clark are also the undertones to Benjamin's *Arcades Projects*, another unfinished piece of work existing as a montage of collected notes and sources. Begun decades earlier in 1927 and remaining incomplete in 1970 when he died, the *Arcades*

Project is Benjamin's materialist philosophy of history, constructed out of visual, tactile, and spatial debris that survived in the remaining nineteenth-century Parisian arcades, which one by one were being demolished. Benjamin demonstrated that slightly outdated objects and spaces of mass culture possess the potential means of spatially unsettling the historical fixity of the past and undermining modernity's emphasis on the always present and ever new. This focus on the materiality of history that has moved just past its function provides a dialectical contrast to the myth of unimpeded social, ideological, and economic progress. In his unearthing of these buried markers, Benjamin exposed progress as the fetishization of modern temporality that is caught repeating the new as always the same.

For Benjamin, the material structures and urban plan of Paris exemplified the ability of the past to haunt the present, while also providing a specific material link between the cultural theorist and the artist.[15] Benjamin's wandering flâneur, like Matta-Clark's modern-day urban dweller, traversed the city as a kind of "colportage phenomenon of space," spanning past and present and therefore identifying a spatial and temporal conflation that was embodied in the flâneur's movements and that was also contained within the commercial activities and commodity exchanges that took place within the arcades.[16] Positioning cultural material within an expanded temporal register before and beyond the present, Benjamin qualified progress as enacted by bodies in motion through and back to specific sites, and in relation to specific structures and objects. Here the ties to Matta-Clark's practice are strong, and thus the larger stakes of his *Fake Estates* project may become clearer once aligned with Benjamin's intellectual project. Spatial accessibility, and by extension the social legibility afforded to those offered access, are together based on the reuse, revisitation, and replacement of specific objects and constructions—a system that is activated and reactivated by embodied encounters. For both the theorist and the artist, these encounters in turn are embedded in a durational process of material reinvention that bends forward and back across sites and through time.

Matta-Clark himself began to address the formation and embodied use of illegible spaces over time through his informal artist collective, Anarchitecture, which most likely served as an inspiration that led him to purchase the *Fake Estates* gutter-spaces. In a letter sent to member Carol Goodden from Paris in 1973, Matta-Clark outlined a list of proposals to be undertaken by the group, one of which was noted as "Fake Estates: property slivers with some projected ideas for them."[17] Although in the end Anarchitecture would not formally participate in the *Fake Estates* project, the working group did consider spaces of collapse, ambiguity, privacy, and inaccessibility outside of the readily demarcated and legislated. In the interview with Lisa Bear, Matta-Clark remarked that the group was "thinking more about metaphoric voids, gaps, left-over spaces, places that were not developed . . . the places where you stop to tie your shoe-laces, pieces that are just interruptions in your own daily movements. These places are also perceptually significant because they make reference to movement space."[18] For Pamela Lee, "a place that is an 'interruption' or a 'movement space' is a liminal space, unbounded by the restrictions of real estate. Leftover because not legislated for use, these spaces refuse ownership because they are illegible, ambiguous, kinetic even."[19] Suggesting that these spaces that are outside of architecture's conventional frameworks could also be reused, Anarchitecture members such as Goodden, Tina Girouard, Richard Nonas, and Laurie Anderson took photographs of holes, horizon lines, fallen monuments, train wrecks, spaces between buildings, doorways, and locked keyholes. They then exhibited their findings anonymously at the Greene Gallery in March 1974. In addition, *Flash Art* magazine published a two-page spread on the group's photographic findings.[20]

While refusing conventional understandings of individual ownership, Matta-Clark's articulation and Anarchitecture's reuse of "movement space" call attention to both the spaces that bodies move through, and spaces that are themselves moving, either changing over time or activated by phenomenal passages through them. Giving momentary pause to the sites over which bodies traverse while emphasizing that such sites both transform and are transformed by embodied pauses and passages, Matta-Clark and Anarchitecture attempted to stage what he called a "perceptual metamorphosis, a model for peoples' constant action on space as much as in the space that surrounds them."[21] This fluid understanding and responsive experience of space in relation to the actions undertaken within or across them resist the economic valuing of fixed spaces, attuning the experience of ownership to the ways people continually and repeatedly come upon each other as either situated inhabitants or passersby. It is through these moments of revisitation and within these sites of reuse that the process of owning space becomes one of reowning materials and actions, and of replacing interactions and encounters.

REUSE AND REOWN

While participating in Anarchitecture's informal gatherings and discussions, Matta-Clark visited his properties several times on his own, taking photographs of the concrete or dirt ground of each small, strange plot. He put these photos in a cardboard box along with the property deeds and city maps detailing their dimensions and location. When Matta-Clark could no longer pay the property taxes, he gave the box and thus turned over the ownership of the plots to his friend, the art collector Norman Fisher. Matta-Clark died of pancreatic cancer in 1978, long before he or Fisher could do anything with the properties or their documented materials. Upon Fisher's death, Matta-Clark's widow, Jane Crawford, received the box, and ownership was again transferred.

In the 1992 retrospective of Gordon Matta-Clark's work at the IVAM Centro Julio Gonzalez in Valencia, Spain, *Fake Estates* was finally born as an exhibitable artwork, ultimately without the participation of the artist. It exists to this day in the form of collages assembled by Crawford from the contents of Matta-Clark's box (Figure 2.1).[22] In 1994, the artworks were also exhibited at the Holly Solomon Gallery in New York, and again in 1995 at the Rhona Hoffman Gallery in Chicago, both under the title of *Realty Positions: Fake Estates and Other Architectural Musings.*

In 2003, *Cabinet* magazine editors Jeffrey Kastner, Sina Najafi, and Frances Richard interviewed Crawford about the development of the initial collages. The black-and-white photos, deeds, maps, and tax slips were arranged

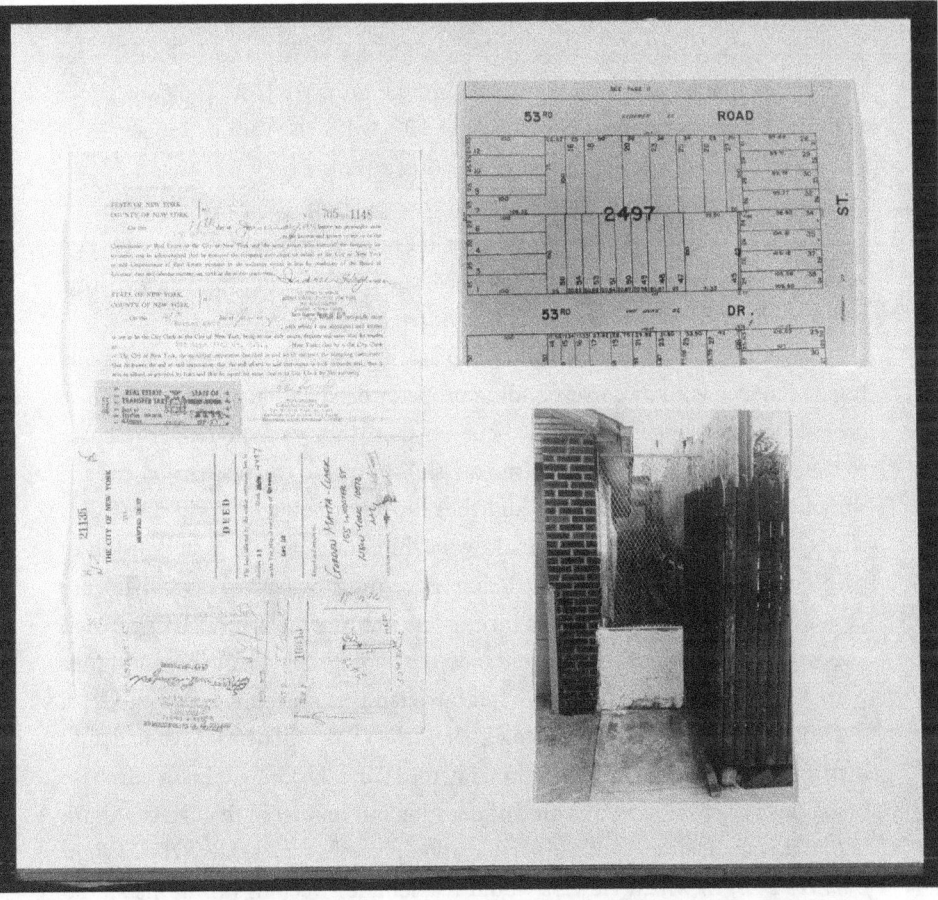

FIGURE 2.1. Gordon Matta-Clark, *Reality Properties: Fake Estates, Little Alley Block 2497, Lot 42,* 1974 (posthumous assembly 1992). Photographic collage, property deed, site map, and photograph. Framed photograph and documents; 20⅝ x 22⁵/₁₆ x 1⅜ inches (52.4 x 56.7 x 3.5 cm). Solomon R. Guggenheim Museum, New York. Purchased with funds contributed by the International Director's Council and Executive Committee Members, 1998.

in the infamous cardboard box in no particular order, so Crawford used the photo negatives that were kept in Matta-Clark's archives to follow the sequences of images that together made up one property plot. Then she drove through Queens trying to match up the sites with the various sequences of photos. Crawford recalls: "Some of the sites running between houses, down the middle of the block, must have just been about impossible to photograph."[23] On many occasions, she had to trespass on private property in order to gain access to a site, which harkened back to Matta-Clark's own experience visiting the plots in 1973 with Davidovich and Sussler.

Crawford used archival tape to assemble the strings of photos, pairing a sequence with its corresponding property deed and map. She decided to exclude the tax slips, because she believed that "they were no longer relevant to the works."[24] The exclusion of the tax slips points to the suspension of each site outside the passage of time and thus beyond the incurring of taxes. But it also signals a negation of formal ownership duties and to a suspension of specific economic factors and restrictions governing ownership as well. The use of archival tape also furthers the incomplete nature of Matta-Clark's project, as it would allow others to undo and redo the photographic sequences and thus marks not only artistic authorship but ownership as unstable. If Matta-Clark did not actually put the collages together, is the work still defined, valued, and ownable as a Matta-Clark artwork? Crawford cited the Guggenheim purchase of a collage as prompting this kind of question but countered that Matta-Clark had in fact made other "puzzle-participation pieces" such as the 1970–72 *Blast from the Past,* in which viewers would reassemble sweepings from his studio floor with a photo and measure as a guide.[25] The collages were not fully authored or owned by Matta-Clark, just as the actual sites were no longer owned by anyone. Yet through the hands of Crawford and later through other artists commissioned by *Cabinet* magazine, and in their combined reuse of his sites and their renewed destabilization of spatial use-value, Matta-Clark's unfinished project initialized a practice of collective art making, dispersed across time and space, that was perhaps best suited to his reimagining of spatial ownership and belonging. Ultimately, such a recalibration would have been impossible to materially realize as a solo artist.

Over the years, materials and sites passed between various hands and were transformed over time, so that any kind of ownership of each formal piece of the project as well as the various versions of the whole was contested from the very start. The inability to easily determine, contain, value, own, transfer, and exchange the artwork as object not only informs a critique of the commodity framework embedded in the institutional system of acquiring, displaying, and preserving artwork, but it also makes formally apparent the elastic concept of property ownership, as proposed initially by Matta-Clark and enacted by others after him. In addition, the process of revisiting, reusing, renewing, and replacing each step of the project put each participant into new contact with Matta-Clark's sites, with his documentations, with the different owners of surrounding properties, with different museums, and with new artists and viewers. In each of these steps, the original properties—however they could be accessed and whatever was left of them—became partially reowned.

"Who would have known beyond a shadow of a doubt how Matta-Clark would have chosen to assemble it?" Jane Crawford attests. "Nevertheless, there's an open-endedness to it, and it's that aspect of his work which I find so compelling."[26] In fact, as the three *Cabinet* editors agree, with respect to their fact-finding mission: "Contingent factual gaps such as these turned out to be not simply an obstacle to scholarship, but rather an invitation to identify further disappearances—of authorship, meaning, intentionality—integral to the very fabric of this persistently 'open' work."[27] But it is not only the work that is kept formally open through the various transformations of each site in the face of property exchanges and city planning, as well as through the proposals initialized by Matta-Clark and the later versions of his project undertaken through the participation of others; it is also the process of owning and reowning sites, materials, and structures that is kept open through embodied encounters.

The means by which this incomplete cycle of ownership confronts the conventions of spatial situation afforded through fixed sites of property gets taken up by the first three artists commissioned by *Cabinet* magazine to revisit three specific *Fake Estate* plots. Their projects reassess the process of ownership through a revaluing of the meetings, departures, connections, and reconnections that occur between users and passersby, in relationship to the property's economic salability and transfer.

Choosing a strip off Woodward Avenue in Queens measuring two feet wide by three hundred and fifty feet long, the artist Jimbo Blachly proposed to install ten parking meters down the left wall of a building (Figure 2.2).[28] The meters' revenue would go toward the purchase of another plot housing the abandoned foundation of what once was a masonry building on West 171st Street in Manhattan. Taking into account the cost of purchase and installation of the meters, their income, the cost of hiring a local gang to maintain the meters and ensure safety, the asking price of the masonry foundation, and the down payment and mortgage, Blachly's financial plan estimated that in six years the Manhattan property would be owned outright.

Implicit in Matta-Clark's initial purchase of unusable plots of land was a vacillation between the useless site and its useful potential. Blachly's work in turn reinforces this concept of ownership experienced as an ongoing process in which the useless site becomes useful only to become useless again, and so on. What one owns, then, is a relation between usefulness and uselessness, always in flux between sites, objects, or buildings, those who own them, and what they do with them. As critical artistic processes ongoing and unfinished, Matta-Clark's and Blachly's projects both take place within already established infrastructures. Matta-Clark gains legal possession of the plots by engaging in city auctions, while Blachly embarks on a plan to procure a mortgage. Choosing to hire neighborhood youths to monitor the parking meters, Blachly even acknowledges the urban legend of the "local gang," whose presence is linked to the low income and high crime rates of the neighborhood. Yet in his temporal continuation and spatial extension of Matta-Clark's initial purchase, Blachly also invokes an alternative sociability implicit in the "workless" site, so named by Pamela Lee.[29] Matta-Clark's workless property,

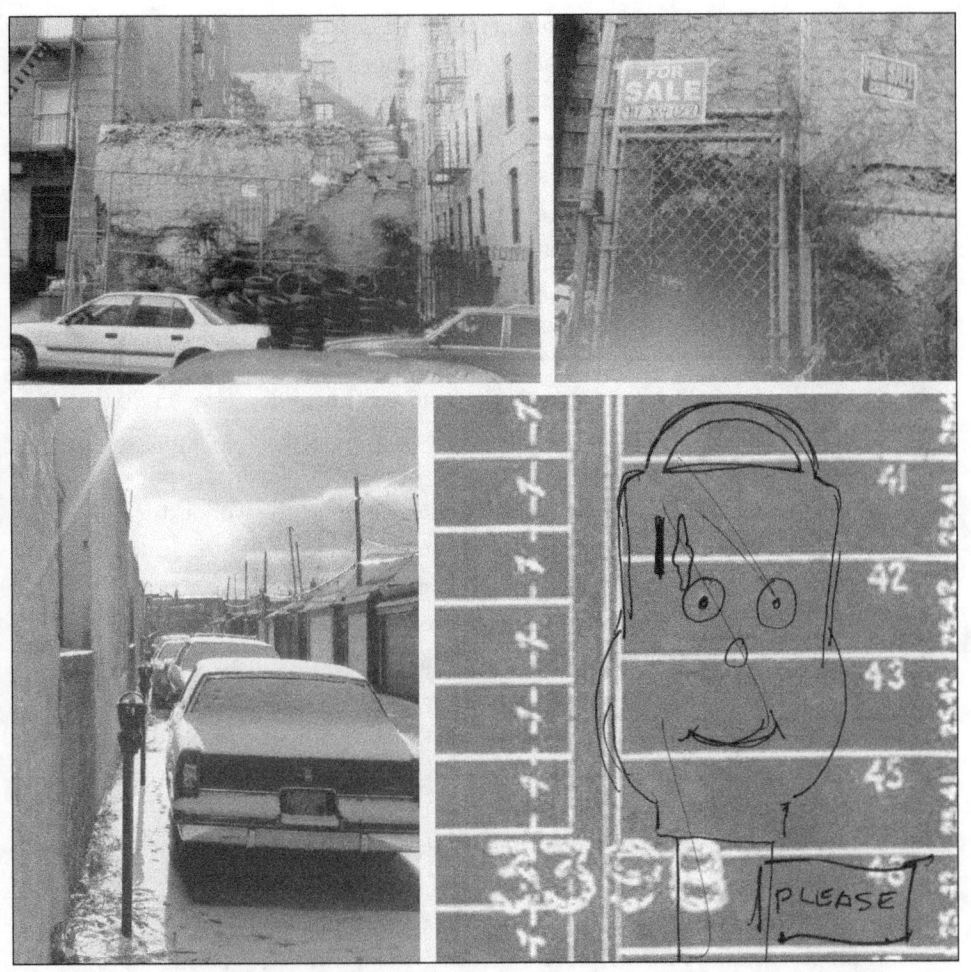

FIGURE 2.2. Jimbo Blachly, Proposal for Block 3398, Lot 116. *Cabinet Magazine.*

workless both in terms of its commercial worthlessness and in light of the artist's subsequent inability to use it, passes into Blachly's hands. In its re-incarnation and reownership, the unusable, oddly shaped site in Queens traces a dialogue between two artists—a dialogue that proposes a networked understanding of use-value founded on the two artists' intertwined processes of ownership over time.

For *Cabinet*'s second commissioned artist, Matthew Northridge, the uselessness of inaccessible plots attests to the fundamental emptiness inherent in the unending impetus to possess property—a critique made explicit in Matta-Clark's envisaged title for his project, jotted in his notebook as *Fake Estates* (Figure 2.3). Northridge chose an unseen square lot, close to Sixty-sixth Street in Queens, measuring roughly four or five feet on each side, large enough only for an anchored pole. At the top of the pole, Northridge proposed to place a tiny blue cottage complete with landscaping. The work exists only as an illustration, which Northridge describes as "an idealized model and still quite fake."[30] The drawing's emphasis on an idealized and fake site of property, impossible to actualize yet still possible to own, revisits Matta-Clark's challenging of the tangibility of ownership. For Matta-Clark, the site of the property is nowhere fixed, neither stabilized between its imagined use and material viability nor between its conceptual and physical dimensions. For Northridge, the site is always vanishing, only to be physically present somewhere among the maps, deeds, contracts, and photographic documentation. In Northridge's piece, the property site is an impossible ideal, only ever to be falsely stabilized as a thing that can be used, transferred, and used up.

For *Cabinet*'s third commissioned artist, Clara Williams, the object of property, always in the process of being sited, ultimately belongs to no one. On the corner of Fortieth Street and Borden Avenue in Queens between the Calvary Cemetery and the Sunnyside residential neighborhood, Williams proposed to install a black residential mailbox on a strip of grass between the sidewalk pavement and a wire fence (Figure 2.4).[31] Across the side of the box is printed the word "NOBODY" in black-and-white letters usually reserved for a resident's name or address. Further complicating Matta-Clark's accordance

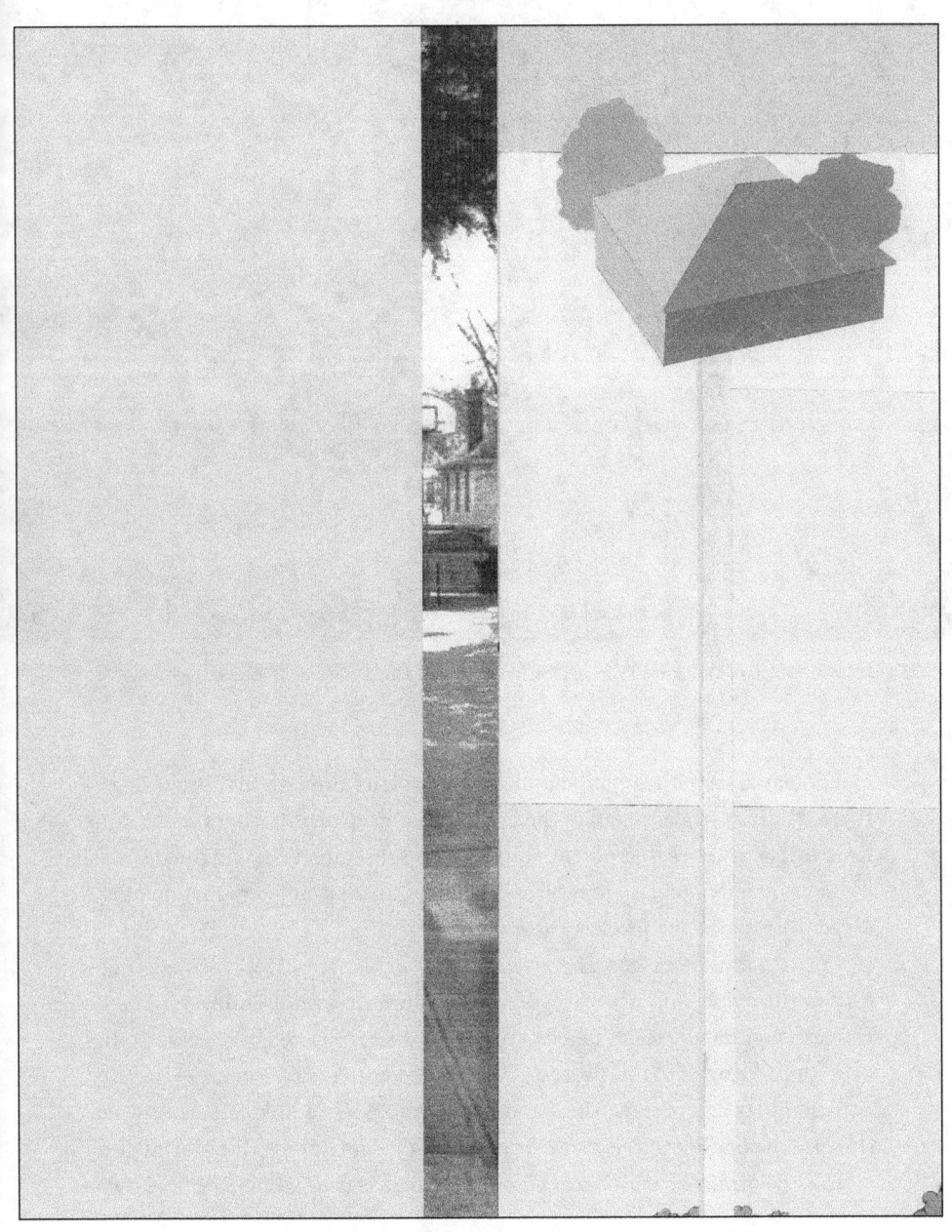

FIGURE 2.3. Matthew Northridge, Proposal for Block 2406, Lot 148. *Cabinet Magazine.*

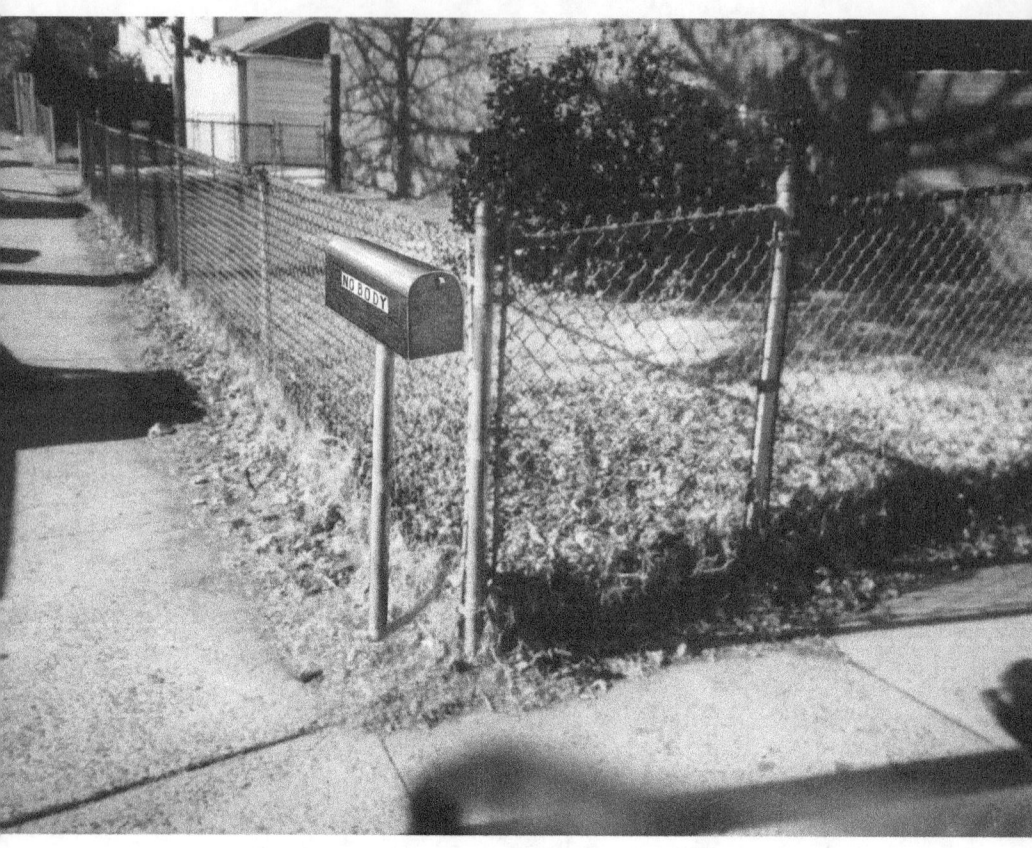

FIGURE 2.4. Clara Williams, Proposal for Block 209, Lot 160. *Cabinet Magazine.*

of a potential usefulness to the useless plots of land through his purchasing of them, Williams's placement of the mailbox points to an inhabitant at the same time as it articulates that potential inhabitant's disembodied, unnamed status. There is literally no body to receive the letters; there is no body that owns the object that marks the property as owned.

Matta-Clark, together with Blachly and Northridge, redefined property as the ownership of a variable relationship between usefulness and uselessness, continually resituated as a material process enacted by specific bodies over time. Attuned to this process, Williams foregrounds a property's material situation between objects, sites, and bodies and poses a link between ownership and belonging that is nonetheless critical of its linking. Her installation reveals the means by which owned objects (such as the mailbox) declare ownable sites (such as the plot of property) while also marking out sites of belonging (such as the house situated on the plot). The object and site seemingly belong to a body, or should. But what, asks Williams, if no body belongs to the owned object or to the potentially ownable site on which that object stands? The mailbox and the site belong to each other, maintaining each other as useful. Williams's choice of a mailbox gestures to the federal postal system that marks points of location and tracks correspondence between them—a system that validates the fixed notion of spatial ownership and makes the inhabitant socially legible. While engaging with rather than operating outside of this system, very much like Matta-Clark's own engagement with the structures and rules of property exchange, Williams draws attention to those who are illegible, are literally nobody, because they are not property owners or renters and are thus not fixed in one place. Seeking to revise this claim, Williams instead declares that in fact nobody fully owns property, implying by extension that nobody is fully in one place.

Reowning the initially useless sites and reframing property as a process in which spaces and structures are used and reused, inhabited and abandoned, Blachly, Northridge, and Williams join together with Matta-Clark to form a collaborative determination of spatial ownership that is not necessarily egalitarian, fail-safe, or enduring. In contemporaneously resuscitating Matta-Clark's *Fake Estates*, *Cabinet* magazine's research and their initial three commissions propose a spatially specific, temporally disjunctive, and conceptually dialogic network of belonging. Linked through the passages and meeting points of makers, viewers, property owners, users, and inhabitants, this network offers replaceable avenues of reconnection that momentarily and vulnerably offer the capacity to be in place, possibly even at home, without allocating, containing, and protecting the spatial sites in question.

REUSE AND REPLACE

For the thirteen new *Odd Lots* artists commissioned by *Cabinet* magazine in 2005 to once again revisit, reuse, and reown some material parameter and conceptual dimension of Matta-Clark's *Fake Estates*, the potential to belong to Matta-Clark, to his sites, to the multiple instantiations of his project, and to each other led to an expanded exploration of the ways in which belonging in place is spatially and temporally activated, as well as culturally contextualized within various urban landscapes. The individual proposals, installations, and practices housed and extending from the pages of *Cabinet* and the walls of White Columns revisited processes of urban flux and expansion, reassessed property demarcation and protection, and reenacted the economic transactions and social interactions necessary to uphold the experience of being in place. As a whole, the new projects together activated moments of spatial situation traced through temporary social formations and interactions unfolding between owners, users, and passersby that were alternately visible or invisible, legible or illegible. The group exhibition proposed that if the experience of belonging was unattached from owned spaces or structures and reattached to the moments and sites of embodied encounters, it could be replaced over a number of reusable and renewable spaces.

Recalling the formation of Matta-Clark's urban sliver spaces, *Odd Lots* artist Francis Alÿs depicted a similar process of spatial transformation in the small Mexican town of Tepoztlan. Alÿs projected a slide of a tiny commercial building that sold thread and buttons next to a drawing that sketched out three stages leading to the structure's creation between two buildings that once stood on either side of it. The informational nature of Alÿs's piece followed the form of both Matta-Clark's initial visual documentation and Crawford's *Fake Estate* collages. A recorded announcement told viewers that the space was once a passageway for animals to access a piece of land located behind the buildings. After the land was sold, the animals were gone, and the passage was thus no longer needed, a new owner built a small structure in the passageway. The owners of the buildings on either side later decided to demolish them, leaving only the thread and button seller. Through these alterations in the urban landscape, Alÿs emphasized the creation of new spatial possibilities in which structures continued to flexibly adapt to the ongoing cycle of destruction and reconstruction. In Tepoztlan, a town quite different from Matta-Clark's New

York City, Alÿs's structure replaced use-value in a site of disuse, resituating the seemingly insubstantial thread and button seller as, the recorded voice tells viewers, "a positive residue of a natural process . . . a metaphor of resistance."[32] While spaces and structures come and go, the spatial flexibility and structural adaptability of Alÿs's small building takes advantage of urban transformation, attesting to the eventual renewal of all kinds of seemingly illegible sites.

For the artist Maximillian Goldfarb, an expansion of the built environment and cityscape bespeaks not an organic growth process tending toward renewal but, rather, what he qualifies as "the unstoppable expansion tendencies of poorly considered city planning."[33] Echoing Matta-Clark's attention to urban expansion with an added focus on the destruction of the natural landscape and thus on the contemporary demands of environmental politics, Goldfarb placed low-power radio transmitters with sound loops emitting ambient nature sounds on FM public radio frequencies during the months leading up to the exhibition. Surrounding homes or passing cars receiving the radio signals would hear the sounds of tree boughs breaking, buzzing insects, or rushing creek water—all sounds associated with an environment very different from the one within which the hearer was situated. The work was presented in the gallery as a series of documentary photos next to a pair of headphones playing the transmitted sounds. This aural punctuation of natural into urban, in both the outdoor sites and the site of the gallery exhibition, also in turn momentarily reversed the sprawl of the urban environment into the natural. Yet although an abstract natural environment was audible, its mode of transmission was technological, rendering its experience secondhand in the gallery. Any reversal of urban expansion is thus made unstable and always already bound up with the technological developments that in many cases help to drive that very expansion.

While Goldfarb's sound piece temporarily replaced the increasing disappearance of undeveloped natural landscapes, Mark Dion's "Gordon Matta-Clark Subterranean Museum" hyperextended the demarcation of usable space by delving beneath one of Matta-Clark's original sites, reusing the only remaining unowned space under the earth's surface. Described as "an event-based experience" and exhibited in the gallery as a mixed-media proposal formally akin to the earlier print proposals of Blachly, Northridge, and Williams, Dion's subterranean museum hypothetically invited visitors down through various geological periods apparent in the earth's inner layers.[34] Plunging viewers underneath one of Matta-Clark's original sites, Dion's imagined museum reactivated Matta-Clark's renewal of unviable, inhabitable spaces while also reinvoking the former artist's attention to the obsessive need to contain and control all kinds of available space. The environments above and below ground alter in time, and both can be subject to a cycle of disuse and reuse driven most emphatically by urban expansion and the ease by which the entire world, surface, and now depth can be accessed and possessed.

While Jude Tallichet offered feng shui as a practice capable of bringing balance back to a consistently changing spatial environment by redesigning the White Columns office space according to its principles, a number of artists created object-based works that considered the materialization of structures and spaces in continual flux. These artists were interested in momentarily spatializing the ongoing processes of ownership. For his part, Dan Price created a Tupperware container with the exact dimensions of one of Matta-Clark's sites, which he converted into volumetric space. Tupperware, which Price noted was introduced the year Matta-Clark was born, contains and preserves leftover food. Like Matta-Clark's use for the leftover parcels of land, Tupperware also proposes a future use for its discarded matter, affording new use-value to what could have been thrown away. Yet while Tupperware preserves and keeps its contents from rotting, Matta-Clark's plots were subject to change and indeed decay over time. Framing a connection between an abandoned site of property and a Tupperware container that envelops its dimensions, Price's objects offered a temporary framing of space that registered past and future time as momentarily and materially situated, not only, as Matta-Clark feared, in order to fix the site but also to slow its disappearance, rendering it potentially valuable and allowing it to be eventually reused (Figure 2.5).

Katrin Sigurdardottir, in turn, enacted the temporal registers of spatial formation with her composite set of objects that came together and apart,

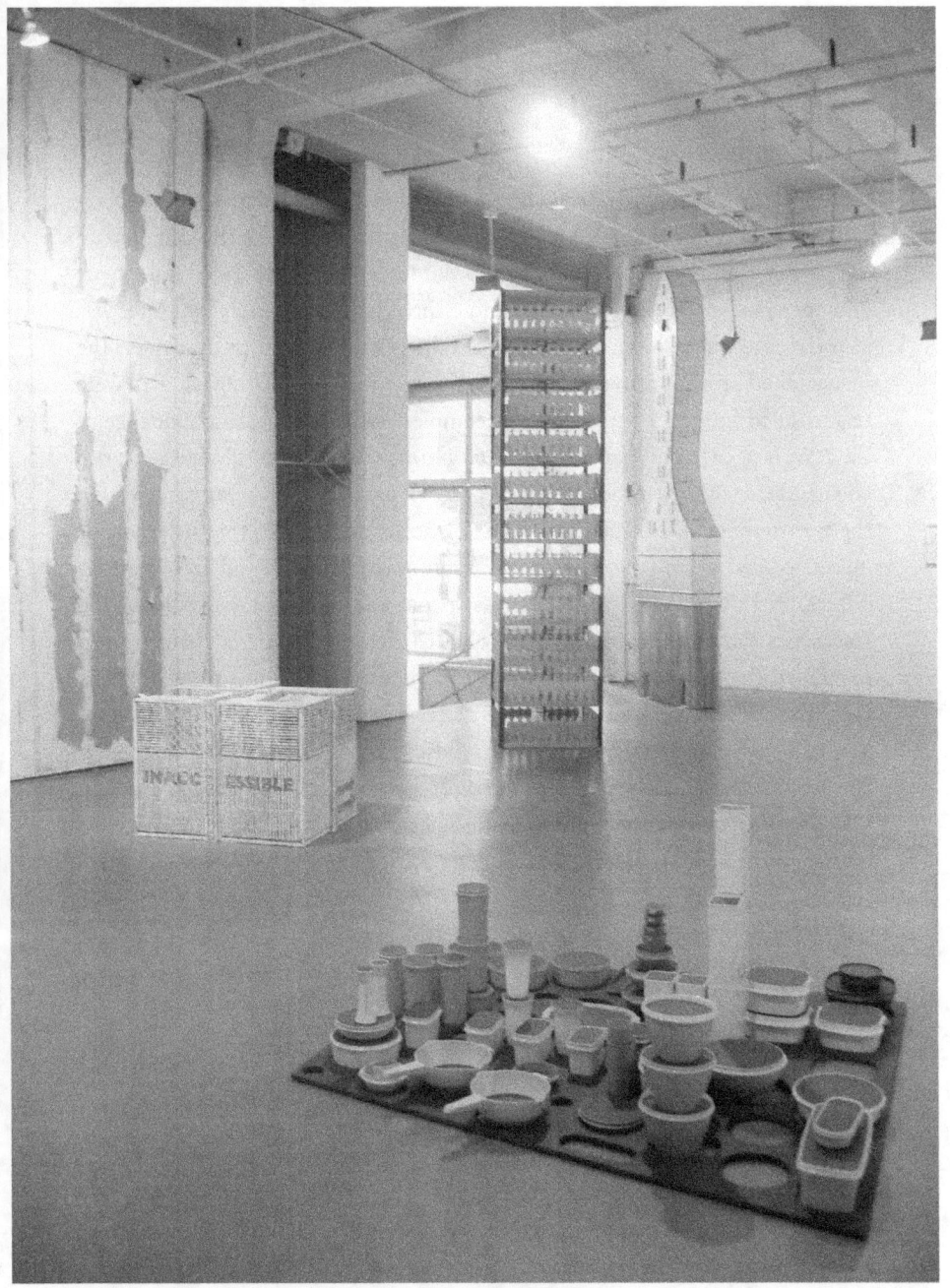

FIGURE 2.5. *Odd Lots: Revisiting Gordon Matta-Clark's Fake Estates,* curated by Jeffrey Kastner, Sina Najafi, and Frances Richard. Courtesy of White Columns Gallery.

materially mirroring the process by which Matta-Clark understood the specification of sites through embodied encounters and passages. Folding out to
map a cityscape, her seven small cargo containers together formed one object
and one continuous environment. Before their exhibition, each container was
sold separately and shipped to a number of previously determined owners. The
owners then sent the boxes back to the gallery in time for the show and all were
reassembled into one unified object, complete with tags bearing evidence of
the travels of each component part. Reminding new viewers of Matta-Clark's
engagement with the property market of buying and exchanging, and also of
the transference of Matta-Clark's box of deeds and photos, Sigurdardottir's
object formed a temporary whole through its passages to and from various
bodies, and therefore through both its spatial and temporal dispersions. The
fragmentation of the initially whole object through the sale of its parts also
paralleled the continual splintering of urban cityscape into sections of property. Yet the reintegration of Sigurdardottir's boxes posed the possibility of
a return to a composite yet cohesive landscape, in which the distances and
coexistent differences between each sector were nonetheless legibly marked.

The coexistence of individually determined spatial sites can, however,
present another scenario of spatial cohesiveness that is instead marked by territorial fixity and thus haunted by a destructive potential. Engaging with the
ways in which boundaries of owned land are defended and upheld at any cost
to human life, Helen Mirra stretched a cotton band with the same dimensions
as one of Matta-Clark's lots across the gallery wall.[35] On the band, Mirra
printed text from an ammunition catalogue, signaling the owning and using
of guns as a form of protection against those intruding onto private property.
The catalogue text introduced a language of territorial violence inherent in a
conventionally fixed notion of ownership, where the unchanging and yet vulnerable lines demarcating one's property against another's must be protected
against incursions of any kind. Mirra's work recalled the accusations of trespassing, the threats, and the enraged demands experienced by Matta-Clark,
Davidovich, Sussler, and later Crawford while they were attempting to access
and document Matta-Clark's properties.

In her own challenge to the sought-after impermeability of spatial demarcations threatened by temporal change, Valerie Hegarty placed a rosebush that eventually tore through a corner of the gallery. Wedging its way wildly in between the unmovable wall, the growing rosebush provided a visual translation of one of Matta-Clark's strangely shaped slivers wedged oftentimes invisibly in between larger, more accessible properties. Hegarty imagined that the change in the sliver plots over time, incurred as planners, architects, and owners continue to divvy up the city, ran parallel to the natural yet still obtrusive process of a rosebush's growth. As it blossomed over the course of the exhibition, the rosebush invasively broke through the gallery wall, resisting its assumed fixity with both flowers and thorns.

Isidro Blasco turned to the photo collage, a familiar Matta-Clark art form, in order to formally depict a break in the fixity of a unified cityscape. Depicting one splintered viewpoint down a street in Queens, individual photos detailing a portion of the view were horizontally and vertically layered on top of each other, visually suggesting that the building and street were simultaneously deconstructing and reconstructing themselves before the viewers' eyes. Blasco explained that she was inspired by Matta-Clark to "break loose the grid at an urban scale."[36] She did so by focusing on one particular line of perspective fragmented over time that is always impossible to hold steady and unified in one's eyes.

In dialogue with Mirra's, Hegarty's, and Blasco's attention to the ramifications of fixing and defending sites of property, Dennis Oppenheim's two models of high-rise constructions warned against the disembodied nature of unified and yet also uniformly designed and embodied buildings. In defiance of his early training in architecture at Cornell, Matta-Clark had himself declared that the nature of his own artistic work, most famously his building cuts but also his interventions into liminal and inaccessible urban spaces, "take[s] issue with a functionalist attitude to the extent that this kind of self-righteous vocational responsibility has failed to question, or to reexamine, the quality of life being served."[37] Modern functionalism equates formal structure with functional efficiency as aesthetic design comes to be aligned with practical and predictable use-value. In Oppenheim's work, tiny yellow figurines, all identical in size and shape, were lined up in rows to form the walls of the rectangular structure. Nearby in the gallery, a large paintbrush shape, replete with more identical figurines, was titled "Building A For Artists." Oppenheim's wall of stick figures and his artists stuck in a paintbrush were serialized and inhuman, inhabiting diagrammatic structures that mimic the functionalist modern architecture with which Matta-Clark found fault. Both artists question the supposedly transparent equivalence between universal user and architectural use-value, calling instead for specifically embodied structures that can nonetheless be variably used (Figure 2.6).

Echoing such a call was Julia Mandle's performance piece that revisited Matta-Clark's appeal to specific, embodied, and variable spatial experiences, in which artist and viewers together participate in the process through which sites are framed and reframed, used and reused, over time. Wearing yellow platform shoes, the soles of which marked chalk lines wherever she walked, Mandle took small groups from one of Matta-Clark's original sites in Queens across Roosevelt Avenue to another. Reenacting a version of Matta-Clark's own chalk tracing of several property lines as seen on Davidovich's video, Mandle's shoes retraced temporary traffic lines that marked each group's renewed discovery of the sites and the connections they made between the two spaces as well as between the two artists and their intertwined projects. The passage of bodies to and from these sites reactivated both past and present spatial demarcations in relation to the movement and presence of another set of users, inhabitants, viewers, and makers who were granted new access. In addition to Mandle's project, the *Odd Lots* exhibition also offered a small number of bus tours to several of the properties in Queens. The tours were led by Matta-Clark's friend Jaime Davidovich, participating artists Jimbo Blachly and Mark Dion, as well as curator Nato Thompson, who directed attention to examples of everyday resistance to fixed spatial norms.

FIGURE 2.6. *Odd Lots: Revisiting Gordon Matta-Clark's Fake Estates.* Courtesy of White Columns Gallery.

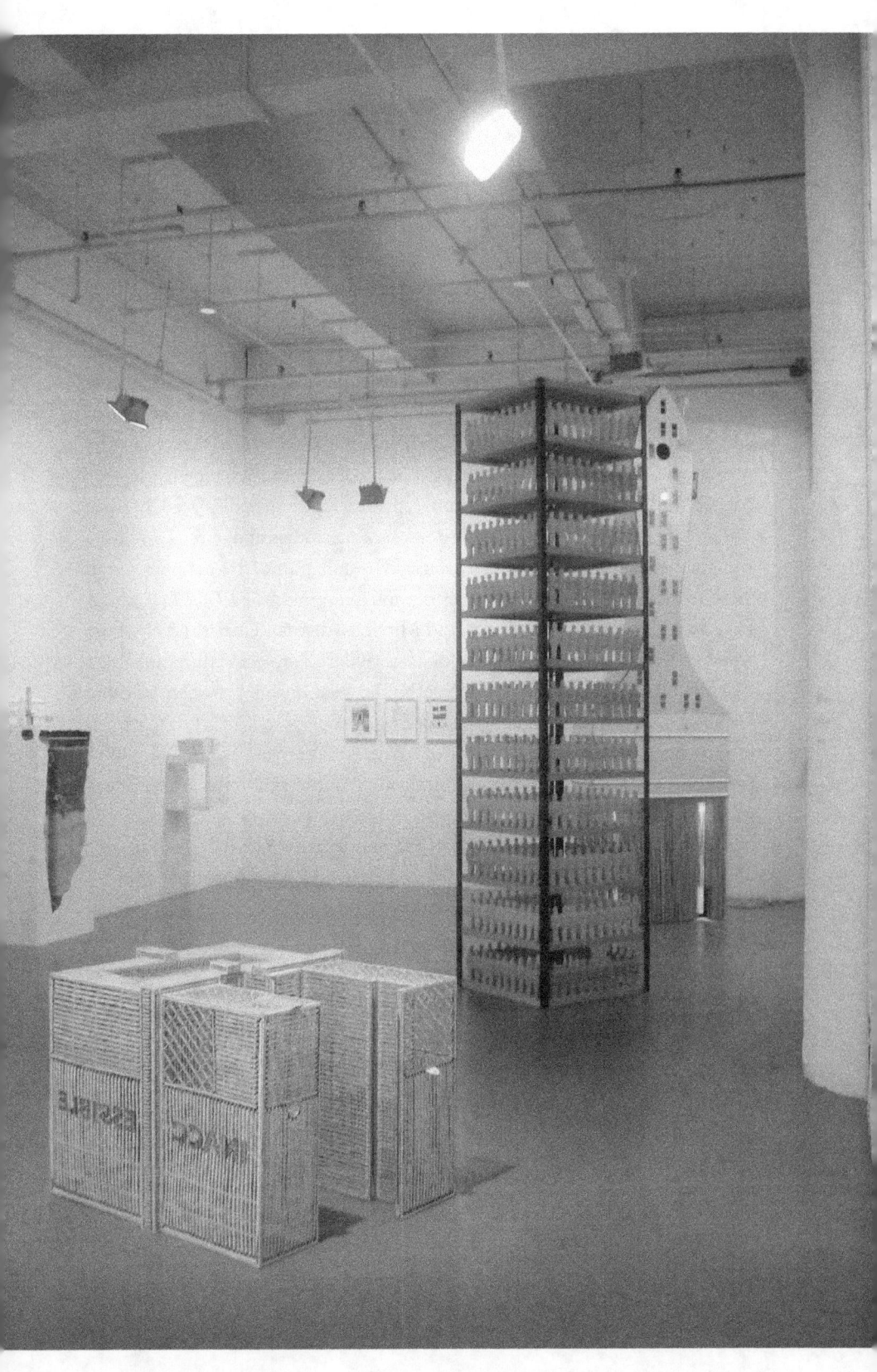

Also tracing the ways in which bodies come upon and ultimately belong within spaces, the artist Lisa Sigal was inspired by Jorge Luis Borge's infamous narrative that describes a map of an empire drawn to scale. Sigal decided to map a single Matta-Clark property, point by point, on the gallery floor. She chose the central courtyard of a building because its size could fit inside the gallery. Initially closed off to pedestrians in its urban form, the sliver space was redrawn in the gallery and resited as accessible. Sigal's replotting also remade Matta-Clark's initial work as accessible to herself, another artist, and to a new set of viewers. Matta-Clark's and Sigal's site thus becomes jointly repossessed and reowned, suggesting a new opening to spatial belonging expanded through embodied interactions replaced, rather than displaced, in time.

The siting of space as a process linking bodies and sites across time was further specified as a social transaction and framed by temporary and localized community formations in the following pieces by *Odd Lots* artists Jane South, Sarah Oppenheimer, and Mierle Laderman Ukeles, all of whose work responded to the replacement of Matta-Clark's project within the White Column gallery space. For Jane South, the relationship between working within studio or gallery spaces and working outside with property sites urged her to consider a similar allotment of "gallery real estate" negotiated within the group show. As each artist's work divided up the exhibition space, South waited to use the leftover spaces, or the gutter-spaces, of the gallery. Her own work, depicting a layout of the gallery marked with each artist's site, engaged with the relationship between neighboring artworks, akin to objects of property, taking as its subject the social and spatial networks momentarily formed by and negotiated through the group nature of the exhibition.

Working transactions that place and replace specific bodies in specific sites were also the subject and material foundation of Sarah Oppenheimer's contribution. Before the exhibition opening date, Oppenheimer contracted Stettner Construction Company to remove sheetrock from the studs on a gallery wall and to reinstall the same sheetrock on the same studs five times. As Oppenheimer stated, the contract and the finished wall, both of which comprise her exhibited artwork, demonstrated that "the form of property results from social transaction."[38] The company's workers, who would remain anonymous to future gallery visitors, were not to use any new sheetrock or other materials during the repeated un- and reinstallation ongoing from August 13, 2005 until September 7, 2005. For their work, Stettner Construction received one thousand dollars from *Cabinet* magazine. The invisible labor involved in sheetrocking one wall again and again was imparted a legibility, if not a visibility, in Oppenheimer's project, suggesting that processes of replacement must acknowledge the specific material residues of past use as well as the social interactions and exchanges that must occur for that work to continue.

The specifically embodied and ongoing work needed to maintain the relationship between the gallery and the environment in and around Matta-Clark's sites formed the basis of Mierle Laderman Ukeles's piece titled "Queens Cookies/Sweet Splits." Prior to the exhibition opening, Ukeles located several bakeries closest to several of Matta-Clark's lots and invited local bakers to use their favorite recipes to make a cookie based on the nearby lot's shape. Along with the cookies, the bakers' sheets showing the holes after the shapes had been removed were exhibited in a bakery store counter housed at the gallery. The cookies were for sale to viewers, with the money earned going toward the baking of more (Figure 2.7).

Ukeles's process connected spatially with Matta-Clark's actual sites through an extended network of new artists, workers, viewers, and buyers linked through consumption and demand. Her project also continually and visibly used up the material bases of such connections and then enacted the subsequent socioeconomic transactions required to keep the process going. While Matta-Clark's practice reused sites that were rendered useless to the buying and selling process, to be discarded like the remnants of a cookie sheet, Ukeles's project in turn reembodied the labor necessary to keep the processes of remaking, transacting, and reusing ongoing. In choosing to pair the act of baking, a skill traditionally aligned with women and homemakers, with Matta-Clark's involvement in the property market, Ukeles also importantly called attention to the invisibility of certain modes of work conventionally gendered as feminine. In addition to reversing that invisibility, her artwork

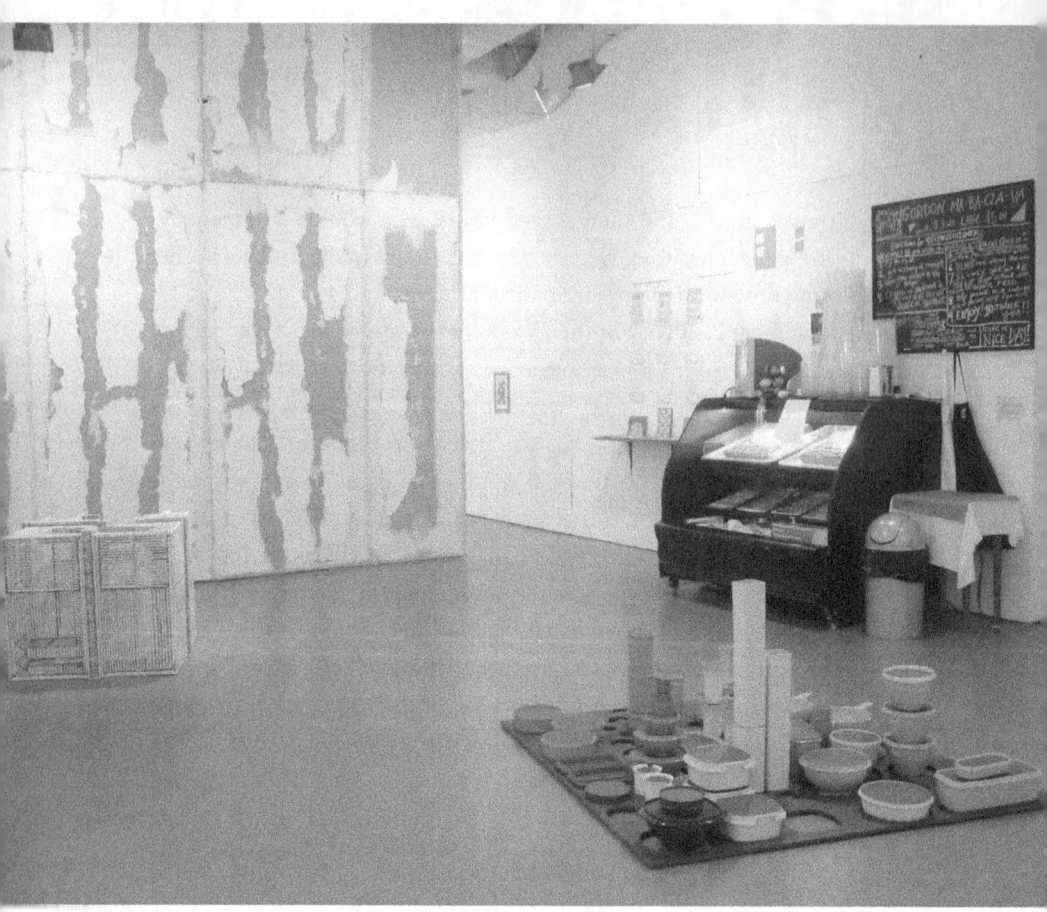

FIGURE 2.7. *Odd Lots: Revisiting Gordon Matta-Clark's Fake Estates.* Courtesy of White Columns Gallery.

overtly claimed its dependence on a local community, its bakeries acting as spatial centers for gathering and its neighborhood recipes revalued as knowledge. Such embodied dependencies, and in turn the spatial determinations they make legible, replace the economic cycle of use and discard by revisiting as well as revising how, why, and who might reuse certain material residues, structures, and systems.

This is where Gordon Matta-Clark's *Fake Estates* comes to an end, for now at least. When viewed as a whole project—however spatially and temporally dispersed, and continually transformed and expanded—all of its imagined and actualized instantiations can be read as a kind of score that activates ownership, situation, and belonging across the various artistic materials and practices enlisted, as well as in terms of the different hands, feet, eyes, and minds that were engaged over time. And while we cannot qualify the intended expectation of these explorations as bringing us closer to a redefinition of home, we can, however, translate the blueprint of these material and phenomenal exchanges into a proposal for a different kind of experience of finding and being at home—one that opens up an owner-oriented and place-bound sense of belonging toward a socially engaged program of replacing home.

Three

IN AND OUT OF PLACE MODULAR
ARCHITECTURE AND REINTEGRATION

A steel pod, able to fit one or two people at most, serves as an isolation tank that can be situated anywhere or hitched to a vehicle and transported from site to site. Inside, owners have personalized the tiny spaces of Andrea Zittel's 1996 *Escape Vehicles* to accommodate their specific needs within a compressed and flexible personal living space. Clients could also opt for a *Deserted Island*, a single-occupancy fiberglass mound that floats above water, its white rocky surface tethered to an anchor but removed from everything and everyone. Alternatively for those others wishing to combine aspects of both escapist and integrated living, Zittel's 2001 *Cellular Compartment Units*, with their small spaces each designated for distinct functions, allow users to transform one room into a multispace habitat. These designs form a part of an ongoing series of *Living Units*, begun in 1992 as compact living systems with built-in dining, washing, and sleeping structures. Zittel's art and design practice, A–Z Administrative Services, specializes in custom-building these kinds of individual modules, made of lightweight plywood panels and steel frames that fold in and out like sides of a box for compact transportation, and that economize space while also affording maximum variation (Figure 3.1).

Structurally similar to Zittel's individualized compartments is Lot-ek's redesign of the shipping container. The architectural duo Ada Tolla and Giuseppe Lignano are invested in the reuse of modern industrial by-products

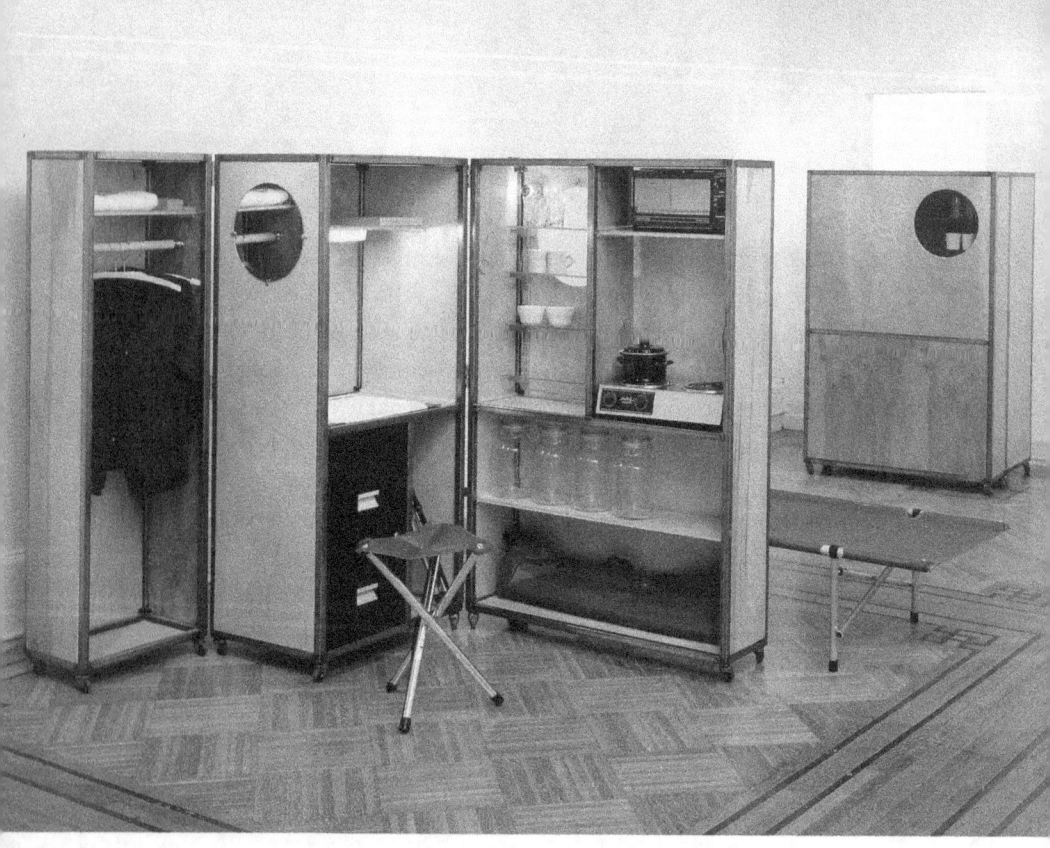

FIGURE 3.1. Andrea Zittel, *A to Z Living Unit*, 1993. Steel, wood, and objects; 60 x 40 x 30 inches (152.4 x 101.6 x 76.2 cm). Courtesy of Andrea Rosen Gallery, New York.

and practices, aiming to reconfigure and transform already available spatial forms so as to integrate those individual structures into already existing and ongoing modes of passage. Their 2003 *Mobile Dwelling Unit* (MDU) simultaneously resurrects the container as a personal dwelling space and engages with its industrial infrastructure in order to propose a global, nomadic habitation system (Figure 3.2). The units can be shipped around the world along

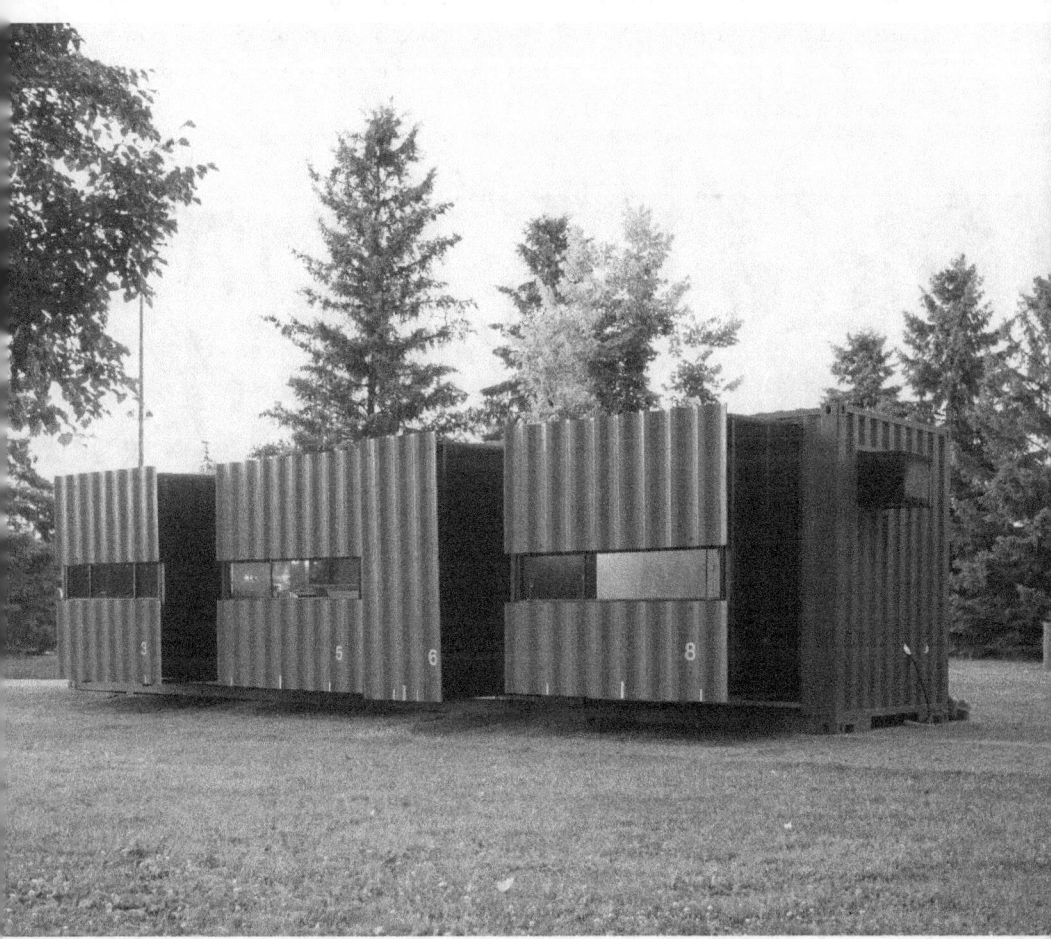

FIGURE 3.2. Lot-ek, *Mobile Dwelling Unit*. Courtesy of Ada Tolla and Giuseppe Lignano.

maritime pathways, meeting their inhabitant at their next destination, already full of their belongings. Cuts in the metal wall of each container allow smaller spaces that are pushed in for transportation to fully extend upon the MDU's momentary situation, allowing all work and living spaces to become functionally accessible by the inhabitant upon demand (Figure 3.3). Once it reaches its destination, the MDU can be loaded into preestablished, open frameworks. Located at maritime ports, these multilevel steel grids afford both horizontal and vertical loading of MDUs in order to temporarily build and then easily dismantle apartment-like tower blocks. Connective corridors contain power, water, and sewage systems, as well as stairs and elevators that allow passage between the units (Figure 3.4).

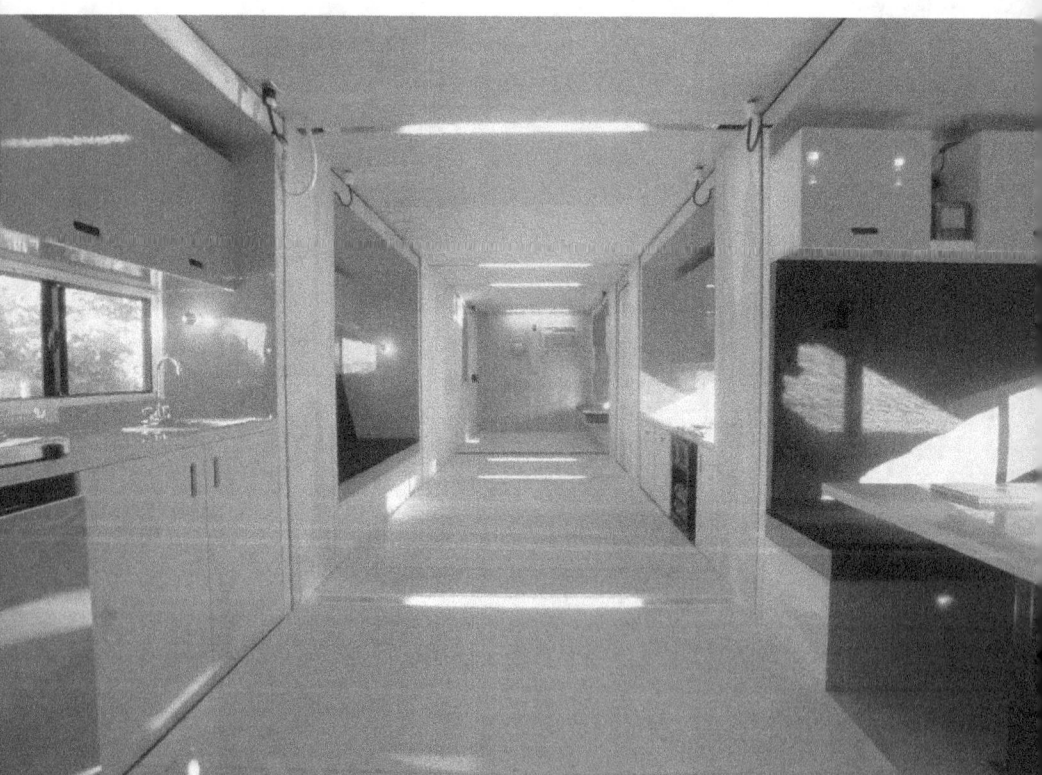

FIGURE 3.3. Lot-ek, *Mobile Dwelling Unit*. Courtesy of Ada Tolla and Giuseppe Lignano.

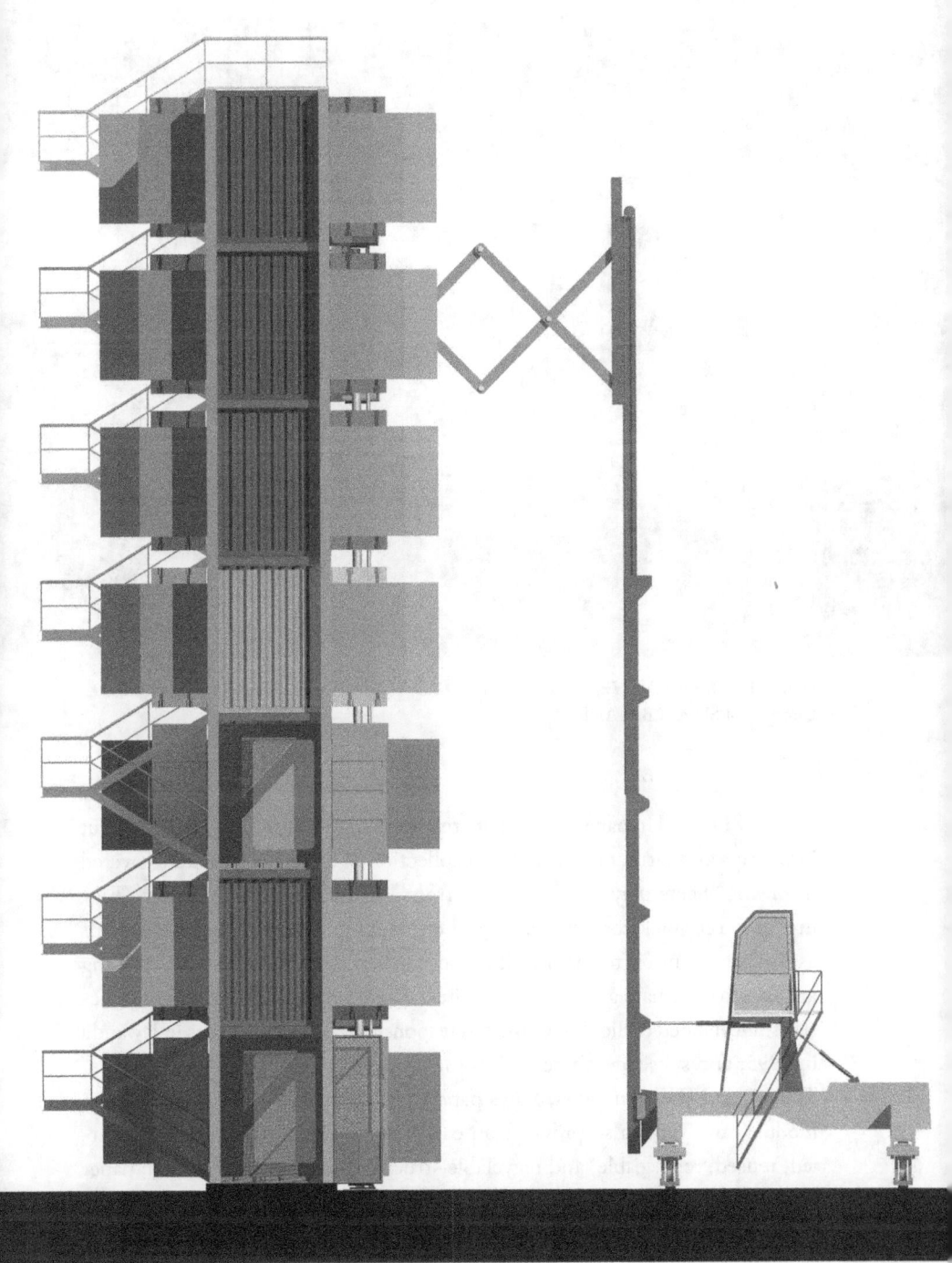

FIGURE 3.4. Lot-ek, *Mobile Dwelling Unit*. Courtesy of Ada Tolla and Giuseppe Lignano.

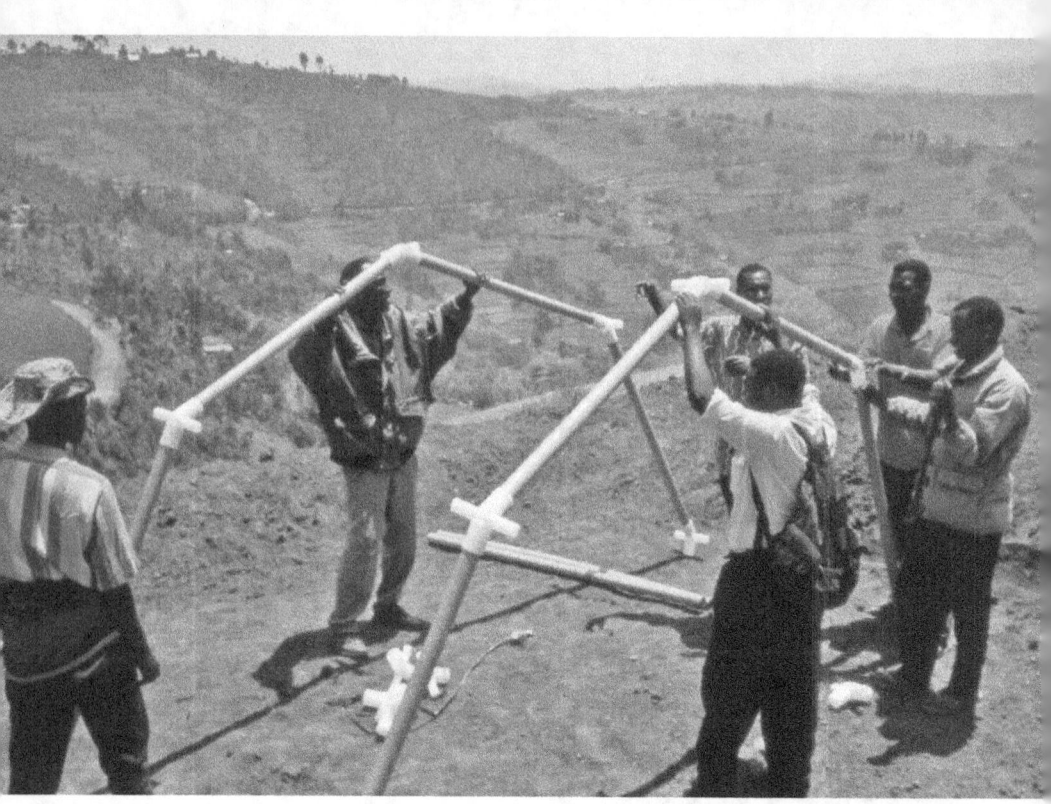

FIGURE 3.5. Shigeru Ban, *Paper Emergency Shelter,* Byumba Refugee Camp, Rwanda, 1995–99. Courtesy of Shigeru Ban Architects.

Framed in paper tubes that are made out of rolls of recycled paper cut into strips and saturated with glue, a collection of emergency shelters covered in plastic sheets may seem a far cry from Lot-ek's structural system (Figure 3.5). Yet quick construction based on reusable forms and given materials as well as attention to mobile situation and temporary community building are also the ultimate goals of the architect Shigeru Ban's paper tube constructions. Developed earlier but refined in response to the refugee crisis in Rwanda in 1995, and subsequently reused in the earthquake-stricken zones of Japan, Turkey, and Western India, Ban's paper tube is the most basic construction module, and yet it also provides an easily and inexpensively produced, varied, reused, replaceable, and recyclable structural foundation. As such, paper tubes pose an immediately flexible, environmentally viable response to the necessary housing demands of those in flight, as they are forced to make and remake temporary sites of grounding. Like Zittel's attention to individualism in combination with standardization, the ease with which the shelters can be constructed allows those in possession of these materials to build, extend, detach, connect, and vary their own temporary living spaces. And like Lot-ek's emphasis on existing structures and coordinated pathways, the sustainability of a modular response system structured on these paper tubes is based on its ability to fit into already existing infrastructures of emergency relief, while also addressing present problems and revising material conditions accordingly.

While the previous chapter proposes an opening for a socially engaged program of replacing home through a loosening of entangled ownership and belonging, this chapter—and the ones following—asks what that program might look like and how it could function or indeed fail. I am suggesting that the above structures and practices, while by no means acting as the only examples, map the limits of a territory within which such a program can be activated. Combining functional aspects of unitary detachment and integrated synthesis, modular architecture considers the situated connection of component parts and their means of coming together alongside the independent mobility of disconnected individual containers and their possibility of reconnecting. With return, renewal, revisitation, and reuse in mind, such structures can be reintegrated into already active nomadic systems present within each specific spatial landscape, however industrially or technologically dispersed. As units are attached to and detached from each other and from larger situated frameworks, to be embodied and reembodied over time, the pathways of dwellers in turn determine the plan and construction of modular habitations. So the autonomy of individual parts and the dependencies between them together support ongoing processes of both structural and phenomenal reintegration, through which temporary, contingent, and unexpected social organizations may coalesce, to be replaced over time.

Informing modular architecture's capacity to offer momentary spatial situation, reintegration and replacement together operate through the renewal of established materials across growing global pathways, as well as through the resituation of structures that disconnect and reconnect on each specific site, allowing for both ongoing mobility and temporary grounding. My argument here is that modular structures become viably inhabitable if they are able to engage with preestablished spatial frameworks and social systems, intervening from within such familiar models in order to propose new structures and programs that continually vacillate between stasis and mobility, individual autonomy and social coherence. As bodies, and the individual structures they inhabit, move toward and away from each other, returning to and reforming social networks, modular architecture's challenge is therefore to sustain portability while affording the momentary pause that can be reintegrated and replaced over time within different sites. Whether responding to or anticipating a dispersed spatial experience that is either chosen or forced, modular architecture keeps its inhabitants moving out of place, while also allowing them to pause in place and with others.

DETACH AND INTEGRATE

"The best way that I can define it," Andrea Zittel explains, noting the common thread between her art practice and her life, "is by saying that I am always looking for the gray area between freedom (which can sometimes feel too open-ended and vast) and security (which may easily turn into confinement). I am fascinated by the way a quality which initially appears to be liberating can suddenly turn out to be confining, and vice versa."[1] For Zittel, individual autonomy is implicitly linked to structured standardization—one not possible without the other. Her A–Z Administrative Services, founded in 1991, provides clients with programmed constructions for using and inhabiting space. Her series of *Living Units*, for example, manages and maintains specific functions related to eating, sleeping, socializing, and resting and can be personalized according to individual needs (Figure 3.6). Surfaces, walls, tables, shelves, pillows, mattresses, mirrors, stovetops, toilets, and more fold in and out, appear and contract, transform and stabilize—all within the confines of a small wooden box that can fold up into a trunk. The units can be then transported as a whole living space but also are small enough to be situated inside a room in one's home or workplace in order to organize, coordinate, and expand its functional uses. To be at home, Zittel's projects suggest, is to be given a set of parameters that are standardized and familiar on the one hand, and flexible and variable on the other, so that being in place mediates between autonomy

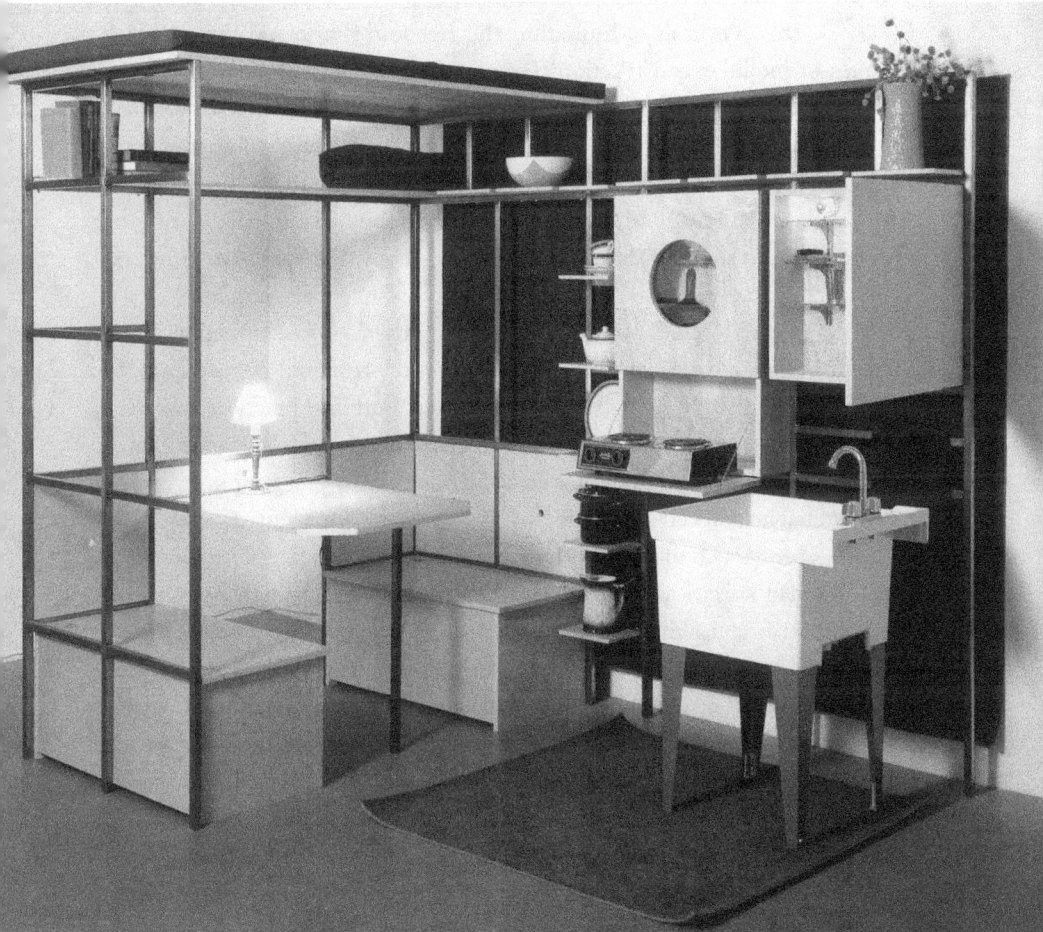

FIGURE 3.6. Andrea Zittel, *A to Z Management and Maintenance Unit: Model 003*, 1992. Steel, wood, carpet, plastic sink, glass, mirror; 86 x 94 x 68 inches (218.4 x 238.8 x 172.7 cm). Courtesy of Andrea Rosen Gallery, New York.

and integration. Zittel's work suggests that both independence and a sense of belonging to a larger whole are necessary as each imbricates the other. "What makes us feel liberated is not total freedom, but rather living in a set of limitations that we have created and prescribed for ourselves," she has remarked.[2] In Zittel's designs, compressed spatial volume is optimized through streamlined organization, so that spatial limitations can be transformed into specified systems for individually efficient habitation.

This synthesis of limitation and freedom is afforded through techniques of modular construction that are coordinated with design variables personalized for each client. The term *modular* now refers most broadly to the standardized, usually factory mass-produced, structural components that systematically come together to form a built and unified whole. Based on standardized dimensions linking spatial plan and embodied use, modularity thus proposes a systematic framework to connect body and spatial environment that can activate temporary and flexible models of inhabiting space as well as economically efficient means of producing them. Often linked with prefabrication, or the off-site factory production of structural components that are delivered and assembled on site, modular building practices materially initiate a cycle of structural connection, disconnection, and reconnection, as bodies are able to negotiate their spatial dispersion by plugging in to and out of interchangeable and adaptable variations of situated infrastructures.[3]

Modular building, as theorized by modern architect Le Corbusier, was founded specifically on the measurements of the human body and its standardized replicability. At the outbreak of World War II, when his studio was forced to close, Le Corbusier turned his attention to proportional measurements utilized in architectural planning and design. Looking to ancient Egyptian and Greek methods of elaborating measurements according to dimensions of the body, Le Corbusier aimed to reinstate the body as the central modern planning device. In his theoretical treatise *The Modulor,* translated into English in 1954, Le Corbusier repudiated the conventional meter and inch as distanced from architecture's objective of providing "containers of man or extensions of man."[4] Instead, he mathematically developed a grid system, based on a human figure with an arm raised and expanded fully through the figure's occupation of space either seated or standing, that could be used in the design and organization of both interior spaces and exterior facades. Newly afforded through industrialization, standardized component parts scaled and ordered according to a universal human body could, Le Corbusier argued, "unite, harmonize, mutually adapt the work of men which is now in a state of disunity."[5] If modern material and technological advancements offered a multitude of new design and construction possibilities, Le Corbusier's measurement system proposed an ordered way to build habitable structures whose form was intimately applicable to its function of housing the body.[6]

The prominence of the body in the standardization of organically cohesive building units determines how structural interchangeability, adaptability, and exponential replicability together generate the design and construction of modular buildings. Indeed, modularity enacts a system in which parts expand and contract, and in which phenomenal mobility interpreted structurally into an organically emergent built form guides interchangeable units into and out of larger situated frameworks. This flexible and cost-effective system, which relates component parts to a structural whole, not only efficiently generates mass-produced housing that is able to respond to variable user demand and function, but it also can structurally anticipate the mobility of individual inhabitants across different sites as they remake spatial and social environments over time.

We must then consider both bodily dimensions and the flow of multiple bodies as they together influence modular architecture's mobile operations, introducing fluidity, permeability, and temporality into the plan and program of built structures. In fact, it was modern architect Frank Lloyd Wright who first conceived of an "organic architecture" that was based on the experience of the body in motion.[7] As modern industrial developments and economic interests threatened to impose a mechanical circulation within and through built structures, Wright determined a new concept of inhabiting space that would allow for greater individuality and freedom of movement alongside modernity's material advancements. In order to move beyond the constraining order of architectural and urban-planning mechanization that Wright called "Centralization," he proposed instead an architecture of "democracy" that would subordinate mass economic concerns to the concerns of the individual human being.[8] Wright's concept did not aim to return to a premodern spatial experience of the built environment but instead sought to integrate modern materials and industrial developments with an emphasis on individual mobility.

Individual mobility, as Andrea Zittel's projects propose, points toward an ideal conception of separation and distinction from others, and a release from social mores and restrictions. Taken to its extreme, it means living off the so-called grid, under one's own terms alone—an ultimate narrative of freedom prevalent in the United States since settlers began imagining the open frontier. After working on more conventional trailer units, Zittel began exploring modular architecture's capacity to support individual disconnection, creating her series of *Escape Vehicles* in 1996 (Figure 3.7). Paola Morsiani, curator of Zittel's 2005 retrospective at the Houston Museum of Art and the Museum of Contemporary Art, Los Angeles, describes these units as fulfilling "the role of fantasy in the notion of a home disconnected from the fabric of the city and yet fully participant in it."[9] Fantasy runs rampant, of course, because inhabitants can choose when, where, and how to isolate themselves, and when they wish to return. So autonomy and integration are dually afforded through these aluminum pod-like structures that are stationary when in use, giving the occupant the option of social contact. But they are also supplied with operable wheels for semi- or completely isolated mobility.

Offering another fantasy of escape without the material realities of sustained or forced social isolation is Zittel's *Deserted Islands,* created around the same time as the *Escape Vehicles* (Figure 3.8). Whereas composite parts typically come together to form larger modular structures or community housing projects, Zittel's individual islands transform the component itself into a whole unit that remains disconnected and unplugged from its situated docking site. In Zittel's words, the transportable escape unit is a "100-cubic-foot refuge from public interaction."[10] Again, refuge here is chosen and social reintegration is

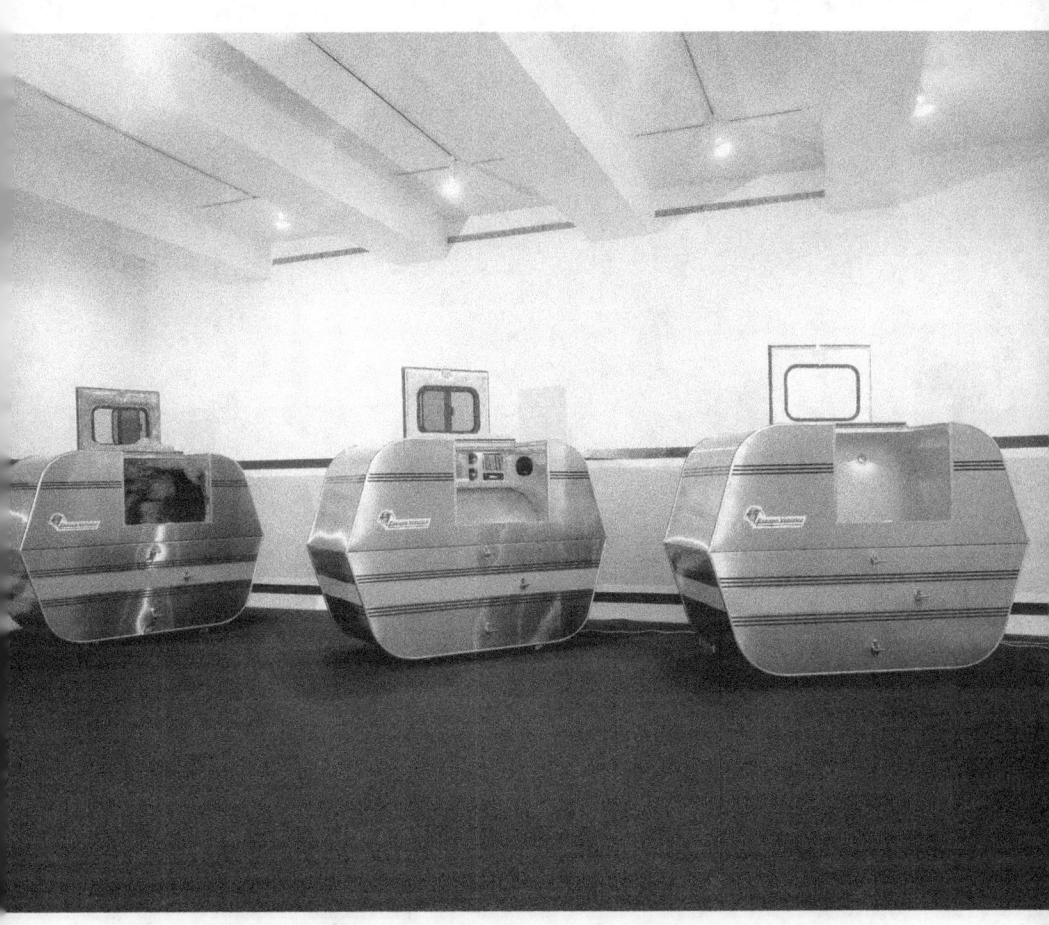

FIGURE 3.7. Andrea Zittel, *A–Z Escape Vehicles*. Shell: steel, insulation, wood, glass; 62 x 40 x 84 inches. Installation view: Andrea Rosen Gallery, New York, 1996. Courtesy of Andrea Rosen Gallery, New York.

always an option. Yet what is most important to recognize is Zittel's acknowledgment of the simultaneous impulses to individualize and cohere, detach and reconnect—impulses that we must also understand as the privilege to get away and to come back, but that can be supported architecturally in many different scenarios through modular flexibility.

Like Wright's concept of spatial and structural democracy, Zittel's projects emphasize personal choice and the security of one's own uniquely contained space. Indeed, Wright himself located the center of democracy and

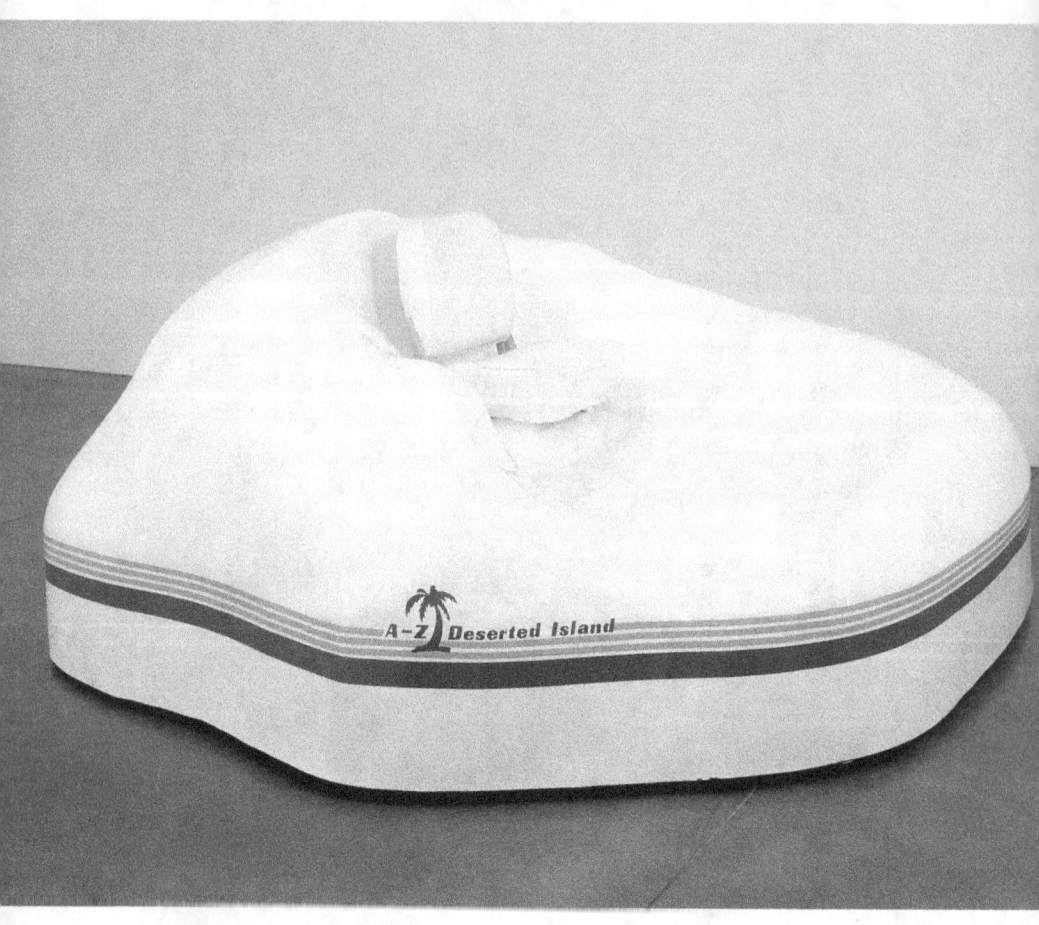

FIGURE 3.8. Andrea Zittel, *A–Z Deserted Island,* 1997. Fiberglass, wood, plastic, flotation tank, vinyl seat, vinyl logo; 36 x 90 x 90 inches (91.4 x 228.6 x 228.6 cm). Courtesy of Andrea Rosen Gallery, New York.

the focus of organic architecture in the individual home. Although concerned with the plan of the modern city center, Wright's architectural democracy rested on the individual structure's ability to negotiate both its surrounding environment and the ongoing flow of inhabitants and urban traffic through and around it. Embedded in the landscape and yet replete with personal choices, the home encompasses the unifying impulses of spatial as well as social integration along with the degrees of differentiation on which democracy must be based. Indeed, differentiation occurs because of and through the possibility of integration and is, according to Wright, the basis for a modern and democratic spatial experience. Wright's concept of organicism, which is the foundation for his concept of architectural democracy, mediates between individual mobility and integrated standardization, both initially established through the body's relationship to a changing spatial environment.

As both Zittel and Wright make clear, the ways in which autonomy and synthesis function alongside each other remain a challenge for modular practices, and the process of coordination between the two is often imagined as either mechanical or organic, or some combination of the two. We can expand on Wright's mechanical analogies of flow and integration by turning to the Metabolists, a Japanese architectural collective formed in 1960, who remain central to the development of architectural modularity, as well as to the experimentations in structural dematerialization and spatial networking developed by Western architectural collectives such as Archigram and Super-studio, as we will see in chapter 5. The Metabolists conceptualize spatial organization and use as a biological process involving the constant regeneration and destruction of organic tissue. Metabolism emphasizes an ongoing variation of a whole structure, in which an individual unit is renewed and replaced, detached and reintegrated, rather than used and discarded, as prevalent in a consumer society. Instead, writes Kisho Kurokawa, one of the Metabolists' founders, "if spaces were composed on the basis of the theory of the metabolic cycle, it would be possible to replace only those parts that had lost their usefulness and in this way to contribute to the conservation of resources by using buildings longer."[11]

Taking Wright's organic concept of individualization and integration alongside Kurokawa's metabolic system of renewal and reintegration as a historical backdrop to Zittel's practice, I want to suggest that her projects challenge us to consider the relation between detachment and coherence, and the potential to be spatially situated in either case. While modular component parts are primarily designed to fit organically within a larger structural framework, Zittel's self-enclosed, spatially compact container units offer alternative modes of disconnection. But we must also recognize that the potential for disconnection is offered while bracketing out the return to phenomenal re-connection and spatial resituation, and *bracketing* does not mean erasing, just temporarily suspending (Figure 3.9).

Looking to the Metabolists, we cannot help but structurally align Zittel's *Cellular Compartment Units* with Kurokawa's standardized and meta-bolically replaceable module of choice, the capsule (Figure 3.10).[12] Each allotted a specific function, these capsules, like Zittel's compartments, come together

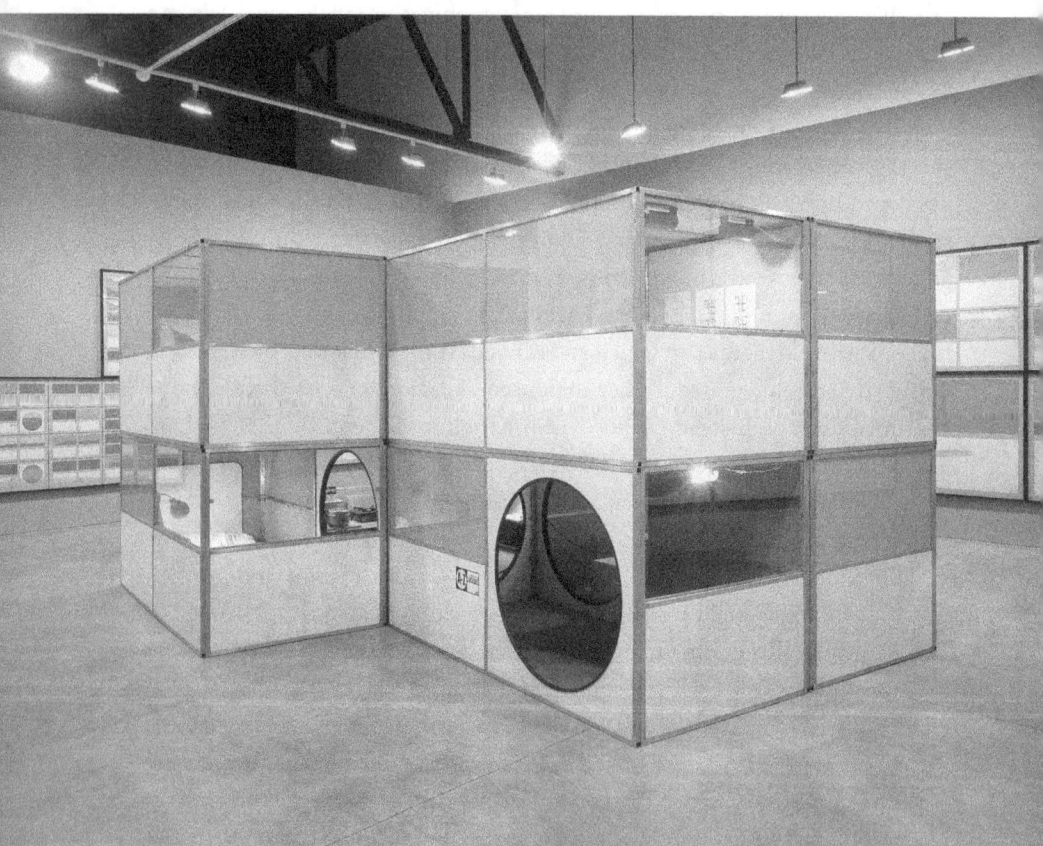

FIGURE 3.9. Andrea Zittel, *A–Z Cellular Compartment Units,* 2001. Stainless steel, birch ply-wood, glass, and household objects; overall: 96 x 144 x 192 inches (243.8 x 365.8 x 487.7 cm), each of ten units: 48 x 48 x 96 inches (121.9 x 121.9 x 243.8 cm). Courtesy of Andrea Rosen Gallery, New York.

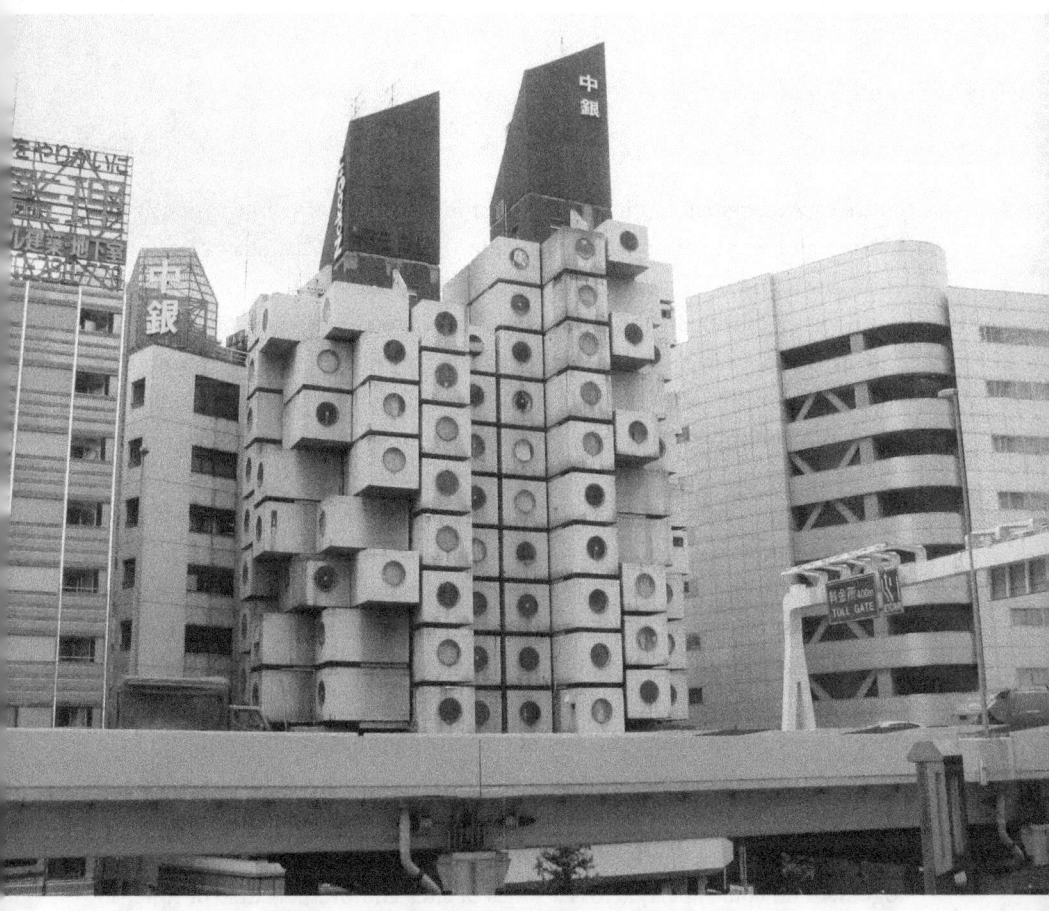

FIGURE 3.10. Kisho Kurokawa, *Nagakin Capsule Tower*. Shimbashi, Tokyo, Japan.

to afford part-time dwellers individually functional spaces adaptable to their own temporal patterns of aggregation and disaggregation. Thus Kurokawa's capsules also attend to the flexible formation of communities, however accidental or contingent, that occurs amid the principles of detachment and reattachment. Proposing a concept that marks an implicit foundation to Zittel's practice, Kurokawa reimagines a "time-community" that is not bound to one fixed location but is primarily determined through embodied activities performed over different courses of time.[13] So as community is redetermined according to the passages and pauses, departures and returns of dwellers, the entire capsule system has its own kind of movement, with units variously inhabited and empty at any given moment. Although in Kurokawa's case the entire structure is situated, the relation between unit and system suggests a morphology of reemergence and reintegration, as inhabitants come together and apart separately and create groupings that are housed in an outwardly unchanging, conglomerate structure.[14] While Zittel's pods and units emphasize internal specifications that personalize spaces of being and belonging, nonetheless they must be understood to operate both in the face of and because of the potential to reconnect socially and spatially—reconnections that Zittel's structures specify as tentative and precarious.

Initiating a system that enables detachment and integration quickly and continuously across different sites, modular building practices must consider the relation of movable, uniform parts to a variably situated and often temporary whole. As nomadic architectural structures attend to the individualized mobility of their inhabitants and the continuous reframing of their relation to variable community and spatial formations, the means by which such mobility is materially afforded correlates structurally with phenomenal experiences of return, renewal, reuse, and replacement. For as bodies come together and come apart, across a series of sites and over a course of time, so too do the modular components of nomadic habitations. Keying in to an ideal concept of social and spatial detachment, where one can choose to just get away from modern urban chaos, Zittel's mobile constructions not only materialize escapist fantasies but they also serve to remind us that if individual persons and units can come together, then they also can come apart, establishing the whole modular structure as only vulnerably integrated and temporarily unified.

DETACH AND REINTEGRATE

If we accept our fleeting spatial situations, at times welcoming our detachments while at others bracing ourselves against our dispersions, then what kind of spatial and social integration can we experience, and how? For Lot-ek's Ada

Tolla and Giuseppe Lignano, detachable modular structures must explicitly engage with, and not escape from, modern spatial experiences of dislocation and temporary situation. Named in opposition to the high-tech operations that continuously discard and upgrade their materials, and instead invested in the rehabilitation of modern industrial and technological by-products, Lot-ek reuses structural frameworks and reintegrates them back into already functioning modes of passage. "That is the world we take from, the world we import into our architecture," Ada Tolla affirms. "The interaction of the human body with that world is something that we started investigating from the beginning. It comes from playing with these objects that are not designed by us, but that are sort of given."[15] Lot-ek's emphasis on the given suggests not only an environmentally responsible mode of being and building in the world and an acknowledgment of our implicit embedment within nomadic infrastructures. It also recognizes all the ways in which we can intervene from within those systems of mobility to reintegrate spatial situation within moments and structures of dwelling.

Lot-ek's given form is the shipping container. First introduced in the 1950s and measuring twenty feet long by eight feet wide by eight feet tall, the International Standards Organization (ISO) shipping container is a steel box that can be efficiently stacked to transport goods around the world on standard freight ships, themselves an exponentially expandable container for containers. Acknowledging the influence of these standardized units on prefabricated modular building, architectural historian Colin Davies remarks that "every major seaport of the world is fitted with the necessary gantries, saddle-carriers, and quay-cranes to lift and shift containers. Huge multi-story container megastructures, absolutely regular and temptingly architectural, are continuously constructed and deconstructed like modular cities of the future."[16] Lot-ek's *Mobile Dwelling Unit* proposes exactly this, on both sea and land, by reconfiguring the spatial container into an individualized habitation and then reintegrating it within a global transportation network. Each unit can be hypothetically shipped via established maritime pathways, along with other goods and dwelling units, following the travels of their inhabitants, and then loaded into larger structural frameworks located across various international docking sites (Figure 3.11).

By depending on as well as intervening tactically within already existing mobile networks, Lot-ek offers the conditions for continuously mobile dwelling that include temporary spatial docking and momentary community formation. Their modular and nomadic dwelling system provides a fixed, yet open, public frame in flux according to the comings and goings of individually functional private units. Here again, we have echoes of Kurokawa's spatialization of a time-based community. "Like pixels in a digital image," Lot-ek describes, "temporary patterns are generated by the presence or absence of MDUs in different locations along the rack, reflecting the ever-changing composition

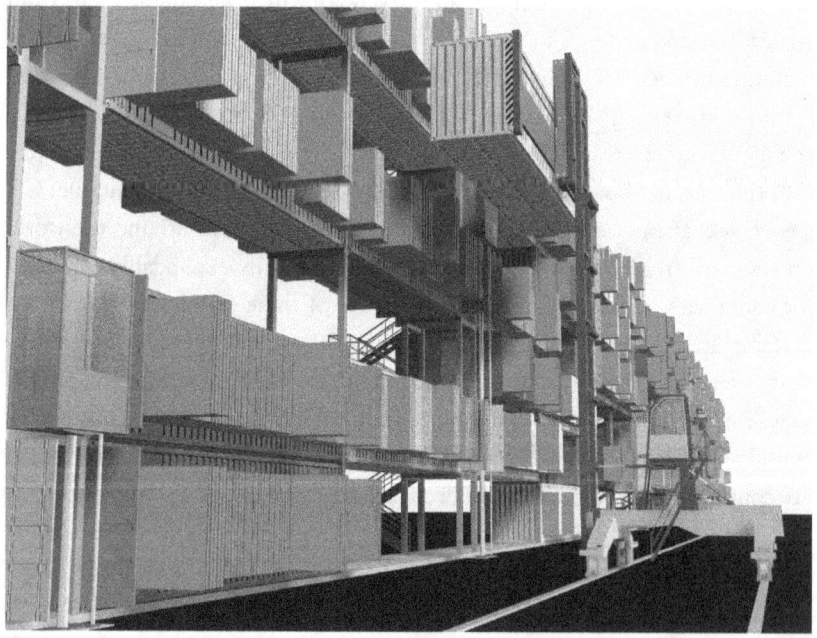

FIGURE 3.11. Lot-ek, *Mobile Dwelling Unit*. Courtesy of Ada Tolla and Giuseppe Lignano.

of these colonies scattered around the globe."[17] These larger structures are greater than each of their parts, since Lot-ek's project emphasizes the potential for community formation, temporarily unified and vulnerably whole, in the face of the flickering presence and absence of different individual habitations at any given time.

In the end, however, Lot-ek's systemic vision was not realized for functional purposes. Instead remaining a nomadically site-specific art installation, a model of the *Mobile Dwelling Unit* and its docking framework were exhibited at University of California at Santa Barbara's Art Museum in 2003 and again at the Whitney Museum in New York in 2004. "The way we see architecture," Lot-ek partner Giuseppe Lignano explains, "is as a giant installation."[18] Working across both art and architecture, Lot-ek negotiates creative imaginings with practical necessities, whether dealing with the materials, structuring, or legalities of either installation art or commercial projects. In fact, their association with art galleries affords Lot-ek a testing ground from which certain key concepts are recycled and reinterpreted into the design and building of fully habitable structures. For example, their *Container Home Kit* (CHK), first exhibited at Syracuse University in New York in 2005, is now on the commercial market and can be custom ordered. Without engaging continuously with an existing nomadic pathway, CHK reuses the ISO shipping container, with easily expandable, modular, open-plan units ready for shipping and on-site assembly. Although situated and thus not capable of activating the installation's proposed nomadic system, the *Container Home Kit* nonetheless returns to the *Mobile Dwelling Unit*'s material foundation, engaging commercially with the MDU's reliance on by-products from the existing industrial infrastructure.

Material and structural reintegration, as well as systemic dependence, therefore provide the basis for the connection and reconnection of component parts, individual units, and larger communities, all of which come together and apart in response to bodies in motion. Modular structures are individually nomadic, as well as dependent both on each other and on established modes of mobility; they are thus flexible to structural change, to the variability of sites and the pathways of inhabitants, to the surrounding spatial environment, and to existing economic and social infrastructures. As nomadic, modular building practices are continuously reintegrating the sites, structures, and networks of an inhabitant's mobile experience of home. Dependent on the variable movements of their inhabitants along existing pathways and by extension dependent on the contingently resulting community formations, modular structures must in turn find ways to both sustain mobility while also providing temporarily grounded spatial situations, allowing inhabitants to return and replace home even as they continue to move on.

REINTEGRATE AND REPLACE

The stakes of modular building and reintegration could not have been higher, when in the spring of 1995, the Japanese architect Shigeru Ban contacted the United Nations High Commission for Refugees (UNHCR) to propose a modular system for temporary, easy-to-assemble shelter to use in Tanzania and Zaire for the more than two million Rwandans fleeing genocide in their homeland. Responding to the worldwide call for refugee shelters, Ban refigured his paper tube buildings that he had previously developed for high-end commercial designs. Attending not only to the privilege of chosen mobility, the proponents of modular architecture and their quick, standardized, and efficient response to forced dislocation systematize the interspersion of moments of grounding within ongoing movements, whether voluntary or involuntary. Yet within the context of emergency relief, modular operations affirm the spatial reintegration and replacement of social formations specifically by others for others. For once access to the existing infrastructures for being situated either in or out of place is denied, then modular practices must be rerouted beyond one's own individualized use and reimagined for another's passages and pauses. Pushing designer-client relations to an urgent extreme, social engagement and responsibility must therefore be translated into material actuality, as modularity's mediation between structural autonomy and dependence meets the need for immediate shelter and temporary community.

Ban's modular paper tube is made out of recycled paper, cut into strips, soaked with glue, and wound around a metal rod that, once released, creates a hollow core. Paper tubes are inexpensive, can be easily produced in a variety of diameters, densities, and lengths, are quickly replaceable, and can themselves be recycled, thus producing almost no material waste.[19] Although not initially chosen to respond to environmental or political crises, Ban's paper tubes first appeared in his exhibition designs.[20] Eventually in 1989, Ban experimented with his first paper tube structure, the temporary *Paper Arbor*, an outdoor pavilion for the World Design Expo held in Japan. At the end of the expo, the tubes were tested, and despite the harsh weather, their compression strength had actually increased as the internal bonding glue began to harden and as the tubes were exposed to ultraviolet light. Following two other temporary structures, in 1991 Ban built the permanent, though internally housed, *Library of a Poet*. Two years later, in 1993, paper tubes were finally authorized and legislated as a standard building material in Japan.[21]

Although Ban first developed his paper tube designs with the formal aesthetics of modernist architect Mies van der Rohe in mind, his system of modular building also has found a vastly different social reuse. For Mark Rakatansky, one avenue of Ban's architectural practice cannot be distinguished as more or less socially engaged than the other. Instead, Rakatansky argues, "what might make architecture social is that it enacts what is social in its condition, within its architecture, not just in its circumstance."[22] So it is not that paper tubing became social in the context of the Rwandan refugee crisis but, rather, that social engagement was already implicit in the formal condition of its design and implementation. Modular architecture, as I have been suggesting, carries the potential to both respond to and to anticipate individual autonomy and social formation, and to configure both as vulnerable, tentative, temporary, and capable of being reformed and replaced over time. This potential to respond and configure for oneself, as well as for others, carries within it an impetus for social reintegration that Ban explicitly revisits in the context of emergency relief.

After the UNHCR agreed to go ahead with Ban's paper tube shelters, the design and prototype construction began in 1995 at Vitra, the Swiss furniture manufacturer, where three versions were tested for durability, cost, and termite resistance. The chosen prototype was the largest of the three, which utilized three plastic sheets and thus afforded the most usable floor area. The paper tubes were connected by small plastic joiners, and additional ropes and pegs provided necessary tension. Each shelter could also be connected to others of the same type, providing variably extendable space for larger facilities such as field hospitals. In February 1997, on-site production was explored. Specialists from a paper tube manufacturer went to the Médecins sans Frontières center, another international aid organization sponsoring Ban and located in Bordeaux, France. The Médecins sans Frontières staff learned to operate the machinery so that they could take over the quick production of large quantities of tubing on site. The final phase took place in 1999, as Ban traveled to the Byumba Refugee Camp in Rwanda in order to lead and oversee the construction of fifty paper tube shelters by refugees and volunteers (Figure 3.12).[23]

Utilizing the standard four-by-six-foot plastic sheet issued to all refugees, Ban's paper tube structure also addressed the prevalent problem of local deforestation instigated as refugees cut down wood to replace the valuable aluminum poles initially provided by the UNHCR but sold by the refugees instead. Paper tubes are inexpensive, made from recycled pulp, not sought after, and thus unlikely to be sold. They could also be produced on-site, reducing transportation time and allowing dwellers to take part in the construction and individual variation of their expandable structures. By intervening in the UNHCR's already existing infrastructure while also responding to particular on-site conditions and making the appropriate adjustments, Ban integrated material operations with contextual specificities, thus offering the potential for temporary social reintegration (Figure 3.13).

While Ban was responding to the Rwandan refugee crisis, he was also working on paper tube housing for victims of the massive earthquake that struck Kobe, Japan in January 1995, leaving hundreds homeless. Ban's criteria remained similar to those outlined for his Rwandan emergency shelters:

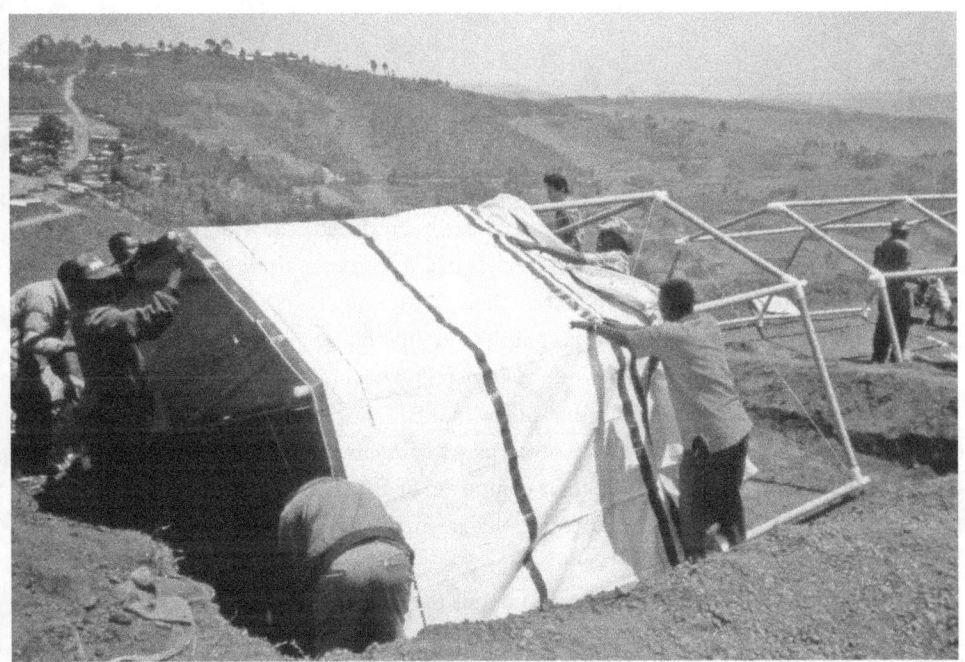

FIGURE 3.12. Shigeru Ban, *Paper Emergency Shelter,* Byumba Refugee Camp, Rwanda, 1995–99. Courtesy of Shigeru Ban Architects.

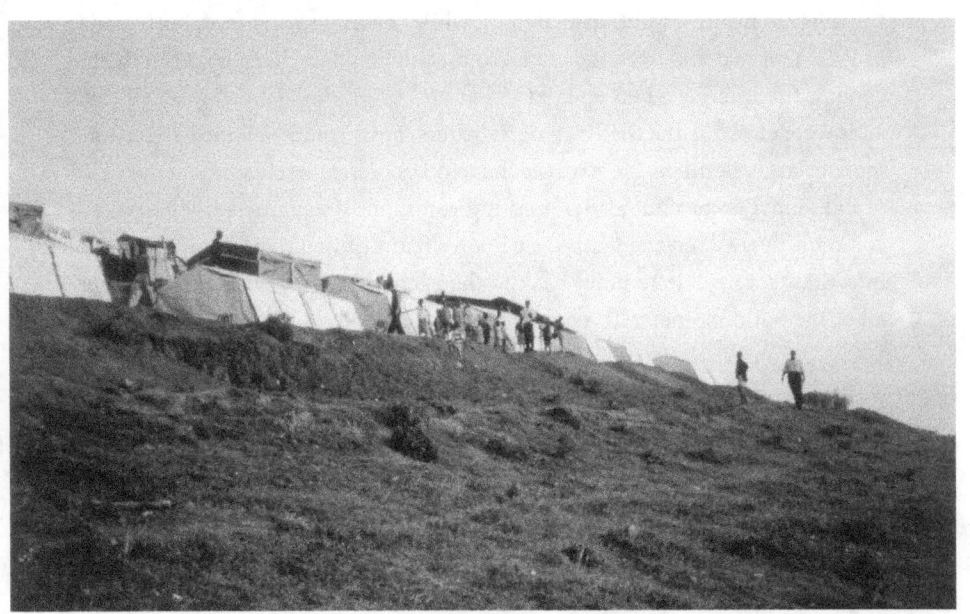

FIGURE 3.13. Shigeru Ban, *Paper Emergency Shelter,* Byumba Refugee Camp, Rwanda, 1995–99. Courtesy of Shigeru Ban Architects.

materials had to be inexpensively and easily produced, constructions had to be quickly and simply built, and models had to conform to the specific needs of the inhabitants in the context of their environment. In comparison to the shelters, these more substantial and less mobile houses were adjusted to the particular climate of Japan while also meeting a contained crisis that was far less spatially expansive than that of Rwanda.

By July 1995, twenty-seven paper tube houses were already in construction in Kobe with more to be completed by September. Built in the vicinity of the destroyed homes, the four-square-meter houses had walls made out of paper tubes and a foundation of borrowed beer crates filled with sandbags. A group of volunteers, earthquake victims themselves, constructed the houses from paper tube component parts that were partially constructed by other volunteers working on Ban's *Paper Church,* another paper tube replacement of a church that was also destroyed by the earthquake and rebuilt by Ban and community members.[24] Self-adhesive, waterproof tape was placed in between the tubes to insure a tight, insulated fit, while the ceiling and roof, both made of PVC tent material, were separated so that air could circulate between them, cooling the interior when open at either end or retaining warmth when the ends were closed. Like the Rwandan shelters, units could be joined to accommodate larger families. Here we see the reintegration and replacement not only of individual homes but also of existing community structures by those very communities. When the temporary houses had fulfilled their need, and their inhabitants were able to move back to their rebuilt permanent homes, almost all of the building materials could be recycled (Figure 3.14).

Four years later, in August 1999, another massive earthquake hit western Turkey, leaving more than twenty thousand dead and approximately two hundred thousand homeless. Ban slightly revised his Kobe paper houses to suit the different needs and climate in Turkey. Though quite similar in design, these shelters were more spacious than their Japanese counterparts due to the larger size of Turkish plywood forming the floor of the structure—a specific material adjustment that also made the finished structures able to ac-

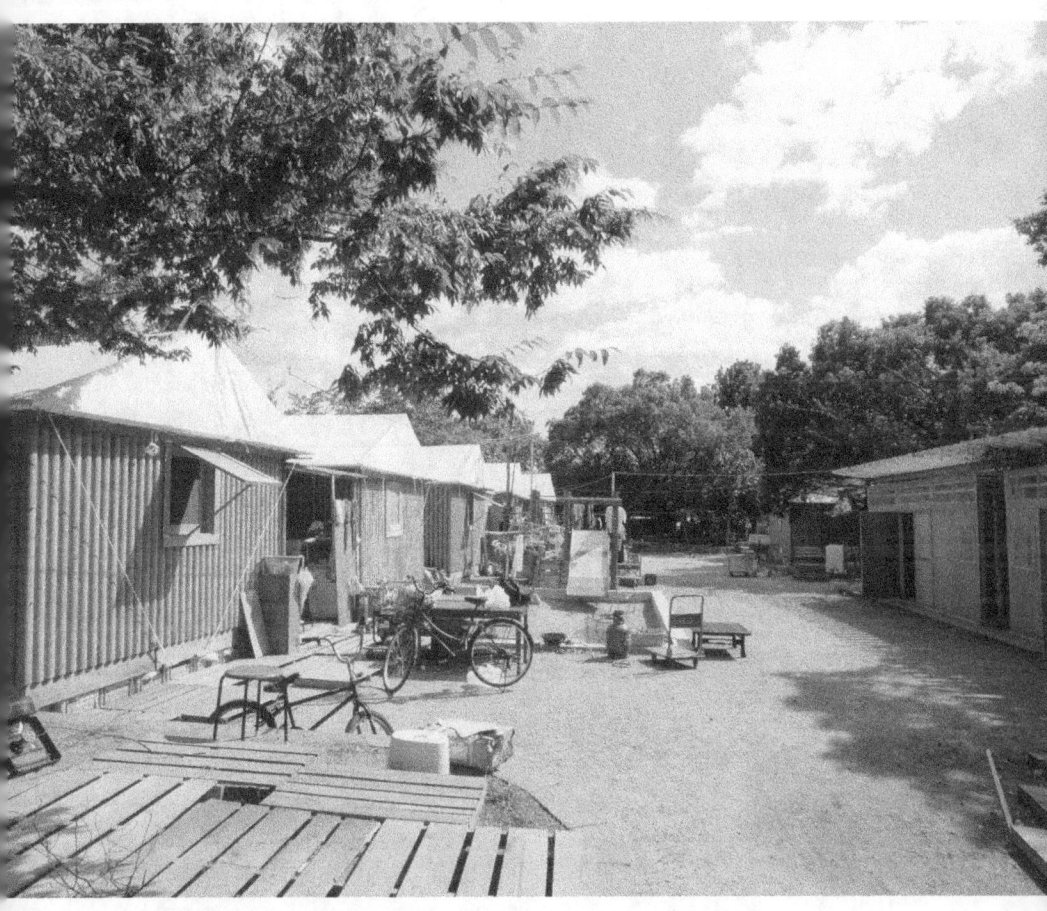

FIGURE 3.14. Shigeru Ban, *Paper Loghouse*, Nagata, Kobe, Japan, 1995. Photograph by Hiroyuki Hirai.

commodate the larger average family size. Ban also provided a higher degree of insulation, necessary for Turkey's weather changes, by inserting wastepaper, cardboard, and plastic sheets inside the paper tubes along the walls. By December 1999, seventeen temporary houses were built with the donation of beer crates and paper tubes from local Turkish companies and plastic sheets transported from Japan. Architecture students and community volunteers provided the labor, alongside the intended inhabitants, who welcomed the prospect of living beneath more than just the conventional emergency-relief tarp (Figure 3.15).

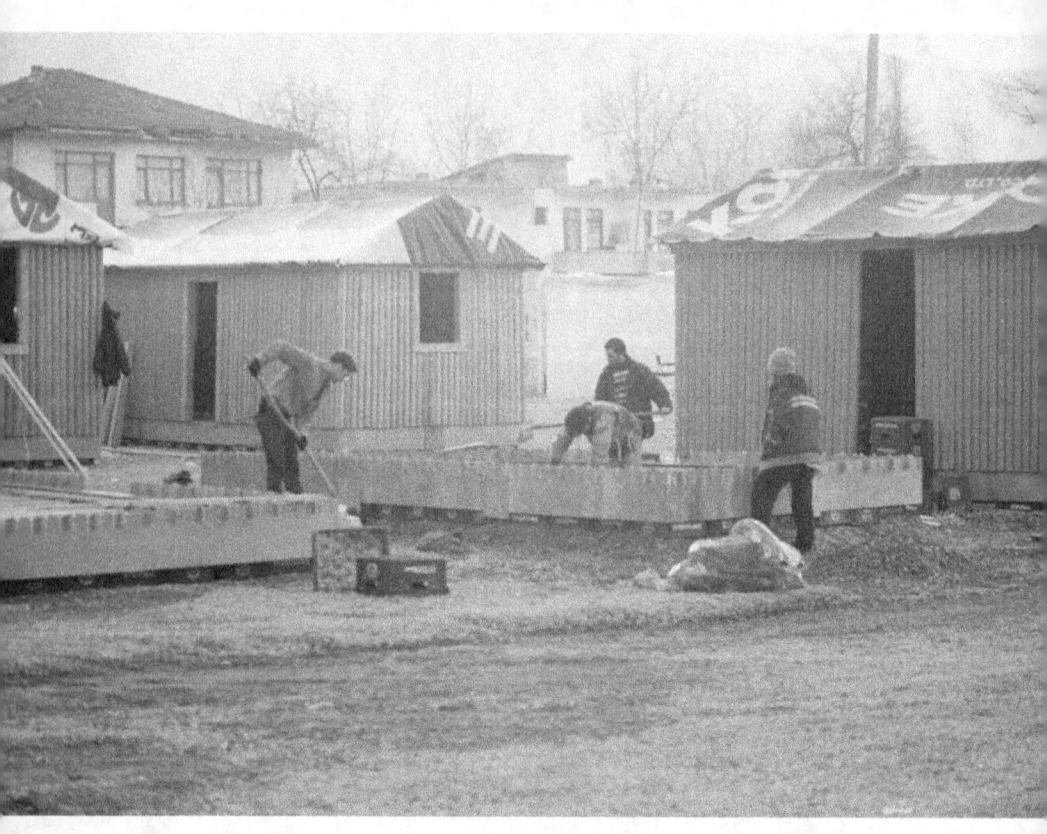

FIGURE 3.15. Shigeru Ban, *Paper Loghouse,* Kaynasli, Turkey, 1999. Courtesy of Shigeru Ban Architects.

When yet another earthquake in January 2002 left more than twenty thousand dead and more than six hundred thousand homeless in Bhuj, Gujarat in western India, Ban reconstructed a version of his paper shelters once more. While paper tubes were again used for the walls, beer crates were not readily available in India, so Ban used on-site rubble from destroyed buildings, covering it with a traditional Indian mud floor. For the roof, Ban assembled a combination of bamboo vaults with locally woven cane mat, insulated and waterproofed with clear plastic tarpaulins. Small holes in the roofing mats allowed air to circulate, providing enough ventilation for cooking to be done inside. Following the paper tube predecessors in Japan and Turkey, the structural, material, and design adjustments in India acknowledged the specific

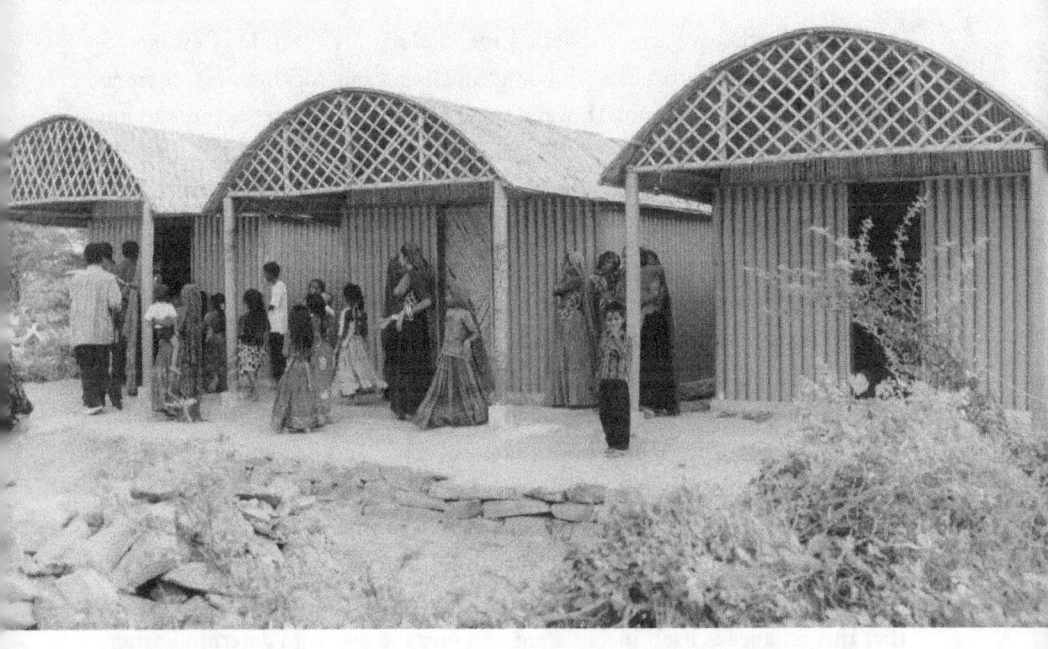

FIGURE 3.16. Shigeru Ban, *Paper Loghouse*, Bhuj, India, 2001. Photograph by Kartikeya Shordhan.

conditions of that new site and the particular needs of its temporary inhabitants (Figure 3.16).

In all three cases, the inexpensive modules, quick methods of construction, and variability of materials within each context rendered Ban's modular building practice capable of efficiently responding to each specific demand for shelter. By reintegrating his materials and methods into available building materials, practices, and cultural plans while also intervening into already present environmental and economic contexts, Ban offered a program of replacing both individual homes and social infrastructures that was undertaken by those who were forced to live within the temporary walls and those who were not.

Whether we are considering the modular architecture of escape vehicles, cellular compartments, shipping containers and docking sites, or emergency shelters, the common thread among all these endeavors is most simply that component parts come together to form and reform whole units, or come apart to afford voluntary mobility or to support involuntary upheaval. Inhabitants seek personal shelter as well as shelter with others, and in some cases from others. Replacing home in any of these scenarios is resolutely a socially engaged process, but the one that conditions and coordinates individual choice through existing materials, technologies, frameworks, and policies for both moving people around and for situating them—forcing, luring, offering that they be in and then out of place. Such a program of replacing home becomes possible if we can recognize how autonomy from and dependence on those infrastructures are negotiated both structurally and phenomenally—a negotiation that operates through the participation of intended dwellers and volunteers, and that relies on both the availability and the accessibility of existing social, economic, and political factions. In turn, we must also acknowledge that this reliance is itself inconsistent and unstable, so as to determine where we can intervene and where we cannot, and to propose what may be capable of reintegration and what may not.

Four

VISIBLY SKINNED BODY ARCHITECTURE AND TRANSFORMABLE CLOTHING

A woman steps into a silver-gray nylon jumpsuit, zips it up, and pulls the hood over her head. Extending from the front, back, and sides of the garment are long nylon tubes that hang like umbilical cords in either silver or bright red. There are forty-nine others like her, stepping into their suits, in a public square in Valencia, Spain as a part of the 2002 *Micro Utopias* exhibition at the Biennale de Valencia. The garments are imprinted in black with words like *nexus, heart, fraternity,* and *life line* along with a grid of interconnected black silhouettes of faces and heads. Once clothed, everyone is connected via the tubes, front to back, and side to side. Then together the group moves across the city, pausing in lines and twisting under and over each other in various formations in front of churches and other public buildings, along sidewalks, and in squares. Initially created in the late 1990s and with various instantiations enacted around the world in places such as Berlin, Venice, Sydney, and Mexico, the artist-activist Lucy

Orta's *Nexus Architecture* seeks to bring people together into a collective matrix and has been used to put pressure on social causes specific to each site. For example, Orta instigated the installation's mass of connected participants to add numbers to an antipollution protest march in Paris as well as to a march against child labor in Lyon. The repetitively structured, connective framework visually emphasizes the mass of participants whose force is activated through the transformation of multiple bodies into resistant displays of public presence in the face of social erasure or illegitimacy. As an ordered structure for enacting specific urban interventions, Orta's *Nexus Architecture* materially and metaphorically links wearers together under a common cause; each stands shoulder to shoulder with others, in support of a common goal or against a shared threat (Figure 4.1).

The individual garments that cohere to form Orta's *Nexus* closely resemble her ongoing series of *Refuge Wear* that transform from garment to shelter. After working as a design consultant for commercial fashion houses, Orta began to use her fashion training and textile research to develop clothing into portable, wearable membranes, constructed specifically for those without access to housing. In response to the outbreak of the First Gulf War and the following economic recession, Orta began in the early 1990s to develop a series of individual body skins, later expanded into multiple interconnected garments, that could be worn as protection against harsh environmental conditions but that also serve as a visual affront to bodily exclusion from social infrastructures. In parallel with the structures and systems presented in the previous chapter, Orta's protective garment-shelters are simultaneously individual and self-expandable, autonomous and dependent. As body architecture, the garments intimately adhere and respond to the wearer's movements, operating modularly through structural transformations. Pulled over the body like a sleeping suit and capable of fully or partially covering the head and

FIGURE 4.1. Lucy Orta, *Nexus Architecture x 50 Intervention Köln*, 2001. Original Lamda color photograph, laminated; 150 x 120 cm. Photograph by Peter Guenzel. Courtesy of the artist.

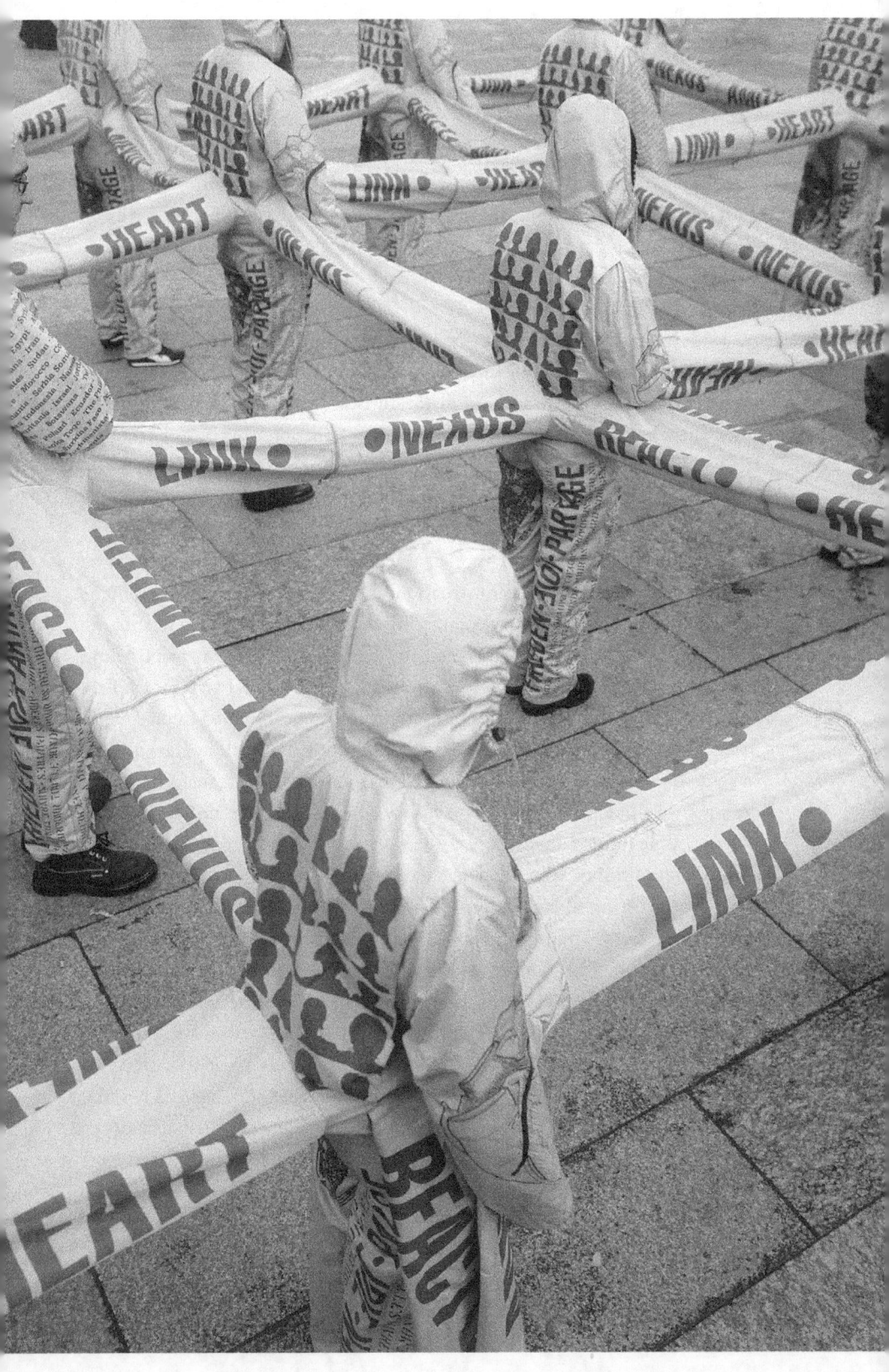

face, the garments are tough and resistant, often incorporating reinforced aluminum, thermo-chromic fabrics, photo-luminescent weaving, and Kevlar. Rendered not only reflective but also vibrant in color, these materials increase the wearer's visibility against the spatial landscape, for once they are cocooned, these bodies stand out (Figure 4.2).

In tandem with Orta's development of garment-shelters, the fashion world has made headway in this area of transformable clothing—a mode of design that, according to fashion historian Bradley Quinn, "hangs in limbo somewhere between Deconstruction and Reconstruction."[1] As borrowed terms from architecture, *deconstruction* in fashion design can be articulated as a process of taking apart and rearranging panels, pieces, layers, and fastenings and putting them back together in order to make visible the garment's construction; *reconstruction,* as defined by Quinn, characterizes garments that "appear to be in mid-manufacture. Like deconstruction, the process of construction is highlighted, but the emphasis is on completing the process rather than destroying it."[2] Transformable clothing thus mediates between these deconstructive and reconstructive tendencies, according to a system of partial and incomplete replacement. Two or more designs are structurally encapsulated in one, while devices like zips, snaps, concealed air pumps, or metal rods allow the garment to come together and apart in varying configurations. Each transformation is designed as a potential form, never fully visible and always conflated within other possible forms and respective functions, to be temporarily assembled by each wearer in response to her particular needs.

Occurring alongside the partial transformations from garment to shelter is the body's transition between invisibility and visibility. But what is made visible, to whom, and in what context? Although high fashion counts only an elite part of society as its followers, a handful of experimental designers have recently begun to use their fashion shows as platforms to question restrictions on public visibility and to offer their wearers the opportunity to be clothed, protected, and seen. For some fashion designers, such as Kosuke Tsumura and Hussein Chalayan, visible individuation, made possible by pockets and appendages that display personal mementos, is a necessary stand

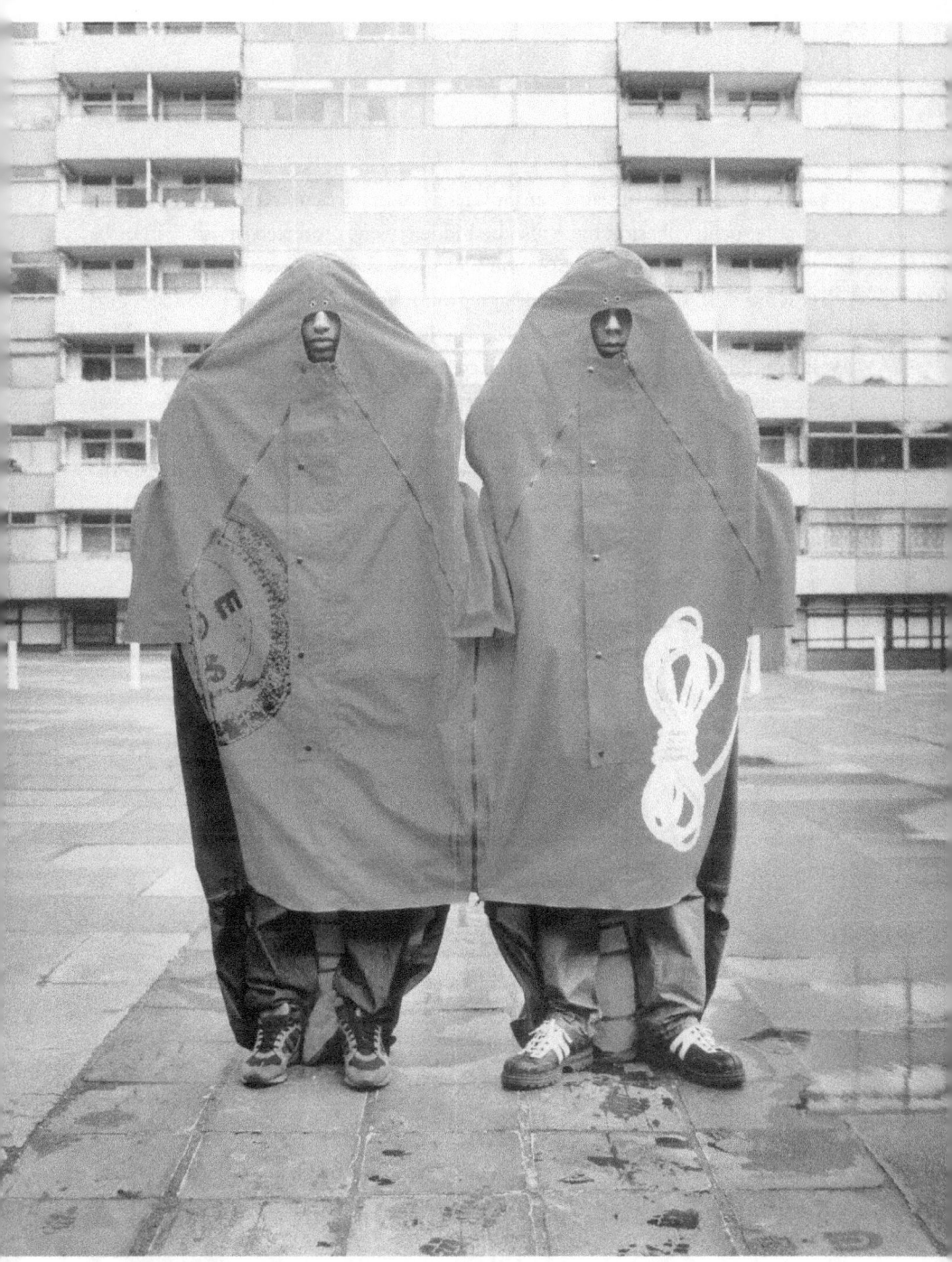

FIGURE 4.2. Lucy Orta, *Refuge Wear Intervention London East End,* 1998. Original Lamda color photograph, laminated, ed. 7; 150 x 120 cm. Photograph by John Akehurst. Courtesy of Galleria Continua San Gimignano/Beijing/Le Moulin and the Artists.

against social illegitimacy. Yet for Chalayan in particular, the structures that enable social cohesion must also be hidden away, protected invisibly in order to remain available for those who have been forced away from their homes (Figure 4.3). In fact, another design group, Vexed Generation, produces garments with the very goal of hiding the individual wearer's features, making him unidentifiable for legal purposes and thus able to inhabit sites in which he may not be allowed to belong. For Vexed Generation, collective resistance can only be enacted through bodily anonymity that allows individuals to come together safely and effectively as a commonly defined yet individually unspecific group (Figure 4.4).

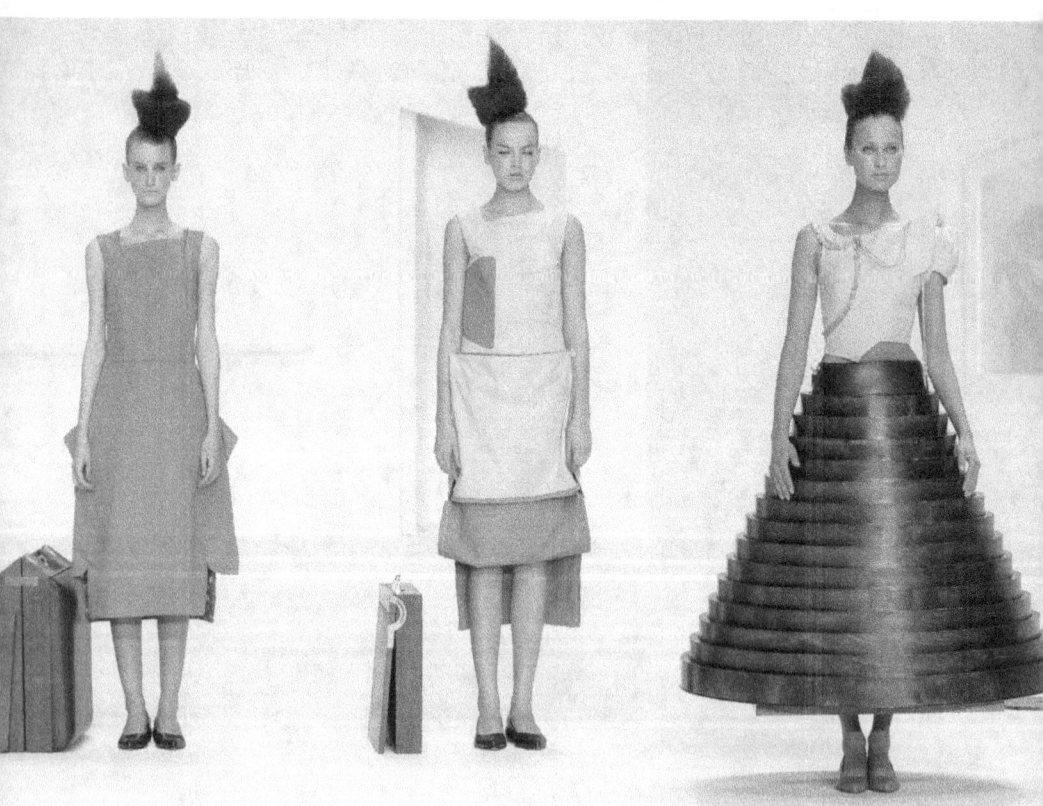

FIGURE 4.3. Hussein Chalayan, *Afterwords,* Autumn/Winter 2000. Photograph by Chris Moore.

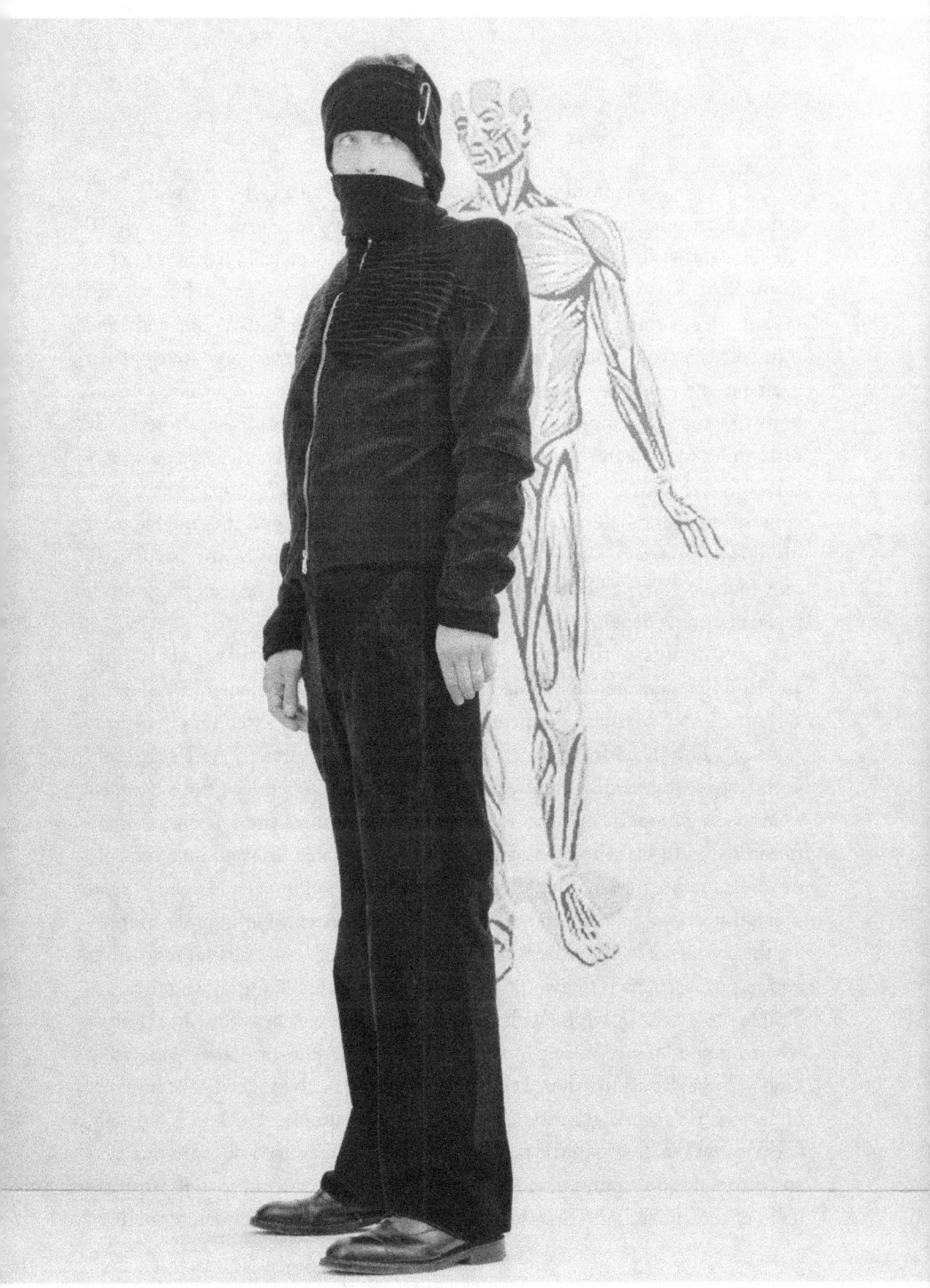

FIGURE 4.4. Vexed Generation. Photograph by Haraldur Hannes Gudmundsson.

I put these fashion designers in dialogue with Orta's art practice in order to consider how the ongoing transitions between garments, individual shelters, and visible public collectives can be variably enacted in order to confront elitist housing systems, discriminating communities, and public spheres that render certain categories of bodies socially invisible. While personal individuation is a concern for Orta, her *Nexus Architecture* and *Refuge Wear* garment-shelters most urgently make visible the effacement of the larger social body to which that individual belongs and has been categorized. Protectively reskinning each wearer as part of a commonly defined collective, the garments thus afford the possibility of publicly situating their wearers in spaces that have conventionally predetermined them as socially illegible, and thus unable to or disallowed from accessing the cultural, economic, and political infrastructures on which, as I argued in the previous chapter, a socially engaged program of replacing home depends.

As much as this chapter will affirm the public calls for social visibility and legibility activated by garment-shelters, I also will problematize collective action afforded by those garments in the public sphere, extending conversations ongoing in both public art and public housing arenas. As I suggested with respect to modular architecture, the negotiation between the autonomy of individual mobility and the dependence on structures and systems of social formation must be conceived of as necessarily unstable. Indeed, intervention, much less reintegration, into already present modes of being and belonging at home is not always viable and certainly never consistent. For in order to initiate the process of collective resistance against existing social-spatial conditions and to propose new frameworks for publicly accessible housing, we must recognize the means by which such collectives are formed, by whom and against whom, potentially resulting in what kind of coherent formation with what kind of force. By asking these kinds of questions, I wish to specify the impetus of Lucy Orta's work, who along with Kosuke Tsumura, Hussein Chalayan, and Vexed Generation in the fashion world challenges us to not turn our eyes away, to not ignore but, rather, to see the ongoing social and spatial displacement of certain bodies. Theirs is an effort to visibly and publicly contextualize, resituate, and rehouse those who are not systematically afforded the materials and methods of belonging at home.

VISIBILITY AND RESISTANCE

Zipping completely over the head and thoroughly encasing the wearer in a protective sack, Orta's first "Habitent" *Refuge Wear* was designed for use in railway stations, squatting sites, and housing settlements. Developing these skin-like membranes that are weather resistant, permeable, and pliable, Orta works with microporous fabrics that she says "attempt to mimic certain characteristics of the skin, such as the transfer of body humidity from the interior to the exterior."[3] As a founding member of the Paris-based Casa Moda, a group of designers and artists interested in linking textile research and experimental fashion design, Orta creates garments that technologically enhance the organic capabilities of skin, replacing its vulnerability with durability (Figure 4.5).

The concept of an architectural second skin can be historically associated with experiments in the late 1960s and 1970s that aimed to dematerialize the solid, fixed walls of conventional building, and thus to render architecture as and of the body. One prototype, imagined in 1966, consisted of a portable sack, carried on the back of its owner and capable of being transformed into a pliable membrane encasing the body in a temporary cocoon-like home. So envisioned Michael Webb, a founding member of the British experimental architecture collective Archigram. Unconvinced that volumetric solidity should be the material foundation of building practices, Archigram turned to the architectural potential of adaptable forms and fluid networks that extended the built site "beyond architecture," as the title of one of their newsletters announced.[4] Beyond architecture, Webb imagined an environment of dematerialized transience where his expandable "Cushicle" sack and inflatable "Suitaloon" membrane would replace the static and solid built structure with the organic form of skin. "Skin," another Archigram member Peter Cook contended, "can be treated as an environmental totality."[5] The body's surface, then,

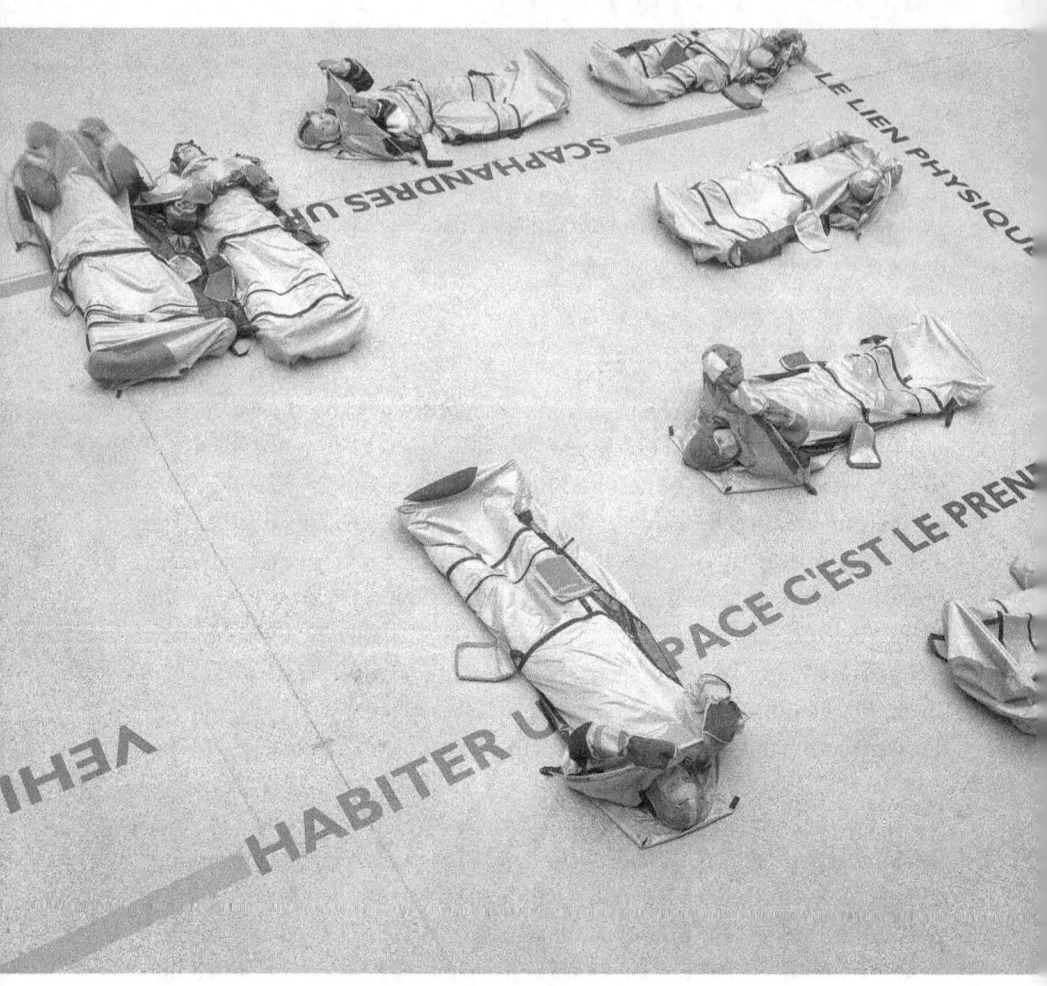

FIGURE 4.5. Lucy Orta, *Modular Architecture—The Unit x 10*, 1996. Extract from 40' Dance performance, Soirées Nomades. Photograph by John Akehurst.

could be both the site and operation of a new kind of architecture that is intimately responsive to both its spatial situation and to the body it houses. While remaining a proposal diagrammed on paper, Webb's "Cushicle/Suitaloon" nonetheless challenged the material foundation of modern architectural organicism, suggesting that the biological form of a body could literally take the place of a built site. Thus, Archigram's notional experiments enacted a disciplinary critique and can be thought of most significantly as a reimagining of the boundaries that determine and classify architecture. Indeed, the transformable "Cushicle/Suitaloon" urged a transformation within the field of architecture itself, challenging its objects and practices to remain open and flexible. From Archigram's retooling of architectural form and function, then, we begin to imagine an architecture that is out of place, that disappears, and is formed as a protective layer only once engaged by its users.

Orta's skin-like garments, in turn, not only upend the conventions of a fixed and stable architecture but also seek to specify the causes and outcomes of their wearers' out-of-place status. The curator Robert Pinto has suggested that her material development and critical use of fabric, in particular, is "a form of re-socialization that acts on various levels."[6] In fact, the *Refuge Wear* fabrics are not only materially innovative and visually alarming, but the surface of the garments are often silk-screened with textual manifestos and images applicable to the specific physical situation of its wearer. For example, one garment reads: "Living without a shelter for prolonged periods rapidly destroys physical and moral health. The lack of inadequate sleep increases stress, weakens the immune system and accelerates the loss of identity and desocialization." Another garment shows a map of Rwanda and a compass, while yet another depicts a pair of open, begging hands, literalizing the mode of each wearer's existence like a "tattoo," to use Pinto's word.[7] So Orta encourages us to see the homeless, as well as take time to pause and read them. These bodies may be socially marked as outsiders to be dismissed, but clothed in Orta's second skins, they become re-marked in another way. As linguistic signs that call out to viewers and confront passersby, Orta's textual tattooing contextualizes the garments as both immediately functional shelters and as critical public displays that call first for our attention, then for potential action and eventual social reintegration.

Although the garments remained prototypes that were not widely distributed, in a series of "City Interventions" occurring from 1993–1996 across London, Paris, New York, and later in Cuba for the Ninth Annual Havana Biennale, Orta's designs were road-tested for short periods of time by homeless individuals and volunteers from the Salvation Army and other shelters.

Yet as much as Orta develops her fabrics and designs with practical utility in mind, she remains primarily committed to her garments' function as social critique. Such a critique poses questions about the ways in which we are currently responding to the large-scale lack of shelter in specific locales around the globe—questions that are, at least in Orta's work, hard to ignore. Although her *Refuge Wear* was developed and constructed as custom-built initiatives primarily exhibited as art installations and urban interventions, she did work on an industrial prototype that would enable the commercial production of her *Habitent* for widespread use during natural emergencies or refugee situations. After several years, the final industrial version bore only a physical resemblance to Orta's garment, existing primarily as an object of shelter. Orta recounts: "I took the decision at this point to dedicate my energies to 'initiatives' and 'pilot projects.'"[8] Nonetheless, Orta has happily admitted to finding certain practical components of her garments present in transformable clothing ranging from convertible coats to wearable backpacks.[9] Ultimately, however, Orta wished to emphasize her work's mode of critical intervention instead of focusing on the large-scale marketing and production of solely functional designs.

This intersection between functionality and critique has a harried history within the realm of public art practice, to which Orta's garment-shelters can also be associated in their effort to both offer public platforms for resistance and provide viable options for public housing. In the 1980s, U.S. federal arts agencies started to support an "art-as-public-places" model in which design-oriented urban sculptures would function as usable furniture, architecture, or landscape, since utility could, in the minds of the funding agencies, be equated with social benefit.[10] Thus as art practices merged with public urban design, so did aesthetic intervention and functional necessity. Yet the collaboration among artists, architects, and urban designers on which this model of public art is based supports a conflation between aesthetics and function that unproblematically marginalizes the kind of critical social-spatial intervention that Orta's garments encourage.

Urban and art theorist Rosalyn Deutsche offers a productive and compelling framework for understanding the often invisibly intricate ways in which public art initiatives merge with larger urban plans for the functional redevelopment of public space—a move that results in the casting out and pushing aside of the homeless bodies that Orta's garments target. I turn to Deutsche because she unveils the conflation in the languages of functional and critical interventions, which when acknowledged allows us to reconsider how specific moments and sites of visible, public resistance may be possible within projects such as Orta's. Deutsche details the coincidence of urban redevelopment, intensified rhetoric about the value of new public spaces, a rising civic interest in the aesthetics of urban planning, and an increase in public art commissions, which for the specific purposes of her research she locates in New York in the 1980s. In the drive to halt the so-called urban decay evidenced by the increasing visibility of masses of homeless people, civic officials began to support public art projects in the name of a "supreme act of unification," bringing together artists, architects, landscape designers, and engineers to construct the image of a well-managed and beautiful city.[11] Public art as functional design, creating rather than questioning the coherence of public space while concealing the conflicts that constitute such space, served as both support for and justification of the city's plans for gentrification in the face of a pressing need for low-income housing. Thus art was integrated within newly developed public spaces in the name of public unification.

The kind of functional public art with which Deutsche finds fault—and against which Orta's work operates—envelops an understanding of the public sphere as open and accessible, and the deliberations occurring within it as egalitarian and capable of achieving consensus. This understanding relies on Jürgen Habermas's concept of the public sphere defined as modern society's site of political participation in which debates on issues of common social concern occur. Habermas's definition of the public sphere has since been revised by political theorists such as Nancy Fraser. Building on scholars like Joan Landes, Mary Ryan, Elizabeth Brook-Higgins, and Geoff Eley who each noted that the public was constituted through and because of a number of gendered, raced, and economic exclusions, Fraser argues that the conception of a public sphere depends not only on Habermas's momentary bracketing but on the significant elimination of social inequality through which deliberations can unfold. Without such an impossible elimination, we must recognize a multiplicity of publics that address all kinds of issues that may or may not qualify as common or public under the conventions of Habermas's bourgeois masculinist ideology. According to Fraser, a new critical theory of the public sphere "should render visible the ways in which social inequality taints deliberation within publics in late-capitalist societies."[12] She also argues for a more active role for these multiple public spheres, which goes beyond merely opinion formation and moves toward political decision making and social policy change. This refiguring of the definition as well as the responsibility and activity of various publics is central to any potentially resistant social intervention.

Contention, hybridity, inequality, and fragmentation are all therefore rife in both the formation and experience of the public sphere and its framing of public spaces. For as Deutsche makes explicit, "social space is structured by conflict."[13] And yet such conflicts are often overridden, in many cases with the help of public art initiatives that seek unification, by the official assertion that public spaces are produced in the name of universal usefulness and accessibility.[14] Absorbing the dominant ideology about a unified city and upholding a desire to build a coherent public sphere, proponents of functional public art may dangerously relinquish its potential for political intervention. By launching an oversimplified impulse to positively unify neglected communities, such art practitioners often fail to recognize the extent to which they instead collaborate with the dominant forces that wish to secure the erasure of social conflict. Time and again, the increasing need for low- to moderate-income housing and the increasing visibility of the homeless are met with gentrification plans that spatially reinforce the marginalization of poverty and the centralization of wealth and commerce, pushing out of sight the effects of civic development.[15]

Orta's garments instead seek to dismantle this ideal of public unification, which art historian W. J. T. Mitchell has named "utopian" in its imaginary construction of universal public access that hides the violence required to uphold it.[16] For Deutsche, interventions that occur in the public sphere and that aim to provide both a critical and a utilitarian function have much to learn from an association with urban studies, in its respective exploration of the specific and concrete mechanisms by which power relations are framed in spatial terms. If we follow Deutsche, then, we can also acknowledge that the relationship between critique and function hinges on social and spatial specificities that must constantly be produced and reproduced, placed and re-placed, taking into consideration each new circumstance of intervention, and thus guarding against utopic abstraction and universalism.

After backing away from the commercial production of her *Refuge Wear*, Orta continued to vary her garment-shelters, designing them as specific acknowledgments of global incidents requiring but not always receiving sufficient visibility and international emergency aid. *Survival Sac with Water Reserve*, for example, was her response to the crisis in Rwanda. Drawn to Orta's work for this kind of "situational nature," cultural and media theorist Paul Virilio finds within them a counterpoint to "delocalized" art that is constantly uninstalled and reinstalled across the globe without specific reference to each new context. In its specific material response to pertinent threats to the body, Virilio argues that Orta's *Refuge Wear* "becomes a kind of witness to what threatens it."[17] With their visible texts and images combined with their microporous durability and reflexivity, Orta materially reskins those bodies under threat of visual and social disappearance, resituating them as visibly present and contextualizing their erasure by marking a response to a particular situation.

VISIBILITY AND INVISIBILITY

While both her protest and dwelling projects are collectively specific to a situation or event, Orta's garments also offer the wearer a certain means of bodily individuation. In addition to their colorful and protective fabric innovations and textual tattoos, *Refuge Wear* includes pockets, pouches, and other connected appendages that act as variable design elements, to be determined differently by each wearer and capable of storing and protecting personally meaningful photos and objects. Accessed by the interior of the garment, they can also provide a means of transporting water, found items, and daily used objects. When the shelter is no longer needed, or when the wearer must move on, the pockets also have a functional dimension, acting as the garment's packaging into which the temporary second skin is folded for easy transportation and future reassembly.

In fact, in a number of recent transformable high-fashion designs, numerous external and internal pockets have been added to particularize the garment-shelter against the tide of bodily anonymity and to partially differentiate each individual wearer, though only on closer inspection. For example, the Japanese fashion designer Kosuke Tsumura, who counts Lucy Orta as an inspiration, launched his own label, Final Home, in 1993. His collection's signature piece, the Final Home Jacket, is a transparent nylon sheath equipped with a combined total of forty-four external and internal pockets that maximize storage capability while offering the wearer the ability to customize the design by inserting objects or images to be carried and viewed by others. Providing a protective external shell and supporting the storage of personal items, Tsumura's Final Home envelops each wearer in his own way, affording him a self-defined specificity. Indeed, wearers have used the pockets to showcase photos, postcards, artwork, and other memorabilia; the jacket's internal pockets are also capable of being padded with newspaper for extra warmth or filled with food rations or medicines. Although Final Home is a high-fashion label whose garments garner high prices, the surplus stock of jackets was sent to disaster areas and distributed to the homeless through international aid organizations.

While the visible pocketing of personal items attests to the specification of the wearer and his or her context of use, such bodily individuation also intervenes into the reframing of public spaces by countering anonymous public resistance with specifically embodied and visible action. In order to lay some groundwork for this kind of possibility, I want to turn to another high-fashion designer, the Cyprus-born, London-based Hussein Chalayan. His autumn/winter 2003 menswear designs, *Place/Non-Place,* consisted of jackets and shirts with transparent external pockets and multiple internal compartments so that, in Chalayan's words, "you could collect your memories and take them with you."[18] Yet the photos and objects that a wearer could transport with him not only materially marked his past history but also proposed openings for future moments and sites of interaction with others. In fact, the buyer of a *Place/Non-Place* garment was invited by the label's text to come to London's Heathrow airport in May 2004, eighteen months after the collection debuted.[19] Chalayan envisaged a scenario in which wearers would talk to each other about the specific experiences represented by the objects that they had decided to carry with them.

The airport as Chalayan's chosen meeting place was inspired by anthropologist Marc Augé's distinction between places and nonplaces. Chalayan's collection examines Augé's claim that the airport is a paradigmatic supermodern nonplace, structured as transitional and supporting the movement of people and things through space. According to Augé, places are spatially circumscribed and embedded with historical, symbolic context. Nonplaces, on the other hand, are "transit points and temporary abodes."[20] They designate spaces of travel and movement between two points, charting the relations between individuals in terms of transport and commerce. With its invitation to reconnect his garment's wearers in such a nonplace, Chalayan's collection proposes a momentary and incomplete transformation of a public site by way of a temporary event. Chalayan notes that he "was questioning whether holding an event in a particular space could turn a non-place into a place."[21] Pocketing an item affords a future social interaction that in turn offers the possibility of replacing a neutral, transitory spatial experience with another that is just as transitory but that is nonetheless specific to each body and contextualized through the objects visible on the garments.

Although Chalayan's designs remain in the realm of high fashion and are not meant to take over public sites in the name of resistant action, there are a few points that I would like carry forth from the collection and that bear light on Orta's efforts to offer a functional home as well as to critically confront the accessibility of social infrastructures for home. Chalayan's proposal to temporarily transform a spatial experience gestures to the distinction between a wearer's individuation and his independence. For while the design of a garment's compartments may be aimed at rendering one wearer different from another, in order for garments to propose modes of being and belonging in place they must ultimately instigate future avenues of embodied connection and social dependence. This dual necessity for individuation and collectivity was a key point in the previous chapter. Here, however, the emphasis is on the public visibility of individualized bodies and the coming-together of those bodies in a public site.

Chalayan further suggests that the cohesion of bodies and the exchange of objects, images, and narratives are capable of transforming the experience of the public site itself, reframing public space through the visibility of specific embodied connections. Yet when we imagine these future meeting points, we must also consider the uneven mechanisms of collective action. So we must be critical and specific not only about the ways in which we define public space and sites of resistance, but also about the ways in which we define the public and the means by which only certain bodies are able to cohere—a conversation that I have noted is already ongoing within public art practices, as well as within theories of the public sphere. Who gets to come together, who does not, and under whose eyes? Indeed, visible individuation can never be privileged, as in many cases it is in fact a social privilege.

Another collection by Chalayan speaks to an imagined scenario in which personal anonymity affords protection as well as the possibility for social cohesion. Occurring around the same time as photographs from the war in Kosovo were heavily disseminated through the various news media, Chalayan's autumn/winter 2000 show *Afterwords* translated modes of flight into the design and use of his clothing by allowing familiar settings to be replaced in new locales, and thus in support of those who must carry their possessions and indeed what they can of their homes with them. Dressed in undergarments, four women walked onto a stage and removed the slipcovers from the chairs around a coffee table, putting them on their bodies as dresses (Figures 4.6 and 4.7). Once clothed, they folded up the chairs into suitcases.

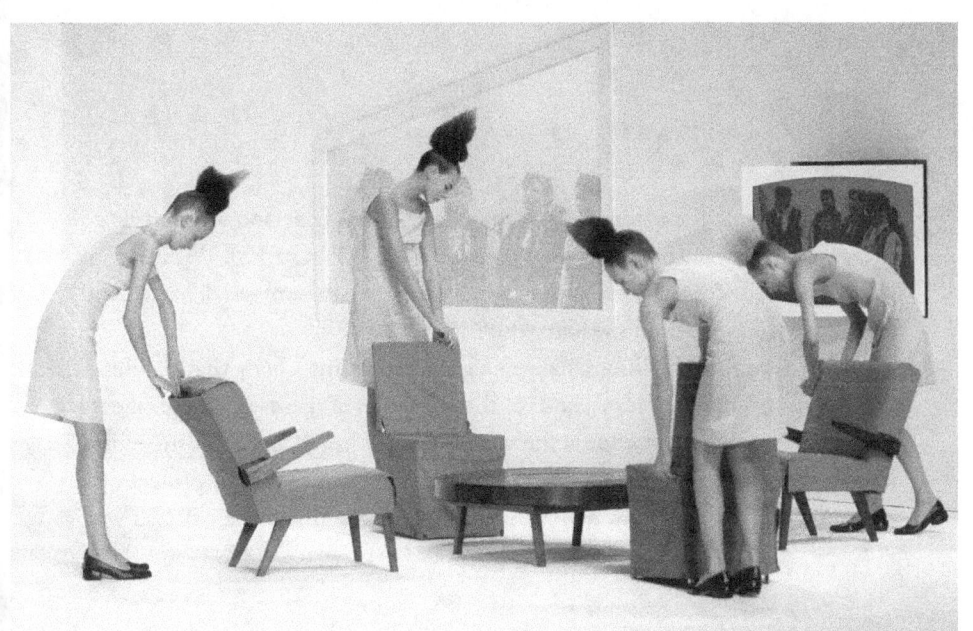

FIGURE 4.6. Hussein Chalayan, *Afterwords*, Autumn/Winter 2000. Photograph by Chris Moore.

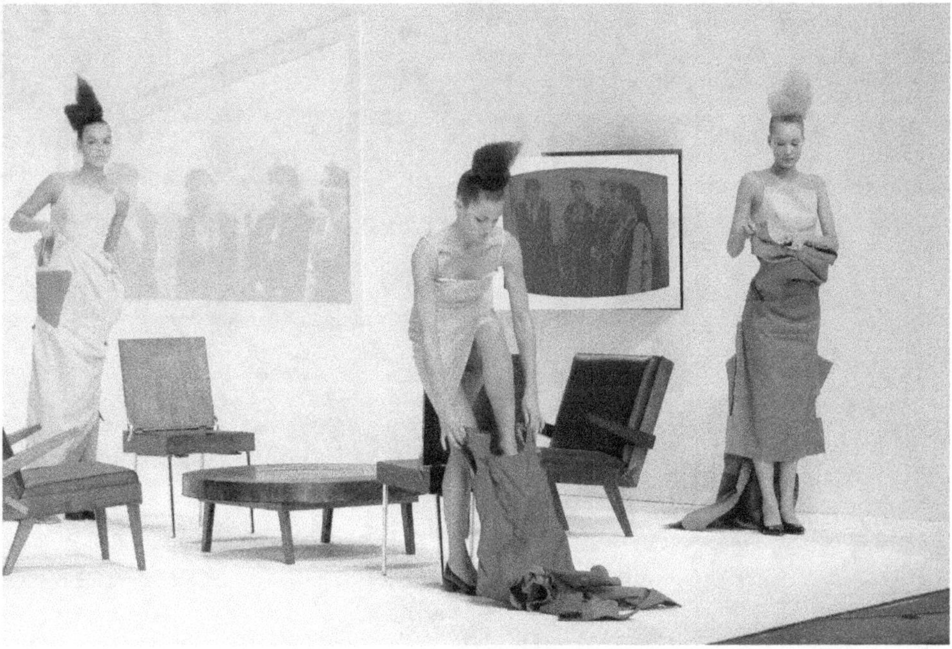

FIGURE 4.7. Hussein Chalayan, *Afterwords*, Autumn/Winter 2000. Photograph by Chris Moore.

Another woman then stepped into the center of the table and raised it up to her waist to form a conically layered, wooden skirt (Figure 4.8). With each of the furniture pieces packed up or worn as garments, the women departed and the lights went down on the bare white stage.

Covering the skin, Chalayan's garments frame a body that is vulnerable, threatened, out of place, and yet the activation of these variable garments by those wearing them affords the wearer the choice to continuously reform a unified spatial situation in any given site. The garments both protect and are protected by the body, as formidable enhancements of the skin, as well

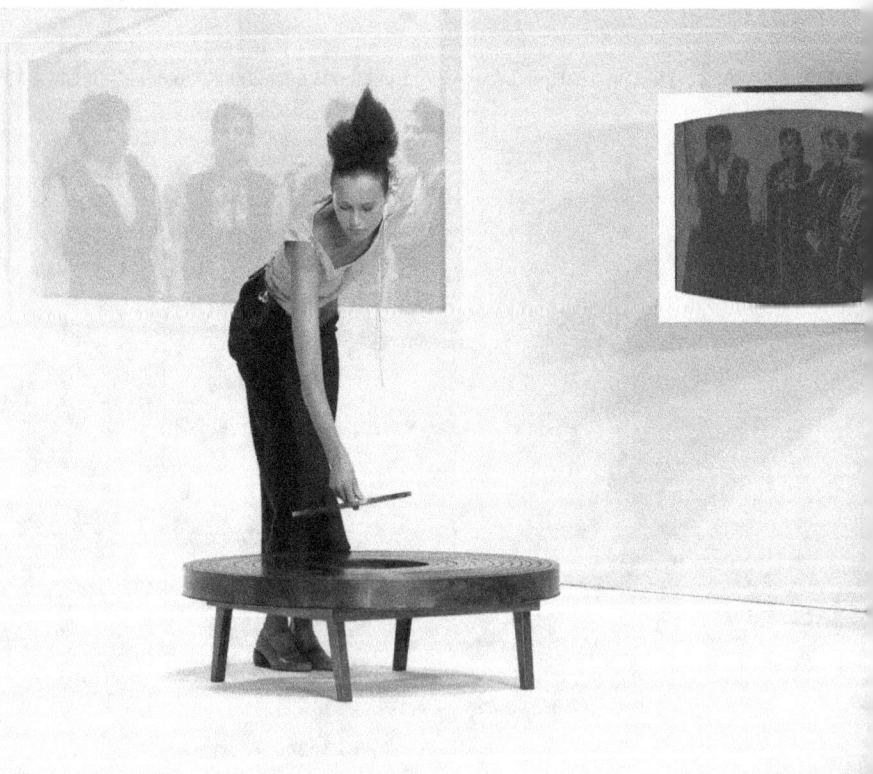

FIGURE 4.8. Hussein Chalayan, *Afterwords*, Autumn/Winter 2000. Photograph by Chris Moore.

as hidden objects and structures. As transformable clothing and as wearable architectural sites, the garments are both structurally solid and permeable, both furniture and second skins, both a room and a collection of bodies housed there. Chalayan's designs therefore not only negotiate between mobility and situation, but they also attest to the necessarily partial visibility of those places in which certain bodies may momentarily belong and for whom home is an unsafe and ever-moving place.

Garments that can transform into shelters are by nature two things at once, and yet they also accommodate two very different positions. They acknowledge the forced mobility of those who have no choice but to seek refuge in the very fabrics that cover their bodies. But these multifunctional designs are also developed by and primarily targeted for those who already have access to permanent housing structures. Chalayan addresses the endless flow of bodies around the world from within the elite field of haute couture fashion, marketed to those who are economically capable of choosing a transient way of life in which on-the-spot decisions to move or stay can be flexibly accommodated. Yet his fashion designs and showings also critique the growing phenomenon of global dispersion, both celebrating and challenging the freedom of individual mobility, as well as calling attention to the ramifications of both chosen and forced migration. As Caroline Evans writes in the exhibition catalogue to Chalayan's 2005 retrospective at the Groninger Museum in the Netherlands, "the theme of travel so prevalent in Chalayan's work can be understood, both literally and figuratively, as a journey of alienation and loss, as much as it is one of self-discovery and self-fashioning."[22] For Chalayan, the temporary spatial situation of the mobile body within a built environment to which it does not belong is always precarious. Chalayan's designs respond to this precariousness by continuously attempting to rematerialize a connection, however vulnerable, between the clothed body and each new site in which she may pause.

Charting potential scenarios for grounded situation, mobility, and the moments in between, Chalayan's transformable garments propose only a framework for shelter, giving wearers travel clothes, suitcases, chairs, and a table as well as the ability to form a cohesive room together, without fully offering shelter as a complete material possibility. Yet rather than disregarding Chalayan's work based on its impracticality—and indeed a similar contestation can be made against the architectural proposals of Archigram—I want to focus on why home is only partially suggested, and on what kind of home is in the transformative process of either appearing or disappearing. Just as Archigram was challenging the frameworks of the architectural discipline, so Chalayan is testing the limits of fashion design as it meets with architecture and responds to nomadism and migrancy. For Hussein Chalayan, invisibility affords protection; the furniture that makes up the room must be hidden away in and as clothing in order to protect a semblance of home while his imagined inhabitants are forced to flee under the backdrop of something like the Balkan war. Within a scenario in which being at home is consistently denied, Chalayan's garments safeguard the structures of home through the very bodies of their wearers rather than the other way around, in which home conventionally protects the wearers.

The oscillation between the visibility and invisibility of Chalayan's room-as-home, and of the wearers concealing the potential form of home on their bodies, points to another trend in experimental garment design that offers resistant modes of invisibility so that wearers are able to inhabit inaccessible spaces or denied sites of belonging. For London-based fashion design duo Adam Thorpe and Joe Hunter of Vexed Generation, the rise in urban surveillance systems in the 1990s inspired their construction of garments that zip up to cover most of the head and face, leaving only the eye area open and visible. Using breathable, bullet- and slash-proof textiles like Kevlar and ballistic nylon that were initially developed to protect military officers against high-impact assaults, Vexed Generation created defensive "urban armor" in defiance of the British government's restrictions on civil liberties. By introducing garments like their Vexed Parka and their Techtonic Jacket, Thorpe and Hunter were directly responding to the 1994 British Criminal Justice Act, which created a new category of offenses meant to either limit or completely ban public gatherings and demonstrations. Wearers could put on these parkas, zip them up to their eyes and over their heads, and be almost unidentifiable, while remaining even more menacingly and publicly visible.

By hiding facial features and enveloping the body in heavily protective, gender-nonspecific outerwear, Vexed Generation differentiates between visual anonymity and visibility. Thorpe explains that the garments "give people enough protection for them to be able to go out and be active, more involved with their environment in a secure fashion."[23] Anonymity need not counteract visibility; the garments do not act as camouflage. Instead, the transformation from visible to invisible remains incomplete. The parka and jacket afford both visibility and invisibility by allowing the wearer to move safely through public spaces, participating in social or political gatherings while still concealing their specific and identifiable bodily details that, if made apparent, could lead to possible detention or incarceration. Yet although anonymous, the dark, heavy materials also visually define wearers against the urban landscape, accentuating their shadowed forms and overtly challenging their legally determined spatial and social restrictions.

In their autumn/winter 2000–2001 *SABS* collection *(See And Be Seen)*, Vexed Generation heightened their garments' visibility in relation to the wearer's anonymity by inserting highly reflective panels into their overcoats and full-body jumpsuits that would shine as bright as fluorescent lights and thus mask the wearer even more fully in the contrasting folds of dark fabric.[24] Several jackets in the collection included a hood that completely covers the face, allowing wearers to see through a tinted vision strip. Creating the potential for individuals to come together safely and publicly, Vexed Generation's designs render wearers simultaneously invisible and visible, bringing them together as an individually unspecific yet public collective (Figure 4.9).

To be invisible, then, is not always to remain unseen, and it certainly does not always entail isolation. Invisible in the guise of anonymous, Vexed Generation's designs offer a particular kind of cohesiveness for a specific kind of circumstance, and here is where I think the intersection with the concept of belonging offered by Chalayan's garments is most productive. While the dematerialization of architecture toward the surface of the body may have

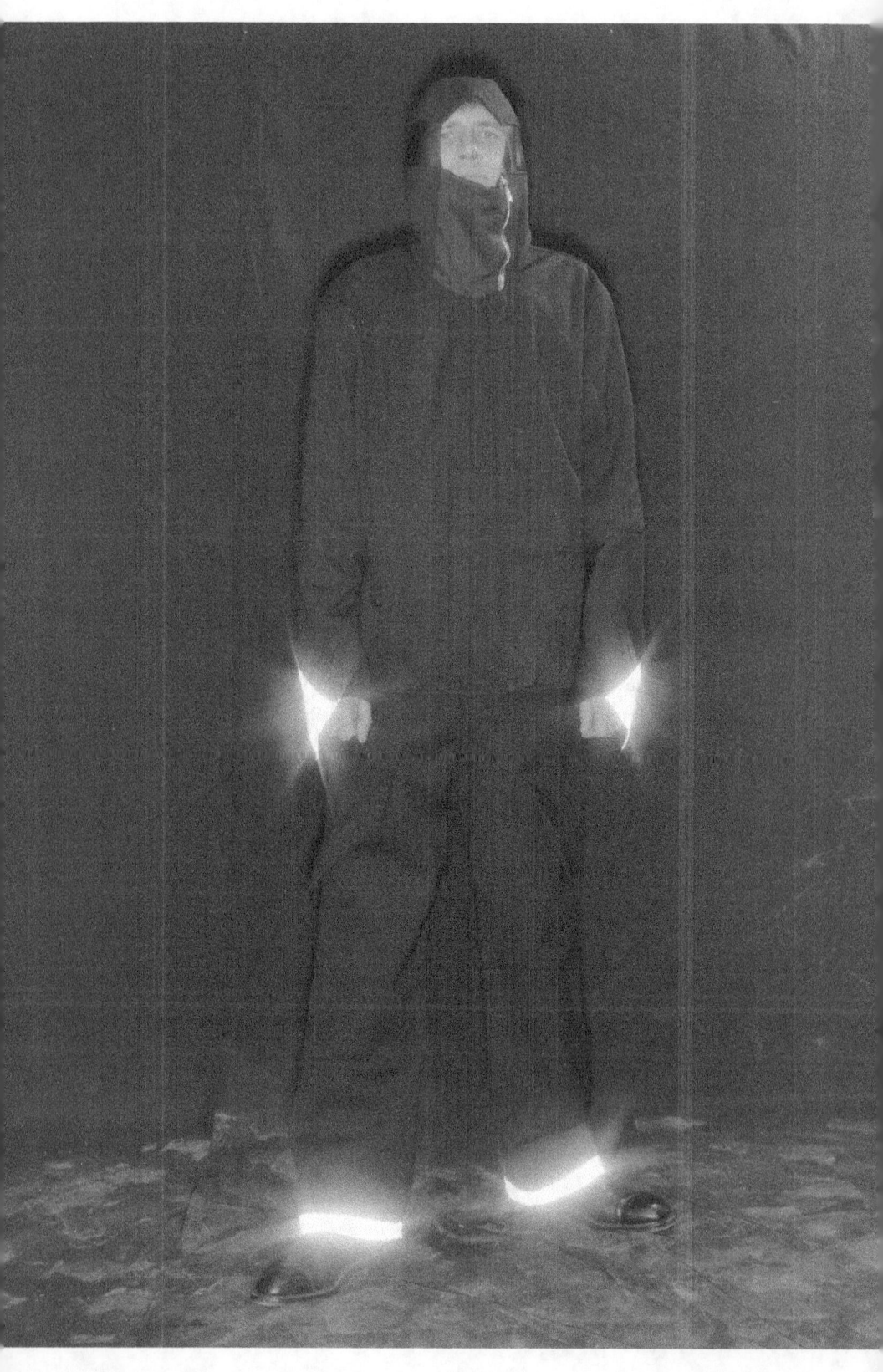

initially pointed toward the self-sufficiency of the individual and the freedom of personal mobility, we can recognize another compelling diversion from that trajectory. Unlike Archigram's individual pod-like envelopments, both Vexed Generation and Chalayan emphasize the ability of bodies to cohere with and against others. Invisibility, as enforced or activated by the garments, supports this coming-together, which in turn encourages the possibility of inhabiting, or at least momentarily taking over, sites in which the wearers do not belong. The coming-together may be fleeting, may be anonymous and illegible, but its purpose is shared by the wearers and protected by the garments. Vexed Generation focuses on the means by which cohesion can be possible, for any kind of reason, and always against the regulations that keep those wearers apart. It is not the end result that is important but, rather, that the approach to a common goal is activated en masse. For Chalayan, wearers come together with the specific purpose of forming a room, which enacts the vulnerable semblance of a home. Such a room is suggested not through a single body but through the collaboration and copresence of multiple bodies, and through the shared responsibility of carrying and transforming the garments into public structures and moments of belonging.

REPLACING PUBLIC VISIBILITY

As political theorist Hannah Arendt contends, the term *public* means "that everything that appears in public can be seen and heard by everybody and has the widest possible publicity. For us, appearance—something that is being seen and heard by others as well as by ourselves—constitutes reality."[25] Appearance, or coming into being by virtue of shared visual recognition in a space of others, is central to Arendt's conceptualization of the public. She utilizes this metaphor of visuality in order to qualify an experience of both the public

FIGURE 4.9. Vexed Generation, *See And Be Seen (SABS)*.
Photograph by Haraldur Hannes Gudmundsson.

sphere and the public body that is based on shared interactions witnessed and legitimized by others. Arendt goes on to explain: "Since our feeling for reality depends utterly upon appearance and therefore upon the existence of a public realm into which things can appear out of the darkness of sheltered existence, even the twilight which illuminates our private and intimate lives is ultimately derived from the much harsher light of the public realm."[26] Thinking through Orta's, Vexed Generation's, and Chalayan's interventions in public spaces alongside Arendt, I want to hold on to the notion that it is not only that we see but that others see and they may see what we see as well, and that these visual actions and embodied interactions unfold in spaces that may not be our own. These commonalities of experience, and by extension the ways in which these commonalities may nonetheless be formed through inequalities of power, are the foundation of our understanding of the world and our various places in it.

The problems associated with finding a place, and ultimately a home, for multiple publics leads me to consider the legacies of public housing, as arguably enmeshed with the contested formation of public spheres and collective public bodies. According to urban historian Lawrence J. Vale, ambivalence toward public housing is directly tied to what it means to be public, who is included and who is excluded, and thus public housing has always been a question of whom to house and where. Beginning in the nineteenth century, as American cities began to be overcrowded with all kinds of "uneasily juxtaposed" people, to use Vale's evocative phrase, civic institutions were given the responsibility of caring for the impoverished.[27] In particular, where to house the socially outcast was more often than not a question of where they would be the least visible, and indeed decisions regarding public housing have historically entailed finding sites and methods of peripherally situating the homeless so as to push them out of sight from the majority of urban dwellers.

What would it mean, then, to make housing both public and visible? If we follow Arendt, what is public is so because it appears as visible to others, and thus by extension public housing that is visible would be legitimized as part of the public, or as one of multiple publics. In living up to its name, public housing must then find ways of visibly cohering various kinds of public bodies in need of a home. Lucy Orta's garment-shelters provide a way to critically reimagine public housing because they attend to both bodily specification and connectivity, and because they also visually disrupt the ideal of both a unified public body and an accessible public sphere. Expanding on her individual *Refuge Wear* series in 1994 and revisiting her linking of individual wearers in *Nexus Architecture,* Orta began constructing shared garment-shelters, as a form of public housing for the homeless. Her *Body Architecture–Collective Wear* connects two or more individual *Refuge Wear* units, joining them together modularly to configure a larger inhabitable structure while also temporarily supporting an intimate family formation.

Orta's self-described "rhizome-like architectural configurations" are both ever extendable and collapsible.[28] The garments' modular system of connection and reconnection can be described, using Gilles Deleuze and Félix Guattari's theorization of the rhizome, as having "no beginning or end; it is always in the middle, between things, interbeing, intermezzo."[29] Indeed, the transformation of Orta's garments from individual to collective structure is always ongoing, always reversible and replaceable. For Paul Virilio, "their primary purpose is to warn us about social decomposition, social divorce."[30] In a conversation with Orta, Virilio tells her: "You are making collective clothing when divorce is on the increase, and are proposing a kind of marriage by garment to prevent people from drifting apart."[31] Even if they have to also support and maintain isolated movements, these garments nonetheless let wearers come back together, their bodies physically and momentarily reattached to each other. Because the collectives are constructed out of the colorful, reflexive, tattooed *Refuge Wear,* individual wearers are rendered visible, but perhaps even more significantly, their momentary transformations into cohesive units occur visibly as well. These processes of transformation, as one wearer comes into contact with others and then leaves again, occur out in the open, in urban locations, under the eyes of others. Thus Orta's connective garment-shelters both guard the individual body and make publicly visible its intimate links with others who are similarly clothed.

Two other of Orta's series also attest to the flexible relationship between autonomous mobility and communal connection, offering the structural possibility for even more wearers to cohere and additionally affording shared spaces whose construction is dependent on how multiple wearers choose to attach. First commissioned in Paris in 1996, Orta's *Modular Architecture* consists of portable, primarily nocturnal shelters that are collaboratively and variably built by the individual bodies that they house and the refuge garments that those bodies each choose to wear. During the day, every garment is completely separable from the others, like *Refuge Wear*, and can be worn and personalized by each specific person. At night, the garments reattach as modular components, transforming into an architectural whole according to the number, needs, and characteristics of the participants. Participants, like the structure, can vary from night to night, coming together in various configurations, introducing new members and accommodating for others who may not return (Figure 4.10).

Similar in structure and system to *Modular Architecture* is Orta's 2000–2003 *Connector Mobile Village* series. Instead of *Refuge Wear* garments, transformable sleeping bags, tents, and ground sheets are attached and detached from each other to form the basis of a larger, portable, built environment. To date, more than twenty groups, from children in Florida to design graduate students in Tokyo, have participated as test occupants of a Mobile Village, each group altering the connection and reconnection of shelter components according to their own particular and often changing needs (Figure 4.11).

Both *Modular Architecture* and *Connector Mobile Village* determine a visibly continuous, participant-driven, publicly enacted flexibility between independence and interdependence, which together are necessary for any long-term program of socially engaged public housing. Orta's work suggests that individual homes, as well as systems of community formation, are based on the ability of bodies to come together not only easily and efficiently, but also publicly and visibly. "To survive," Virilio says to Orta, "one is obliged to form a pack. . . . At a time when we're told that man is free, emancipated, hyperautonomous, a Walkman, you're saying no, wait a minute, we're banding to-

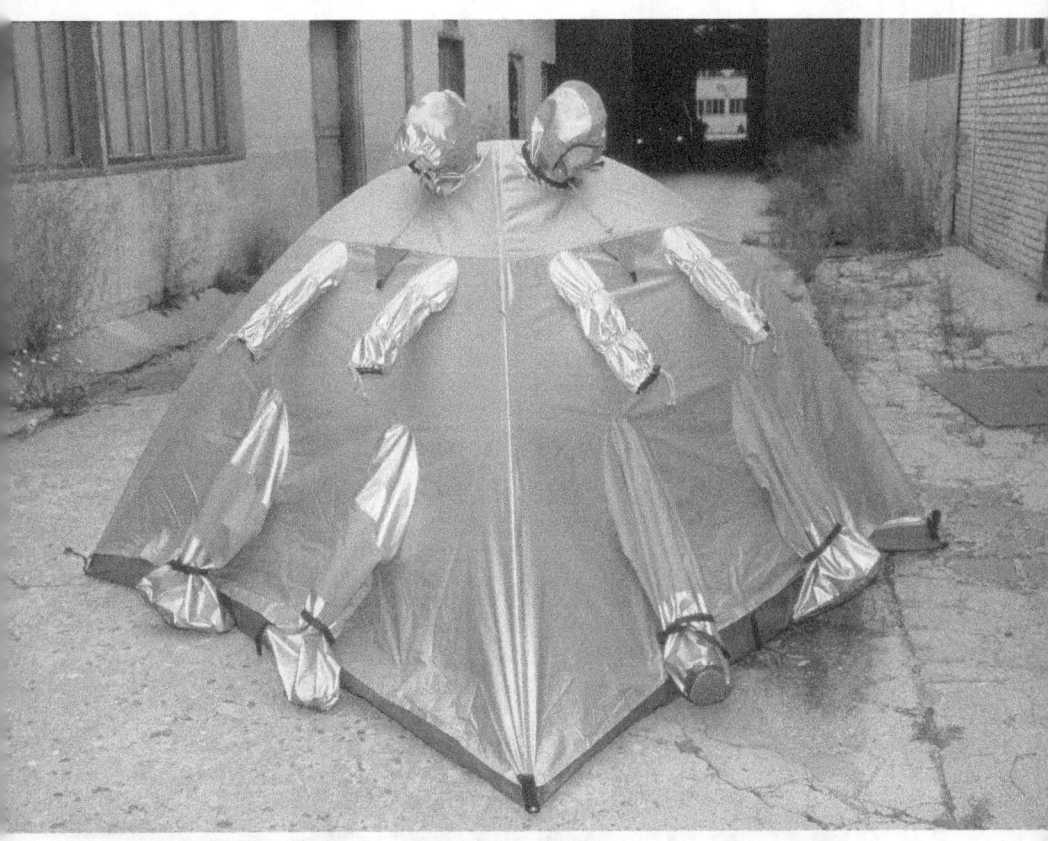

FIGURE 4.10. Lucy Orta, *Body Architecture—Collective Wear 4 persons,* 1994. Aluminum-coated polyamide, microporous polyester, telescopic aluminum armatures, grip soles; 180 x 180 x 150 cm. Photograph by Philippe Fuzeau. Courtesy of Fonds National d'Art Contemporain.

gether again into packs, gangs, and new tribes."[32] In response to the dislocation of bodies from social networks, Orta's garments render the skin as the last possible structure capable of situating the body in connection with others, however precariously. Her visible second skins provide the structural framework that guides the ways in which momentarily cohesive packs may form and re-form, replaceable in each new circumstance, within locations where they do not belong, and with the participation of different bodies over time.[33]

While Orta's garments are situationally specific, the wearer's body oscillates between being partially defined by its pockets and appendages, and yet also acting as one part of a larger group. Just as Vexed Generation's wearers

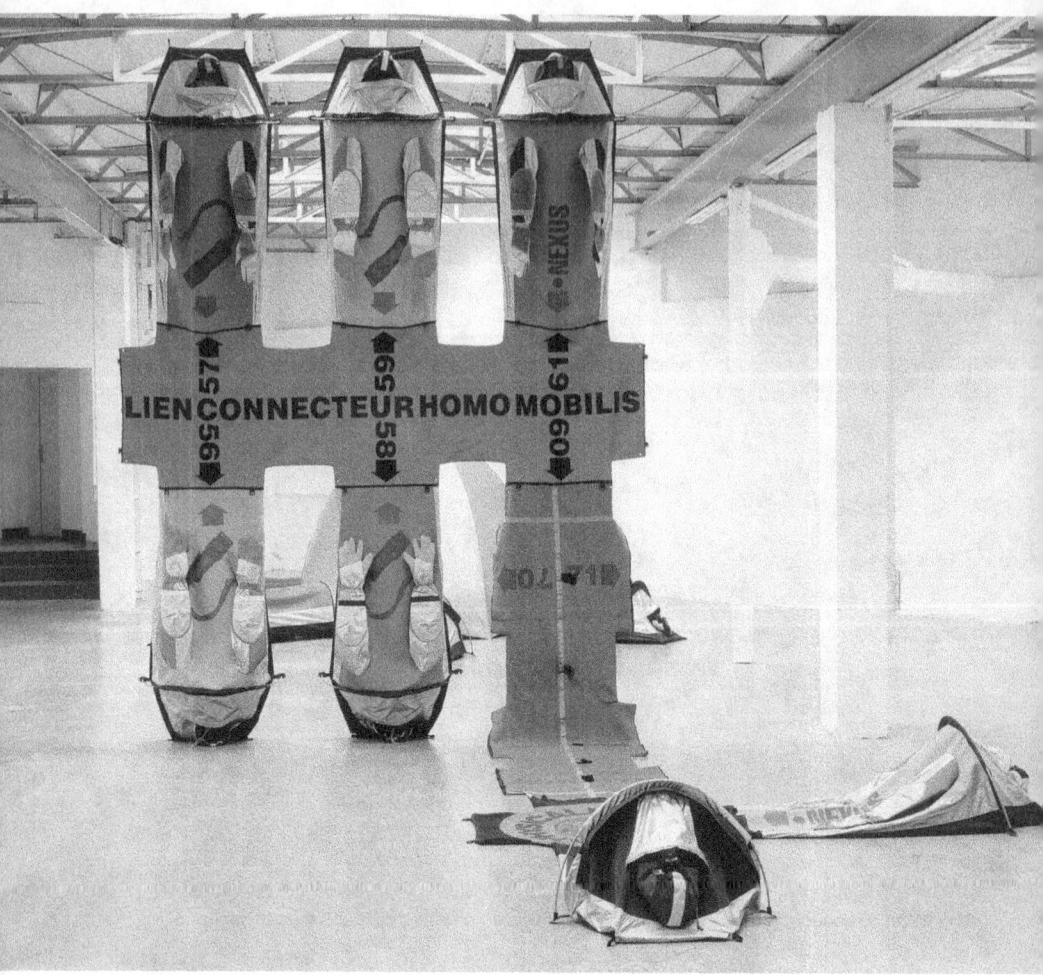

FIGURE 4.11. Lucy Orta, *Connector Mobile Village I*, 2001. Aluminum-coated polyester, reversible Solden Lycra, open-cell polyurethane, silkscreen print, zippers; 570 x 700 cm (variable dimensions). Photograph by Lothringer 13. Courtesy of the artist.

assume an anonymity in order to come together publicly in resistance to their social effacement so, to a certain degree, must Orta's wearers. Unless one looks closely, it appears as though each of the wearers is more alike than different from another. With their quick and easy assembly into cohesive units of multiple wearers, the garments together intervene into specific urban sites by bringing an extendable mass of connected bodies into view. It is this visible mass of intertwined wearers that most strongly belies the social force necessary to activate the move from political deliberation to decision making.

But how can we qualify, much less assess, the garments' collective call for action? The potential for resistant collective action has itself been widely debated within recent community-based public art discourses. Indeed, just as the definition and formation of a unified public sphere have been questioned, so too have the efforts by artists, urban planners, and architects to determine any kind of coherent community within which prescient issues can be collectively raised. Art historian Miwon Kwon has suggested that collective practices must be "projective," "provisional," and "incomplete," where any identification of a public collective is unpredictable and uncertain.[34] However, Grant Kester argues that, even with Kwon's provisions in mind, "it is still possible to define oneself through solidarity with others while at the same time recognizing the contingent nature of this identification."[35] Interestingly, both Kwon and Kester find productive Jean-Luc Nancy's concept of an "inoperative community" in which coherence is not dependent on essential conditions or categorizations but, rather, is formed contingently through interactions with others and with a shared knowledge of ultimate finitude.[36]

Alongside her development of collective shelters, and as a preliminary and ongoing operation to acknowledge the contingencies of community formations, Orta has instigated *Collective Dwelling* workshops in which participants come together to brainstorm new kinds of garments, enclosures, and membranes that can house individual bodies and yet also frame a larger collective enclosure. Established for the first time in 1997 at the contemporary arts center Creux de L'Enfer, in Thiers, France, the workshop drew from teenagers at nearby foster homes and high schools who together discussed the concept of the body as the inspiration for a mobile and connective habitation. In each future instance, a variety of participants were able to discuss the changing relationships among clothing, architecture, and the social exclusions that make certain bodies illegible and housing infrastructures inaccessible within particular sites around the globe, from the Hague to Melbourne, and from Venice to Rotterdam. As Orta's investment in the workshops demonstrates, the ongoing participation of users in the development of their own means of visibly and functionally inhabiting public spaces must involve a coming-together within and outside of the garments, both prior to their development and after their usage. So what kind of public collective do Orta's individual and connective garment-shelters offer? One that is both contingent and coherent, and thus momentarily cohesive as well as temporarily specific to a situation, context, or issue. As both a public housing structure and a community housing system, the garments are visible and variable, and they cohere visibly and variably. Both the materials of individualization and the methods of coming together are capable of being replaced in relation to each wearer, every group of wearers, and within any circumstance.

If, as I have been proposing, replacing home is a socially engaged process undertaken, however inconsistently and precariously, by dwellers for themselves and for others, then we must consider that the very processes of social engagement may remain inaccessible for certain persons. We must also see that recognition as part of a social body requires some kind of visible public legitimization that also may at times seem inconceivable. From Lucy Orta, though Archigram to Kosuke Tsumura, Hussein Chalayan, and Vexed Generation, this chapter has been an effort to reimagine what happens when access to and dependence on social infrastructures for housing are denied, and when efforts to reintegrate certain bodies back into a unified vision of the public sphere are rendered null. To varying degrees in each case, bodily individuation, though still afforded at some level, is subordinated to collective coherence under the auspices of resistant action. Yet a shared desire to confront exclusive housing policies, forced migrations, or illegal public gatherings cannot disregard the immediate need for individually protective, functional shelter in the name of resistance.

Body architecture and transformable clothing aim to simultaneously activate short-term practical requirements and immediately visible critical interventions. But as Orta's ongoing revisions and workshops suggest, we must also make long-term investments in processes and structures that have the potential to turn the momentary intervention into a decisive development, or that at the very least challenge us to think of new forms of public housing and formations of public bodies as a real possibility. The issue at hand is not in assuredly knowing what those possibilities may entail but, rather, how we can make those ongoing investments and what that process would involve. In mobilizing collective action and in affording the material means for bodies to come together, we must continually ask ourselves who is being defined under the banner of collectivity and how is coherence activated and maintained. We must make visible and continuously replace not only the bodies rendered socially peripheral but also the methods of coherence that depend on the interactions of all kinds of participants in a variety of public and private, civic and personal sites.

Five

NETWORKED DEPENDENCIES RAFAEL LOZANO-HEMMER'S *RELATIONAL ARCHITECTURE*

On a clear night between December 26, 1999, and January 7, 2000, those walking through Mexico City's central square, formally titled La Plaza de la Constitución but commonly called el Zócalo, could look up and see a tangled net of piercing bluish-white searchlights stretching overhead as far as ten to twenty kilometers. Some passersby could even say that they had in fact designed a particular light-beam configuration, a new one transforming the night sky every six to eight seconds, illuminating the surrounding National Palace, municipal buildings, the Metropolitan Cathedral, the Supreme Court of Justice, and the Templo Mayor Aztec ruins. Each of these designs formed a part of *Vectorial Elevation,* an interactive Web- and site-based installation devised by new media artist Rafael Lozano-Hemmer and commissioned by the Mexican Culture Council for the city's millennium celebration (Figure 5.1).

Working with designers and technicians from four countries,

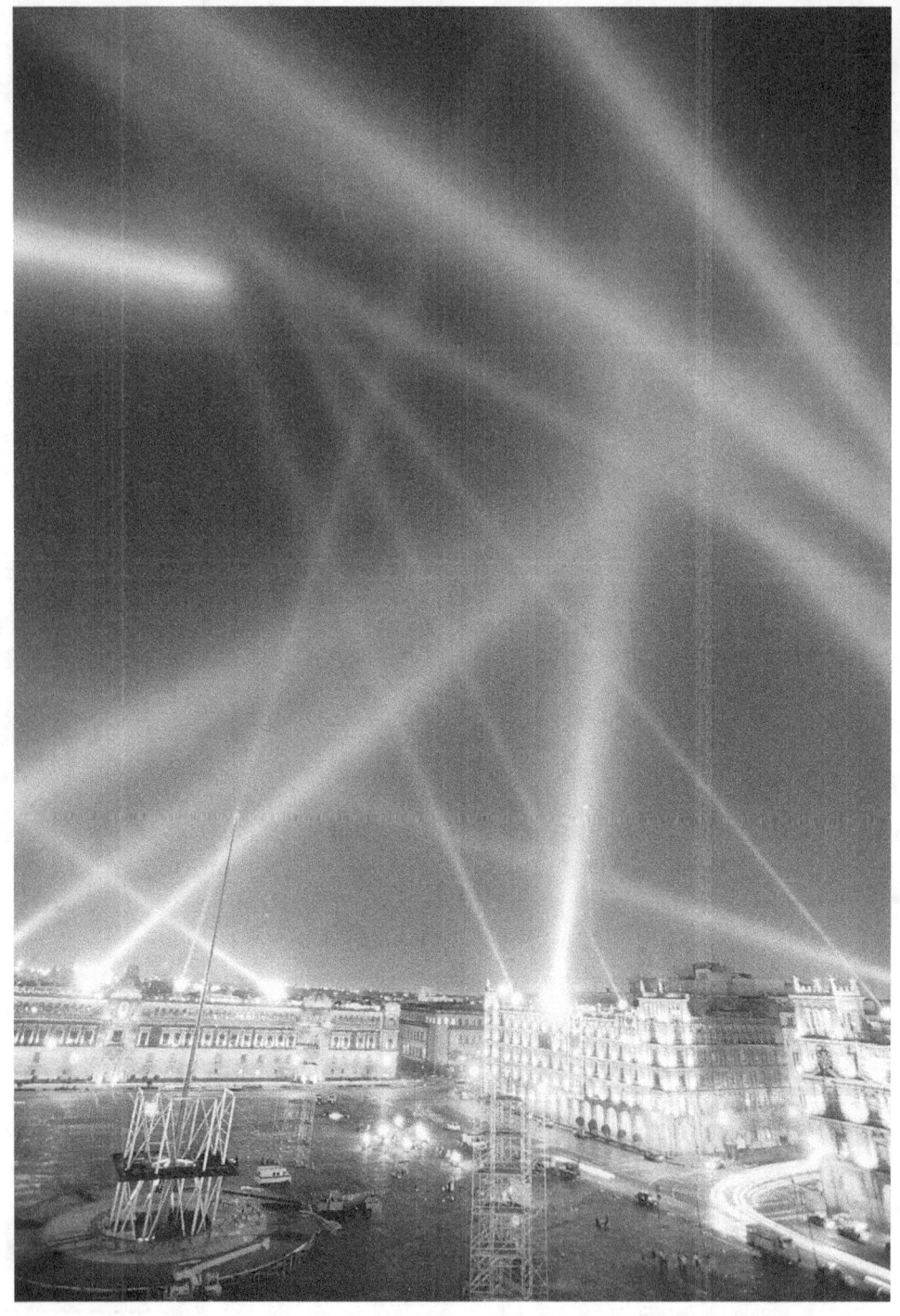

FIGURE 5.1. Rafael Lozano-Hemmer, *Vectorial Elevation*, Mexico City, 1999–2000. Photograph by Martin Vargas.

Lozano-Hemmer developed a three-dimensional interactive simulation of the Zócalo located on the project's Web site, www.alzado.net. In order to afford wider access to the site, Internet stations were made publically available on the Zócalo and around the country, mainly in museums and libraries. The interface offered online participants the ability to remotely control eighteen robotic searchlights placed on the rooftops of the buildings around the square. Participants could select each searchlight by clicking its simulated position, all the while navigating a three-dimensional visualization of their design in process. Target points where the selected light beams intersected allowed participants to move a number of beams at once, as well as to randomize, raise, lower, rotate, and/or invert their patterns incrementally. Once satisfied, the participant would submit the finished design online to be physically rendered in Mexico. Connected by data cables and located by GPS trackers, the searchlights in the square were then positioned by a DMX lighting controller, usually used to manage stage lights, that continually produced each new design before fluidly moving on to the next one (Figure 5.2).

The site, which also included a live video of the changing designs from an aerial perspective and detailed information on each of the buildings, received eight hundred thousand visits from a total of eighty-nine countries, although 70 percent of the participants were from Mexico. Thanks to heavy local media coverage, almost everyone was aware that the searchlights were controlled by computers, and most knew about the Internet participation. Speaking on video to Lozano-Hemmer as he documented the project, those in the Zócalo commented on the work's technological and architectural aspects, as well as on its spectacular nature. Some crossing the square at night thought the lights looked like "a constellation," while others thought the beams formed a "roof" or a "dome" above them. For one woman, the designs turned the Zócalo into a "Mexican Hollywood" (Figure 5.3).[1]

In fleeting instances, the public square thus became many things to many people who moved through different real and virtual spaces, interacting either proximately or remotely in both planned and accidental encounters. Lozano-Hemmer does not predict who will connect and how, and he certainly

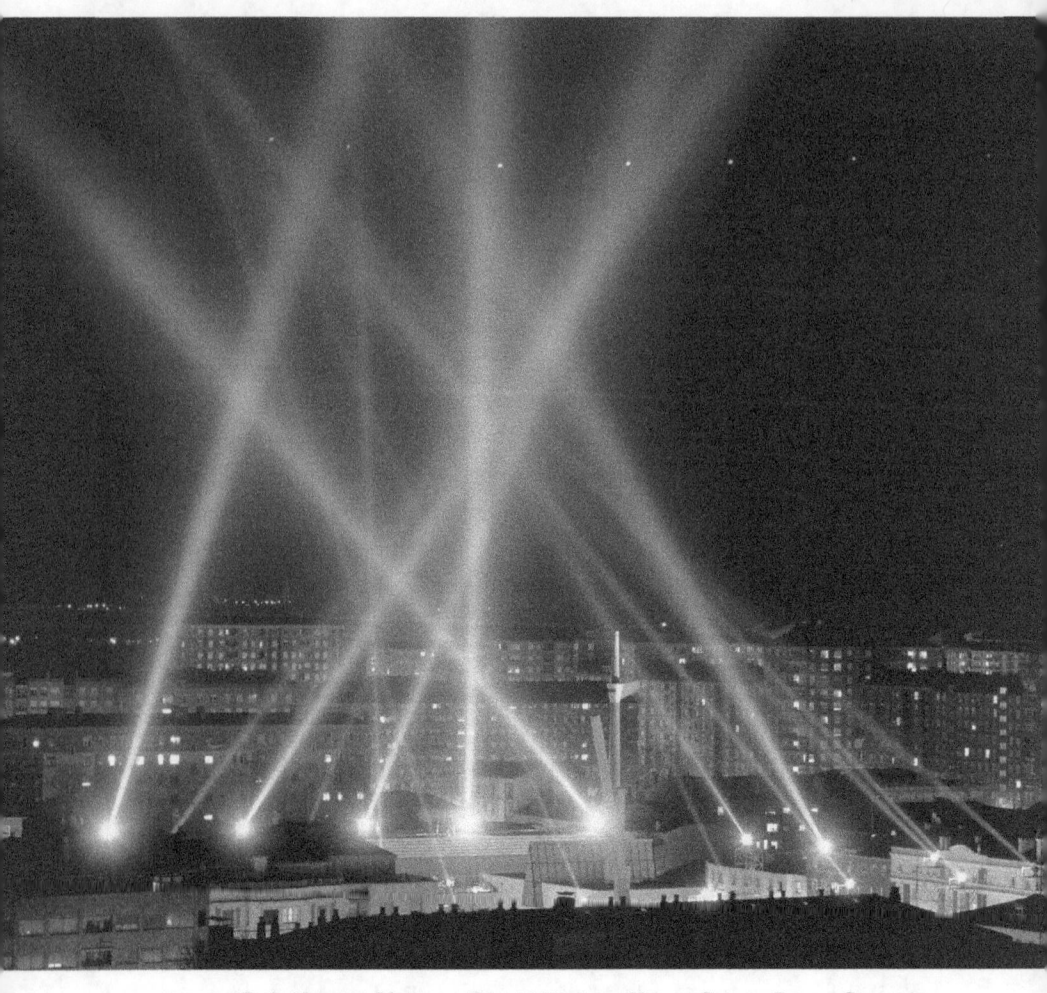

FIGURE 5.2. Rafael Lozano-Hemmer, *Vectorial Elevation*, Vitoria-Gasteiz, Basque Country, Spain, 2002. Photograph by David Quintas.

does not force these connections—that may happen by chance. But his work does provide the initial conditions that open and close a variety of access points, moments of pause, and sites of connection, allowing each of us to find ourselves in place with the help of others. Both individual and collective moments and sites of connection are in turn often coincidental and, more often than not, happen unexpectedly. In projects such as *Vectorial Elevation*, participation in the emergence of a continuously rematerialized, newly accessible

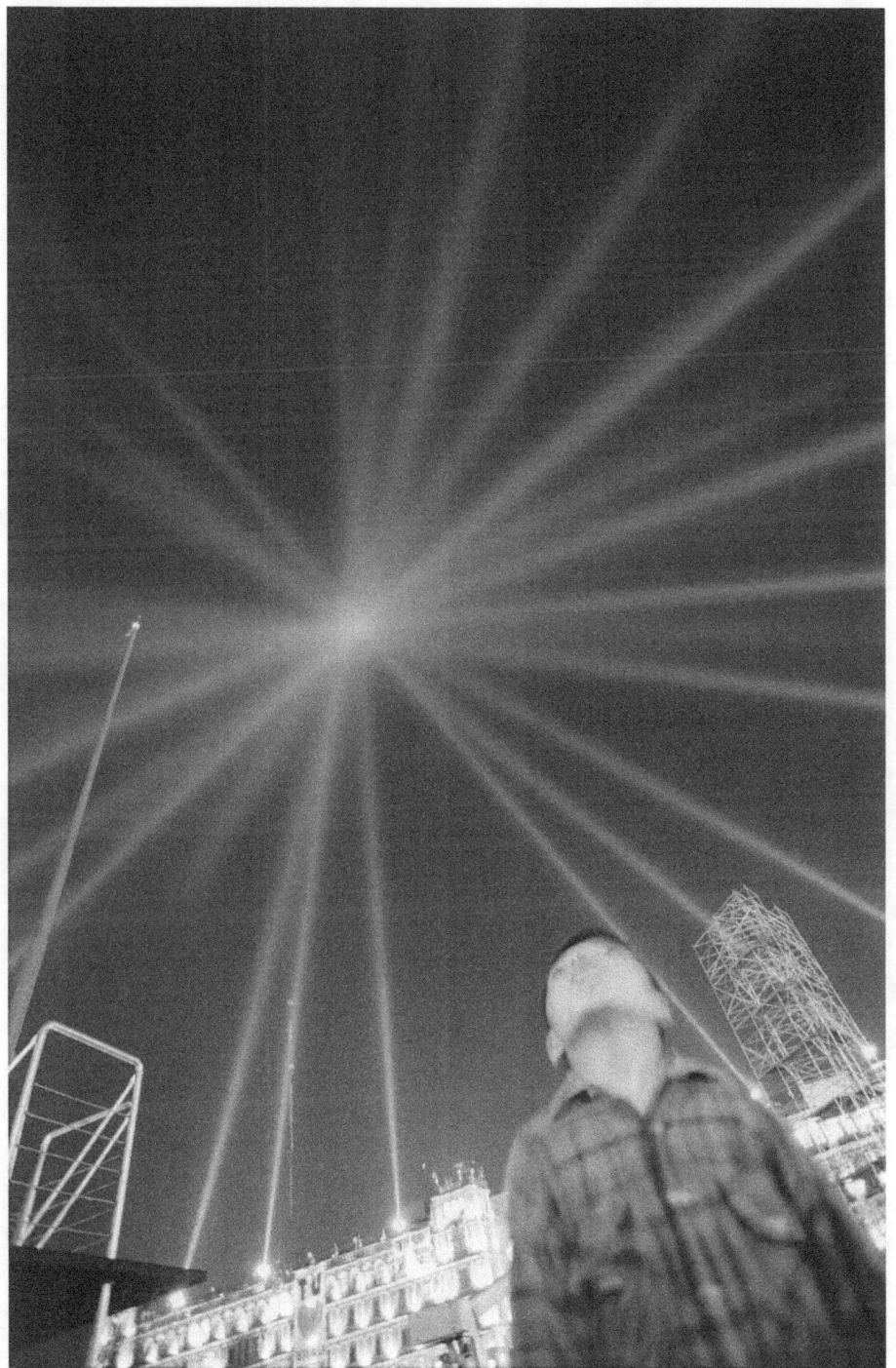

FIGURE 5.3. Rafael Lozano-Hemmer, *Vectorial Elevation*, Mexico City, 1999–2000. Photograph by Martin Vargas.

environment yields these embodied meeting points that are dispersed over time, and over real and virtual spaces. These interactions based on varied levels of participation instigate modes of engaging collectively, though not equally, in the framing of both public and private spaces, and the determination of who gets to use and belong within those sites.

Although Lozano-Hemmer does not overtly attend to or offer structures of home, his attunement to the challenging social efficacy and parameters of participation does put pressure on my concept of a socially engaged program of replacing home to approach a politics of replacing. When considering the ways in which home is offered, such a politics must attend not only to what is being, should be, or can be replaced but must also care for the ways we are able to enact a process of replacing, what that process entails, who gets to be involved, and who does not. While the previous chapter affirms a program of replacing home that depends on public visibility and action as well as on the continual specification and replacing of collectivity, this chapter considers the processes through which social coherence is continuously reactualized. I propose a concept of replaceable collectivity that is purposively asymmetrical and oftentimes accidental, that is made possible by changing dependencies among bodies, environment, and technology, and through which individuals may uncover for themselves and for others the materials and systems of belonging with each other, in place and at home.

RELATIONAL NETWORKS

For the past ten years, Rafael Lozano-Hemmer has been developing large-scale interactive installations and responsive environments that he calls "relational architecture." *Vectorial Elevation* was Lozano-Hemmer's fourth instantiation of relational architecture, debuting in Mexico City and later reinstalled for the opening of the Basque Museum of Contemporary Arts in Vitoria, Spain, in 2002, with 300,000 participants, at the Fête des Lumières in Lyon, France, in 2003, with 600,000 participants, and for a celebration in Dublin of the European Union's expansion in 2004, with 520,000 participants. Using robotics, projections, the Internet, cell phone links, sensors, and custom-made interfaces, Lozano-Hemmer's "architecture" intervenes into public spaces—a parasite that layers itself over existing buildings or embeds itself in expansive plazas, interacting with those bodies who have access to the site and proposing alternative uses for those who may not. Lozano-Hemmer defines *relational architecture* as "the technological actualization of buildings with alien memory."[2] Using alien instead of new to describe his interventions, he avoids the assumption of originality, of a break in which something ends and something begins. Rather, alien memory refers to something that already lingers in the space, that is carried by those who use or misuse the structure, that is traced by those who pass into and out of the space in both past and present time. It is a thought, an action, or a person that does not belong, is out of place, and that can be reactualized through technological networks that engage participants both on and off site, in both close and remote contact with technology and with each other.

Because relational architecture seeks to rematerialize various misplaced objects, persons, or experiences hidden within the site, it distances itself from virtual architecture, even if the two may often share technological constructs and information processes. Although Lozano-Hemmer is careful to admit that relational and virtual architectural concepts are not mutually exclusive or opposing practices, their point of difference hinges on the experience of human bodies within technologically enhanced environments that are a mixed reality of the actual and the virtual. Virtual architecture, rendered for example, in CAVEs (Cave Automatic Virtual Environments) or HMDs (Head-Mounted Displays), depicts familiar landscapes and structures that become accessible to participants either in the same way that they might likely be outside the virtual reality or as fantastic images that afford users extraordinary powers. While the user is within this virtual environment, the outside world also remains the same. Of course this is a crude generalization, but the point I want to make is that Lozano-Hemmer's relational architecture, in contrast, temporarily replaces actual buildings, re-presenting alternative and alien uses through the participants' negotiation of the buildings' virtual sites.

Users become participants, as their accustomed interactions within real spaces are momentarily rerouted and they become linked with others, both online and on the ground.

While inclusive of virtual simulations, relational architecture ultimately aims for a "dissimulation," or a revealing of that which does not belong in the structure or on its site. For Lozano-Hemmer:

> Virtual buildings are data constructs that strive for realism, asking the participant to "suspend disbelief" and "play along" with the environment; relational buildings, on the other hand, are real buildings pretending to be something other than themselves, masquerading as that which they might become, asking participants to "suspend faith" and probe, interact and experiment with the false construct.[3]

Instead of participants pretending to be something they are not, now buildings are the ones masquerading, to use Lozano-Hemmer's word, where the aim is not to mask but, rather, to unveil future uses and misuses of both structure and site. Relational architecture masquerades in order to open up the possibility for new experiences within the spatial environment by providing the conditions for two specific kinds of buildings to pretend to be what they are not. Lozano-Hemmer identifies *default buildings* as architecture that is generic, featureless, and whose structures are cropping up around the globe—one indistinguishable from the next. Relational architecture temporarily localizes the spatial situation and specifies the embodied experience of these kinds of buildings. In addition, relational architecture also confronts *vampire buildings,* so called by the Spanish architect Emilio Lopez-Galiacho. Vampire buildings are those that are immortalized through restoration, and that are monumentalized and protected against erosion.[4] Relational architecture seeks to mask over these buildings to reintroduce life, and thus change, death, and possible reincarnation, into these sites. An architectural masquerade is therefore a performance of concealing and revealing, a process that reimagines and momentarily replaces the spatial environment by reintegrating its participants in real time and across a variety of competing, palimpsestic spaces.

Lozano-Hemmer is also careful to distance his practice from a kind of site-specific art that acknowledges the spatial specificities of the locale alone. Taking on a "temporary specificity" that is not only site-bound, Lozano-Hemmer's architecture is, rather, "relationship-specific," meaning it focuses on the tenuous, temporary relationships between the site and its ever-changing public, and the microhistories and politics that are traced through that space. "I am very committed," Lozano-Hemmer says, "to the idea that a site consists of an indeterminate number of intersecting imaginary, socio-political, physical and tele-present spaces. . . . What is specific is the new behaviors that might emerge during interaction."[5] Relational architecture thus activates static, often ominous public buildings and inaccessible spaces so that, in his words, "the input of the people in the street can provide narrative implications apart from those envisioned by the architects, developers or dwellers."[6] Intervening in these monumental structures, Lozano-Hemmer creates what he appropriately calls "anti-monuments," which are not structures but instead actions that allow people to take part in a revisualization and ultimately a reembodiment of their spatial surroundings.[7] In fact, in 2002, Lozano-Hemmer redefined relational architecture as "anti-monuments for public dissimulation."[8] The antimonument as action suggests alternatives to the fetishization of the static site that Lozano-Hemmer links to status quo representations of cultural and economic power. Refusing to contribute to the immortalization of architectural structures or to the collection and dissemination of art objects, he instead focuses on offering the conditions for social experiences (Figure 5.4).[9]

The nature of these social experiences is what connects Lozano-Hemmer's relational architecture to the relational art that shares its name. Gathering together contemporary 1990s art installations under the name of *relational aesthetics,* art critic Nicolas Bourriaud has indicated a contemporary trend toward art events and procedures such as exhibition openings, invitations, casting sessions, as well as areas for eating, chatting, and dancing. Without considering the social, economic, and political variables that may not afford egalitarian access or participation in such events, Bourriaud's categorization of the art installation as "social interstice" places new emphasis

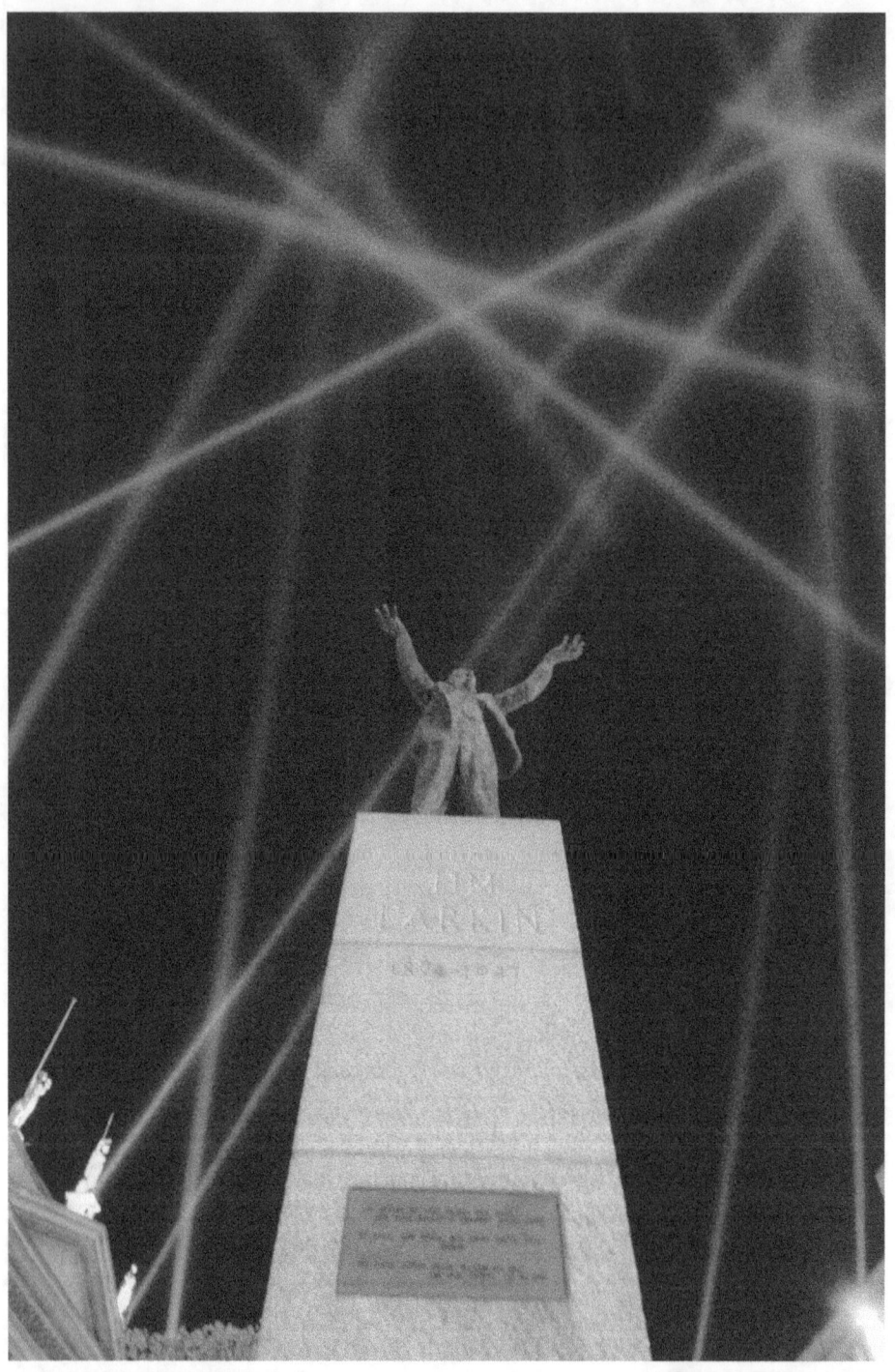

FIGURE 5.4. Rafael Lozano-Hemmer, *Vectorial Elevation*, expansion of European Union Celebrations, O'Connell Street, Dublin, 2004.

on the coming-together and coming-apart of participants across temporarily constructed sites.[10] Lozano-Hemmer's own relational architecture is user-activated and self-organizing, catalyzing multiple interactions with buildings, bodies, real spaces, and digital sites. Expanding on Bourriaud's qualification of relational practices, Lozano-Hemmer's relational architecture provides the conditions for events that happen in multiple fields that in turn resonate in several sometimes unpredictable and usually temporary places within its expanded real and digital network.[11]

Alongside its comparative association with relational artworks, relational architecture is also indebted to the structure and system of self-organizing biological networks. Noted by Lozano-Hemmer as foundational to his practice is Chilean biologists Humberto Maturana and Francisco Varela's study of autopoiesis, which explains the networked unity of structure and function in natural living systems—a unity that is defined through cellular components that continuously regenerate the network of relations that produced the system in the first place.[12] In order to arrive at the contemporary significance of the biological network as model for relationality, Mark C. Taylor demonstrates a movement from networked mechanization, influenced by modern industrial developments, to network culture, as influenced by contemporary communication technologies. The crucial cultural turn is from a mechanistic to an organic system of representation, organization, and experience. Considering Kant's *Critique of Judgment*, Taylor marks a significant moment in the Third Critique in which Kant analyzes the difference between mechanisms and organisms. According to Kant, the cause and effect, along with the means and ends, of mechanisms are externally related. Organisms, on the other hand, are self-organizing and integrated. They emerge from within an interplay of component parts and a systematically unified whole and are thus mutually constitutive.[13]

Indicative for Kant of "self-organized being," the reciprocal relation between parts and the whole has begun to be structurally explored by biochemists and theoretical biologists, such as Maturana and Varela. Their autopoetic understanding of biological systems emphasizes a self-reflexivity in which an organism "continuously generates and specifies its own organization through its operation as a system of production of its own components, and does this in an endless turnover of components under conditions of continuous perturbations and compensation of perturbations."[14] However, the assumption that autopoetic systems are self-contained and therefore closed and complete need not carry truth, as such systems also seem to be necessarily implicated within, and must depend on, other external networks of organization.

In order to elucidate this logical catch, Taylor turns to the writing of sociologist Niklas Luhmann in order to expand on Maturana and Varela's biological autopoetic network, making it applicable to social and communication systems. According to Luhmann, autopoetic systems are both open and closed, and it is this interplay between the two that brings about an interaction between the system and the specific surroundings within which it self-operates. As Taylor concludes: "It is precisely the necessary relation to the environment that keeps the recursivity of the autopoetic system from completely closing in on itself. This is an important point, because Luhmann believes that it prevents autopoetic systems from becoming repressive totalizing structures."[15] Such an argument is applicable to contemporary communications networks and the socially organizing principles that they support. Our ever-advancing present-day technologies also arguably operate like biologically autopoetic systems, in which component parts are self-organizing, self-regenerating, and self-reflexive within a greater whole. Yet similarly in order to retain the possibility of openness and thus of endless variation and adaptability, digitally networked relations must also engage with their social and spatial environments, so as to remain capable of regeneration, revision, and indeed replacement.

This is a direct concern of Lozano-Hemmer's, as he translates organically self-structured and contextually variable relationality into architectural practice. Named architecture though rendered in a form primarily understood as installation art, the work of Lozano-Hemmer is situated disciplinarily between architecture and performance. In its attention to processes of embodied presence, interaction, and activity in real time and across a variety of real and virtual spaces, his relational architecture can be experienced as performance.

But what does it mean for a digitally enhanced, organically structured network that unfolds in time and that is based on spatial and phenomenal relationships to be qualified as architecture? If not offering material structures capable of habitation or protection, then what does this architecture-as-network propose in terms of experiences of belonging? How can digital networks take part in contemporaneously replacing both public and private experiences of home?

A network can most generally be defined as a system for organizing and structuring the relationship between things, whether they are biological components, people, objects, or information. Further specified by architectural and new media theorists Anthony Burke and Therese Tierney:

> Networks consist classically of nodes, or non-dimensional points of connection, and links, equally non-material connections that usually conform to one of several organizational topologies such as centralized, distributed, bus, or mesh, which affect the nature of the relationships they embody and how they may be analyzed and understood.[16]

Networks are thus qualified and differentiated by their ability to perform flexibly, interrelationally, and organizationally. With relational methods of collection and allowances for infrastructural variation provided by advances in mathematics and mobile telecommunications, networks have become the central organizational model of our contemporary moment.

The associations between networks and architecture are not, however, new. As architectural theorist Mark Wigley points out, the associations among networks, spatial organization, and architecture are historically far-reaching, in play well before developments in digital information culture. In order to contextualize Lozano-Hemmer's relational architecture within a wider framework of networked situation and belonging, I want to take a short detour through architecture's theoretical and material intersections with the network in order to plot out prior formulations of networked relationality that have influenced our contemporary structures and systems of being in place with others. Wigley has already taken up this task, and he provides the following overview:

The ancient forms of the word "network" were applied at once to the work of humans and that of animals—as in fishing nets and spiders' webs. In the eighteenth century, it was common to use the word to describe the inside of the body itself, as in the organization of veins, muscle bundles, etc., and in the nineteenth century it was a standard label of systems of rivers, canals, railways, cables, electricity, sewers, etc. Finally, it gets applied to organizations of immaterial things like property and groups of people. The word slides seamlessly from biology to technology to society.[17]

With this trajectory in mind, I would like to focus on the development of mechanistic and organic models of networked relationality taking place from the nineteenth to twentieth centuries, particularly as such developments have affected the structural design and embodied experience of architecture and urban space.

Modern architectural historian Sigfried Giedion identifies nineteenth-century industrial developments as central to a very modern determination and experience of space—one that foreshadows a networked determination of the spatial environment. In fact, Giedion's proposed harmony between architecture and the new realities of industrial, technological, and scientific advancements charts a legacy that still remains important today. Developed between 1850 and 1890, iron changed architecture from a craft to an industrial production. For Giedion, this shift in the engineering process of construction also articulated a shift in architectural vision. The introduction of iron in roof framings and skeletal supports demanded a more complex and fluid balance of forces rather than the previously rigid plan of load-bearing structures. "Iron," wrote Giedion, "opens up spaces."[18] The new material therefore offered new design possibilities, allowing a previously unthinkable partnership with glass to create the greatest possibility for transparency and horizontal suspension.

By foregrounding the shift in aesthetic considerations in the face of the changing material landscape, Giedion also shifted the focus of architectural theory from the nineteenth-century architectural object to the twentieth-century modern observer and user of the built space. For Giedion, both the construction and experience of built forms could in fact be predicated on the moving body of the observer in relation to the built environment.[19] This mobile determination of architectural space, afforded through the use of materials and methods perfected at the end of the nineteenth century, formed the basis of Giedion's most influential modern "space-time" conception. This space-time experience of the environment can, in turn, be linked to a networked organization in which body, object, and landscape are mutually constitutive, self-organizing, and adaptable.[20]

Identifying the movement of the observer around and within a built space as no longer fixed to any linear axis or geometric structure, Giedion's conception results in an experience of space that is also no longer a product of an orderly or rational sequence of movements. Indeed, as early as 1928, Giedion was differentiating between the earlier "rigid-feudal projects" and modern architecture's "living projects" that organically integrated themselves within their surrounding landscape and were designed in response to both the circulation of traffic around their outer facades as well as through their inner divisions.[21] This linking of bodily movement and spatial organization actualizes a relational logic that in turn determines material building practices. For key modern architects Le Corbusier, Walter Gropius, and Mies van der Rohe, whose built projects were central to Giedion's thinking, the body in flux constructs a variable understanding of space as a responsive and adaptable network.

By the twentieth century, then, the horizontally expansive network of infinite flows and meeting points had become integrated into the construction of buildings themselves. As Mark Wigley describes it: "Interiors became circuits. Flow on the outside ever more seamlessly merged into flow on the inside until the line defining the limit of the building became paper thin."[22] But as Wigley contends, it was not until the experiments in architectural dematerialization by such international collectives as Archigram and Superstudio in the late 1960s and 1970s that the network as both structure and system became the ultimate symbol, not only of spatial construction but also of embodied situation within the spatial environment. Both architectural groups aimed to resituate bodies within nodes and lines of linkage by exploring the disappearance of static built foundations and by expanding the conventional parameters of architectural practice away from its unquestioned commitment to the solid, fixed site.

For its part, the British collective Archigram attempted to bring to completion modern architecture's goal of constructing self-organizing and self-sustaining machines for living. Archigram's self-titled newsletter—the nine main issues of which were published between 1961 and 1970—introduced the paper-based designs of core members Warren Chalk, Peter Cook, Dennis Crompton, David Greene, Ron Herron, and Michael Webb. Archigram turned to the potential of emerging technology to imagine deformations and non–object-based networks that lay beyond architecture's structural sites. Their unbuilt projects, such as Peter Cook's 1964 "Plug-In City," David Greene's 1966 "Living Pods," or Michael Webb's 1966 "Cushicle/Suitaloon," as we saw in the previous chapter, revealed "a sublime world of pure servicing, information, networking, transience," in architectural historian Simon Sadler's words.[23] With their interest in systems and flow in ever-emergent spatial situations, Archigram's notations, proposals, and plans sought to dematerialize the walls, floors, and ceilings of architecture, uprooting them, on paper at least, from their ties to spatial enclosure, and initializing a legacy, as Sadler articulates, of "event-based architecture."[24]

Alongside Archigram, the experimental Italian architecture collective Superstudio was also investigating the dematerialized site as network. Led by Adolfo Natalini, Superstudio started in 1966 to produce a body of work that envisioned, again primarily on paper, an antiarchitectural utopia in which repressively fixed architecture and seemingly unavoidable consumer objects would be nonexistent. Instead, Superstudio imagined the world as one continuous circuit board, as exemplified by their 1972 "Supersurface," which rendered the surface of the globe as a horizontally expansive and ever-accessible grid. Natalini aimed, in his own words, for "the elimination of the city as hierarchy and social model, looking for a new free egalitarian state, in which everyone can reach different grades in the development of his possibilities, beginning from equal starting points."[25] This imagined network thus became synonymous with freedom of movement and democratic participation, although as we shall soon see, the material reality of networked organization is always shadowed by other more ominous modes of control. Nonetheless, these unbuilt architectural systems, prevalent in the late 1960s as models of resistance and subversion, visualized the otherwise immaterial ways in which bodies were beginning to relate to each other in the early days of electronic technologies. "It matters little that virtually nothing from all those experiments was built," argues Mark Wigley. "Or to be more precise, what was carefully built was a set of images that remain polemical today, a commentary on the networks we already inhabit rather than a dream of a future world."[26] As buildings became more permeable to their environment, even hypothetically dissolving, architectural attention turned to the evasive yet omnipresent flow of information and bodies through space—a flow that identifies the spatial landscape as network.

Postmodern deconstructivist architecture of the late 1970s and 1980s continued to explore the notion of space as event, where flexibly built sites could respond to and be activated by user movement. "Deconstruction is not demolition," the curators of the 1988 *Deconstructivist Architecture* exhibit at the New York Museum of Modern Art clarified. Instead, "deconstruction gains all its force by challenging the very values of harmony, unity, and stability, and proposing instead a different view of structure: the view that flaws are intrinsic to the structure."[27] Working in both notational form and building construction, deconstructivist architects such as Bernard Tschumi and Peter Eisenman simultaneously dematerialize the solidity of site, displace the stability of structural forms, and rematerialize the site in flux. Eisenman argues that a site, encompassing both the ground and structure, is a function of absence, containing both the memory of previous presence, by which he means both material and corporeal forms, as well as the trace of possible, immanent presence.[28] Thus the site is neither that which was there nor that which will be there, but a complex negotiation of the alternate disappearance and appearance of objects and bodies across space and in time. For Tschumi, there is no space without event, no architecture without embodied program. In his *Manhattan Transcripts,* for example, Tschumi proposes a form of notation that refers to the idea of movement, situating the built site in a network between the past and possible movements of bodies in space.[29] According to Tschumi, bodies in motion "carve out all sorts of new and unexpected spaces," their variable direction and force determining structural form as complementary to embodied movement.[30] For deconstructivist architects, then, there are no pure, stable, or solid forms as architectural tradition would have it but, rather, a system of flows and forces occurring across time.

Now is a good moment to come back to Rafael Lozano-Hemmer since his own contemporary unveiling of the alien uses and misuses of architectural structures and sites appeals to this networked logic of flows and forces, emphasizing the participatory intervention of users, dwellers, and passersby into static buildings. For both modern experimental and postmodern deconstructivist architects, embodied and interconnected movements challenged architecture's conventions of the static place fixed by the impermeable structure, and so architecture's reenvisioned goal was to keep inhabitants in motion and thus out of place. Yet within Lozano-Hemmer's relational architecture, being and belonging in place are instead constantly reassessed and made possible through an organically self-organizing network of live and digital connections whose operation depends primarily on the participation of others across real and virtual environments. In his projects, the digital technology of the real-time interfacing guides the ways in which participants may help each other to use, reuse, revisit, and replace specific spatial sites located on the ground. Specifying the embodied encounters within a built structure, relational architecture calls attention to the uneven processes through which chosen and forced, planned and unplanned interactions take part in experiences of belonging in place.

NETWORKED PARTICIPATION

Posing a challenge to historically utopian visions of architecture as an expansive, connective network, Lozano-Hemmer's development of Web-based interfaces and site-based rematerializations offers multiple avenues for participants to engage disparately, and thus not uniformly or universally, in the temporary determination of accessible public space. Such engagements occur through momentary cohesions that in turn allow some, yet never all, to use and belong within those spaces. As his relational architecture makes clear, this kind of networked participation must acknowledge residues of power and agency, accessibility and legitimacy, that ultimately decide who gets to choose to be spatially situated and who gets chosen for. Who publically participates in the drawing and redrawing of spatial boundaries, or in the self-organization of networked forces and flows, activating the potential for either grounded situation or boundary crossing? Who responds to these participatory networks? Who are the alien persons, uses, and actions that remain out of place, and how are they afforded alternative and temporary modes of individually being and collectively belonging in place? Lozano-Hemmer urges us to begin asking these questions, as he constructs the initial conditions and digital platforms for a variety of interactions among viewers, participants, and technology that together determine the ways in which we gain or lose access to spaces, as we pause in or move through them.

The digital technology that provides the initial impetus for such networked interactions is, for Lozano-Hemmer, inseparable from contemporary identity formation and modern globalized expansions into space. Many of us today cannot seem to imagine what we were like, or how we understood our world, before Web-based technologies. According to Lozano-Hemmer, the process that drives these networks is, however, "not something that has been invented or engineered, but rather that has evolved through constantly changing social, economic, physical and political forces."[31] At our present moment, it is almost impossible to be out of a network, even if some of us may be unaware of, or have no control over, our inclusion.

Invisible, omnipresent, and invasive, networks are now contemporary culture's core organizational structure, as information and new media theorists Alexander Galloway and Eugene Thacker have argued. Their jointly written book, *The Exploit: A Theory of Networks*, details the emergence of networks of both control and resistance within the implicit relationship between political power and technology. As a distributed system, the network emerged as a corrective response to modernity's centralized power hubs and hierarchical methods of organization and control. Once various networks consolidated and engaged with each other, diffusing control ever more horizontally, Galloway and Thacker suggest, "the power centers have evolved downward, adopting the strategies and structures of the terrorists and the guerillas."[32] Widespread connectivity, while conceptually privileged, is now considered a threat by the U.S. government, and networks are even deployed as military systems in the same way as tanks and missiles.

So there is a real difference between the utopian metaphor of the network as democratically accessible and socially communal, and its specific material operations. In fact, in contemporaneously redefining network para-digms, Anthony Burke notes that "the technical liberatory image of networks has been decoupled from the reality of its opposite—that is, networks as a form of ubiquitous control. It is important then to distinguish the image of networks from the networks themselves, for as Thacker points out, 'in the discourses surrounding networks, the tropes of connectivity, collectivity, and participation obscure the material practices of networks.'"[33] Galloway has also urgently called for the material analysis of the ambivalent functions of network structure and organization, in order to understand their effects on political economy. While a network is internally structured to allow an endlessly vari-able multiplicity of nodes, or points of intersections, this multiplicity does not however lead inherently to egalitarian organization. "Quite the opposite," Galloway and Thacker declare, going further to claim that "the liberation of distributed networks, famously articulated by Hans Magnus Enzensberger in his writing on the emancipation of media, is a foil for the real workings of power today."[34] While humans constitute and construct networks, they do so in a way that is unequally distributed and internally inconsistent; there are rules of conduct for the horizontal relationships between computers as well as systems of vertical hierarchy that determine access to domain names.[35] In ad-dition, while individual agency and social formations of connectivity depend on networked interactions, networks are in fact the contemporary medium of power; they exercise control that is both anonymous and nonhuman.

Intersecting with the aims of Lozano-Hemmer's relational architecture, one of Galloway and Thacker's primary goals is to critically analyze and engage with the ways in which network technologies, as both material and immaterial, human and nonhuman, exert political power. Galloway and Thacker point to Michael Hardt and Antonio Negri's concept of empire, which, the former two theorists argue, comes closest to describing the network's operation. Like a network, an empire describes a form of global political organization that is fluid, dynamic, and ever extendable. But what happens when digital information is introduced into the mix? Here lies the significance of Galloway's theorization, and his and Thacker's revisiting, of the material and materializing operations of networked computer "protocol." The concept of protocol refers to "all the technoscientific rules and standards that govern relationships within networks. They are principles of networked inter-relationality, yet they are also principles of political organization."[36] Protocols determine, direct, control, and regulate information flow, as well as embodied and disembodied relationships in real and virtual space, and they also form lines of connections between biological forms and political systems. Indeed, protocols allow for regulation within heterogeneous contingency.[37] For Galloway and Thacker, the network's horizontal, rhizomatic, and distributed organization, as founded on protocol, signals "a new management style, a new physics of organization that is as real as pyramidal hierarchy, corporate bureaucracy, representative democracy, sovereign fiat, or any other principle of social and political control."[38] Just as distributed networks challenged centralized control, now networks themselves must be challenged. A new exploit is needed, the two authors urge—one that is asymmetrical, that is an "anti-Web," and that takes into consideration the nonhuman aspects of the network's control while also addressing the possibly nonhuman aspects of human constituency.

Outlining alternative techniques for temporarily diverting status quo power by momentarily disrupting networked operations, Lozano-Hemmer's relational architecture attempts to respond to such a challenge. On his Web site and in a video-recorded documentation of *Vectorial Elevation*, Lozano-Hemmer calls the work an "ephemeral intervention" that reflects on "urban issues of interdependence, deterritorialization and collective representation."[39] Speaking about his influences for *Vectorial Elevation*, Lozano-Hemmer notes, "Albert Speer and Pink Floyd shows are definitely important precedents."[40] Although viewers and participants in Mexico City may not readily associate searchlights with the threatening antiaircraft surveillance and coordinated sky-scanning patterns prevalent in Europe during WWII, even Hollywood-style searchlights that celebrate over-the-top spectacles send the message that the majority of viewers are small, immaterial, and irrelevant to those producing and participating in these events. *Vectorial Elevation* proposes, in Lozano-Hemmer's words, "new creative relationships between control technologies, ominous urban landscapes, and a local and remote public."[41] Integrating viewers not only as online users but also as the central focus of the project, Lozano-Hemmer rescales the human perspective of the monolithic environment. Instead of being dwarfed by the large square, participants create images and structures that reach far beyond the already massive buildings. By granting control of the searchlights to a variety of participants across the globe, Lozano-Hemmer reveals and then replaces the link between searchlights, surveillance, and authoritarian control.

As a technology of control, the Internet was introduced in Mexico, as in most countries, for military organizational operations but still remains inaccessible to a majority of the nation. Yet for Lozano-Hemmer, technology is unavoidable—its development not necessarily exclusive to developed countries, its actualization capable of both upholding and subverting social inequality and political power. "Think of the software industry in India or the Nortec electronic music movement in Tijuana," he suggests.[42] Lozano-Hemmer's comments do not, however, pretend to erase the tension between social inequality and newly developed technology, whose control consistently and strategically remains in the hands of the already wealthy and politically powerful. Complex technologies certainly run factories in United States–Mexico border towns, but the development of that technology primarily occurs in America, and the underpaid workforce and raw materials come from Mexico. Nonetheless, there may be hidden, microresistant opportunities within these constraints. *Vectorial Elevation*, for its part, reveals avenues through which participants can both gain and lose access to control of digital technologies, offering new spatial and social experiences that are opened up through both the production of one's own and another person's light-beam designs, and often through a confluence of the two.

With participant interactivity as key, a networked dependency emerges among environment, technology, and accidental community, as online participants and on-the-ground viewers come upon each other in a temporarily transformed real and continually transformable virtual space. Interviewing the Canadian theater director Robert Lepage in 1989, Lozano-Hemmer was struck by something Lepage said about computers: while they can communicate efficiently, the director suggested, they do not seem so good at communion.[43] Although Lozano-Hemmer does arguably make a case for alternative moments of computer-generated social communion, the differentiation between communication and communion brings to the fore a central concern of relational architecture. Not necessarily interested in providing the conditions for communication, Lozano-Hemmer's practice instead proposes multiple spaces for people to meet and engage in a shared experience that may in fact be miscommunicated, misunderstood, or unequally shared.

When speaking about his work, Lozano-Hemmer often interchanges *relationality* with *collective interactivity*, by which he means that his projects provide conditions for both "discrete individual participation" as well as "emerging collective patterns of self-organization."[44] Collective interaction need not entail abstractly formulated homogeneity. Instead, to build on arguments made in previous chapters, I am proposing that accidental, temporary, repeated, and revised gatherings, across multiple dimensions of direct and remote interactions, can form potential communities and multiple yet momentary publics over time that are elastic and constantly capable of being realigned. This kind of social coherence is heterogeneously collective and as such attempts to unveil a temporary communion of disparate, individual experiences. The networked sites and systems through which these gatherings cohere and disintegrate offer precarious, vulnerable, and not always viably extendable moments of spatial situation. So if being in place depends on both one's and another's unequal participation in these ongoing replacements of spatial landscapes and structures, then the ways in which we come to be situated and resituated, the ways in which we possibly come to belong and to find home, are not in one or another place but, rather, within the ways we are able to make tenuous connections with others, across a variety of spaces both near and far.

REPLACING NETWORKS OF DEPENDENCY

Acknowledging the uneven distribution of accessibility alongside the possibility of communal coherence within specific spatial landscapes, relational architecture proposes a system of belonging that is not only networked between bodies and sites but that also engages both momentary and extended dependencies between those networked bodies. It is not only that bodies connect and interact with each other, that they relate and that their relations constitute architectural experiences. I am arguing that within these spatial and social relationships we can come to see how bodies depend on one another and how the potential for belonging is opened up through these moments of dependency that are constantly being realigned and replaced. Although *dependency* has become an ideological term most recently pathologized into a morally and psychologically weak identification, the term's root "refers to a physical relationship in which one thing hangs from another," as political theorists and historians Nancy Fraser and Linda Gordon have articulated.[45] Emptied of its deviant connotations, dependency acknowledges social, economic, and political relations as necessarily uneven, interconnected, and relational. Only by considering how one experience of being and belonging in space hangs from another, how one body's spatial situation leans on another, and how those relations of hanging, leaning, cohering, and distancing are framed and repositioned, can we begin not just to propose but to viably enact a socially engaged program of replacing home.

As a way of visualizing these networks of dependency in action, I want to end by turning to another of Lozano-Hemmer's relational architecture projects, *Under Scan*. In that work, thousands of video portraits taken across the East Midlands in England were projected onto the ground of the main squares and pedestrian passageways in Derby, Leicester, Lincoln, Northampton, and Nottingham, from November 2005 through March 2006. The project was commissioned by the East Midlands Development Agency to enliven the public spaces of those cities, and to provoke viewer interaction within the otherwise anonymous sites. Local videographers and producers spent several days in each city gathering and filming a diverse group of people who answered calls to participate in an interactive art project advertised in local papers, schools, and onlines sites. The willing participants, who included students, actors, artists, art viewers, dancers, and members of various local community organizations, were filmed from above while lying on their backs and were free to move around and express themselves however they liked. The only stipulation was that each was asked to make eye contact with the camera at least once during the filming. Their activities varied from resting in one pose, dancing, sleeping, laughing, speaking, and motioning toward the camera while appearing reserved, confrontational, welcoming, or aloof (Figure 5.5).

At first, these video portraits could not be seen under the simultaneous projection of bright white light akin to the power and color of high-noon sunlight and produced by lamps capable of generating 110,000 lumens of intensity. But as people walked around the area, their shadows gradually revealed the video portraits that began to surface as if coming up from water (Figure 5.6). This occurred as a camera-based tracking system linked up with a main computer that was tracing the direction and measured the speed of the pedestrians. The system then would point one of fourteen projectors at the locations where the passersby would most probably intercept a video portrait. The projectors were able to encompass a maximum area of 2,500 square meters, layering up to fourteen different portraits within that framework. The video portraits, in turn, were stored in custom-designed servers that could be activated by a wireless link and were capable of being corrected, rotated,

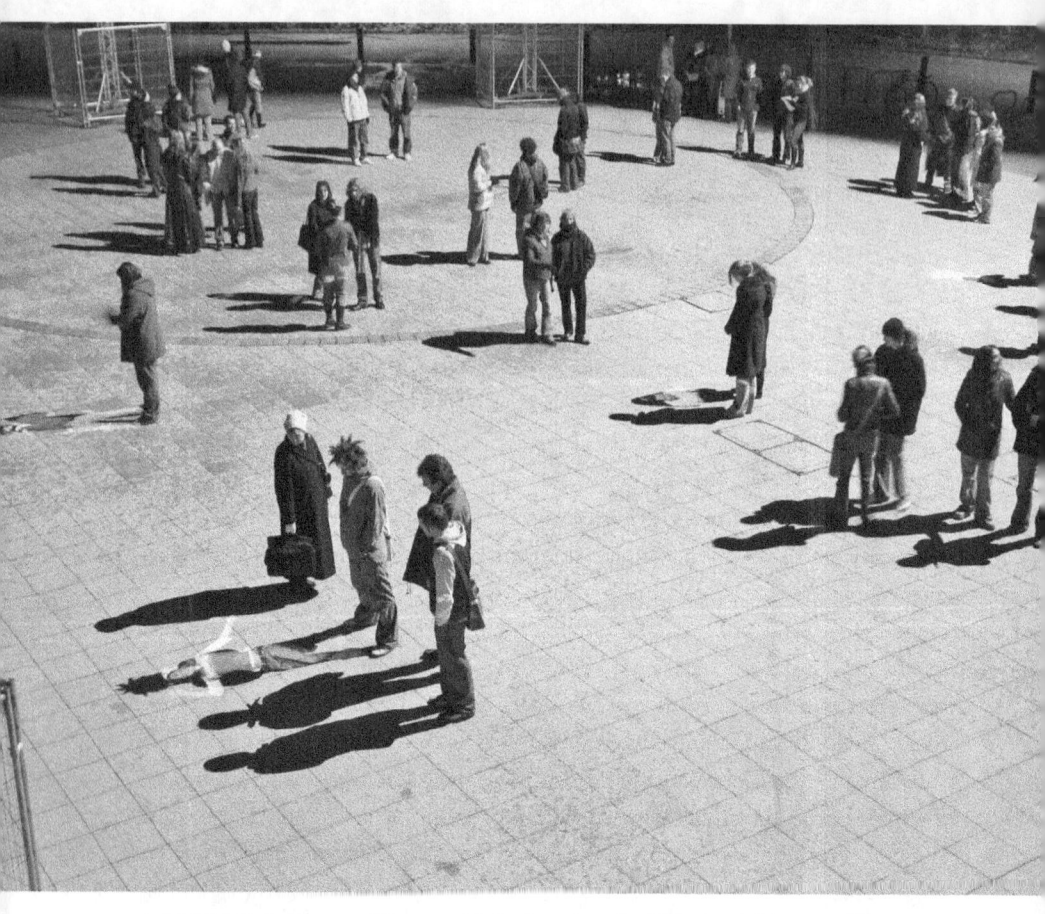

FIGURE 5.5. Rafael Lozano-Hemmer, *Under Scan*, Lincoln, U.K., 2005. Photograph by Antimodular Research.

inverted, and geometrically scaled to approximately match the size and scale of the passing bodies.[46] The short sequence of video portraits began with the subjects in a still position turned away, but as they appeared within the shadows, their bodies moved and their heads turned to look straight at the pedestrian, as if about to engage with him. When a shadow moved away from a portrait, the portrait also looked away, motionless again (Figure 5.7).

In Lozano-Hemmer's video documentation of the project, viewers became increasingly aware of the project's ability to provoke people to start talking to each other, as multiple passersby stood together in temporary

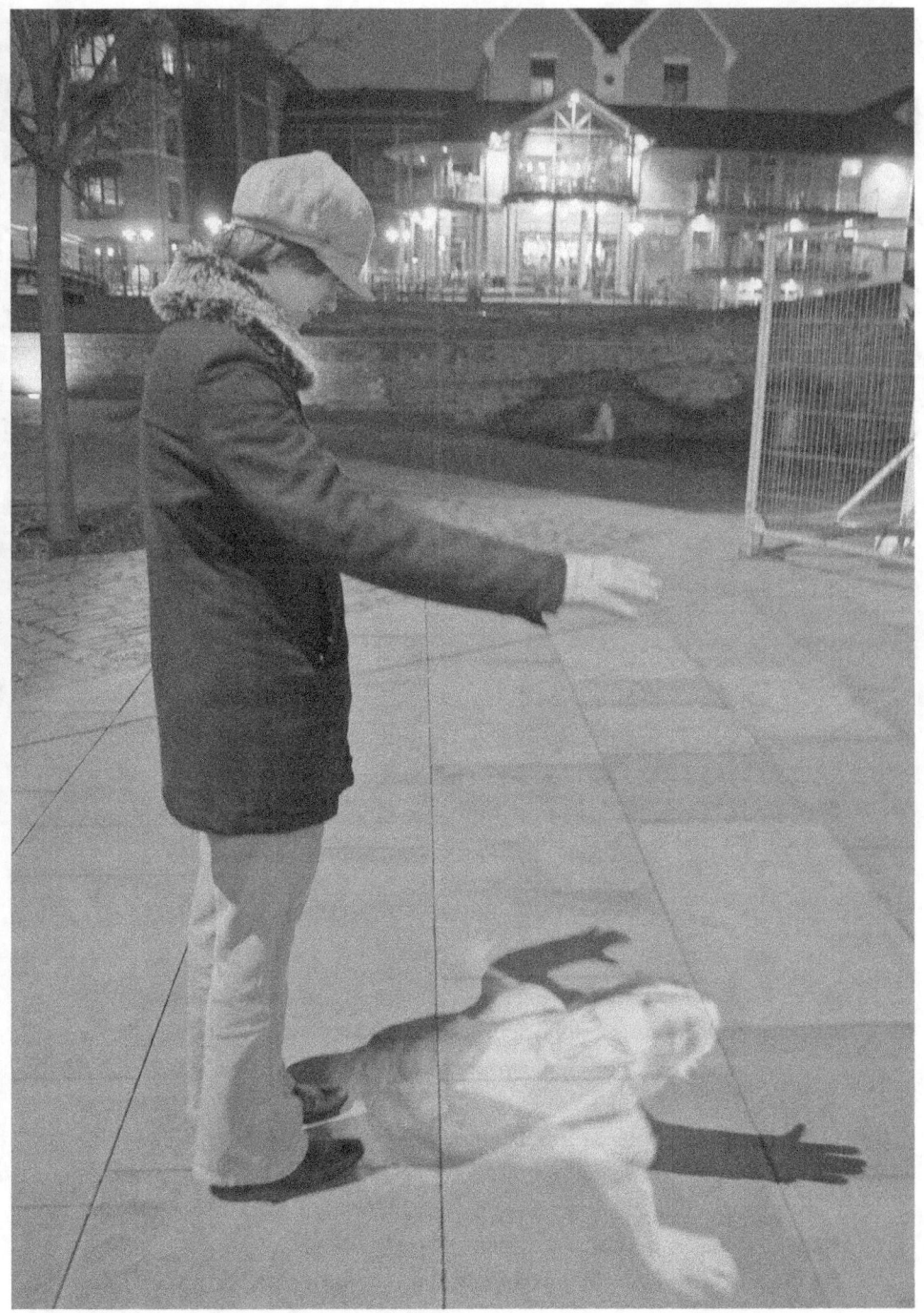

FIGURE 5.6. Rafael Lozano-Hemmer, *Under Scan,* Nottingham, U.K., 2006. Photograph by Antimodular Research.

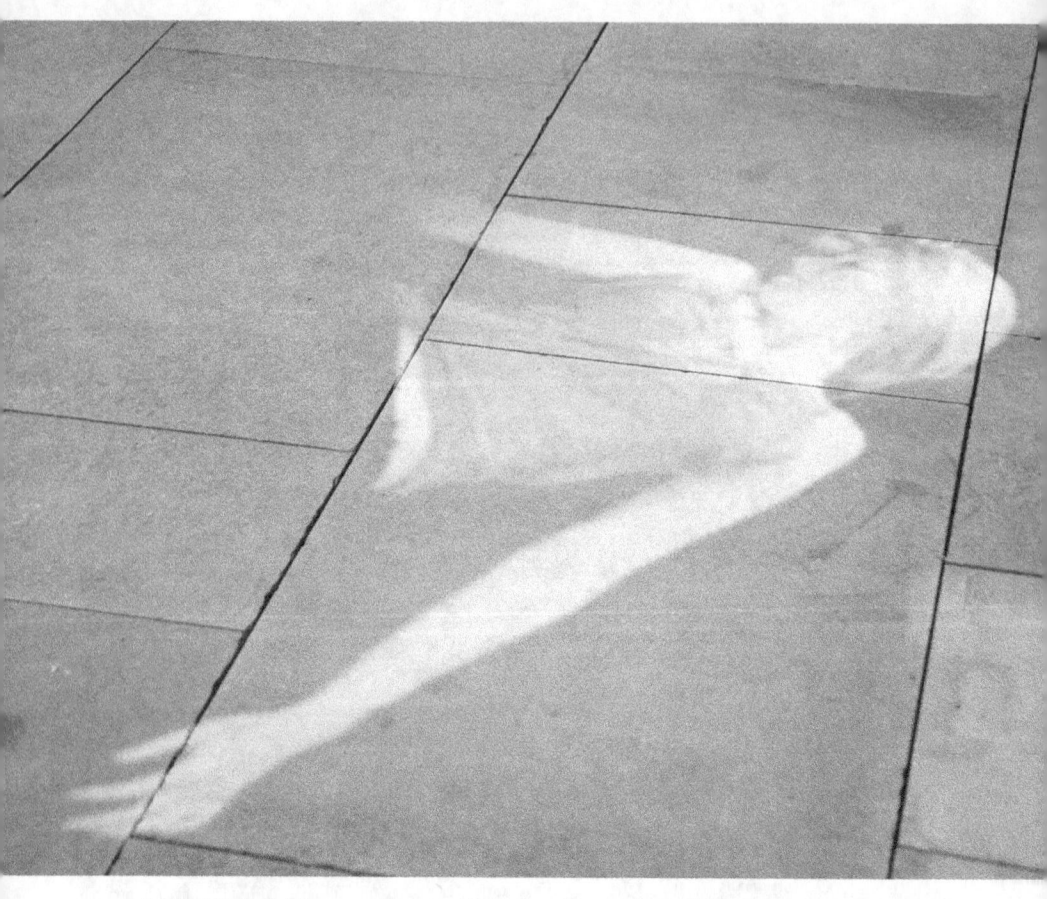

FIGURE 5.7. Rafael Lozano-Hemmer, *Under Scan*, Nottingham, U.K., 2006. Photograph by Antimodular Research.

groups helping each other engage with a video or watching others unfold.[47] Interrupting these interactions between viewers and video portraits was the tracking mechanism—its regular grid projected down onto the site every seven minutes (Figure 5.8). For many viewers, this particular effect was eerie, forcing them to continuously recognize that they were already implicitly placed within a surveillance system that knew what everyone was doing and could also predict what they would do next.[48] Lozano-Hemmer's relational architecture thus tracks its users, as the pathways and activities of passersby are systematically and digitally monitored. But as the tracking system is regularly revealed, his

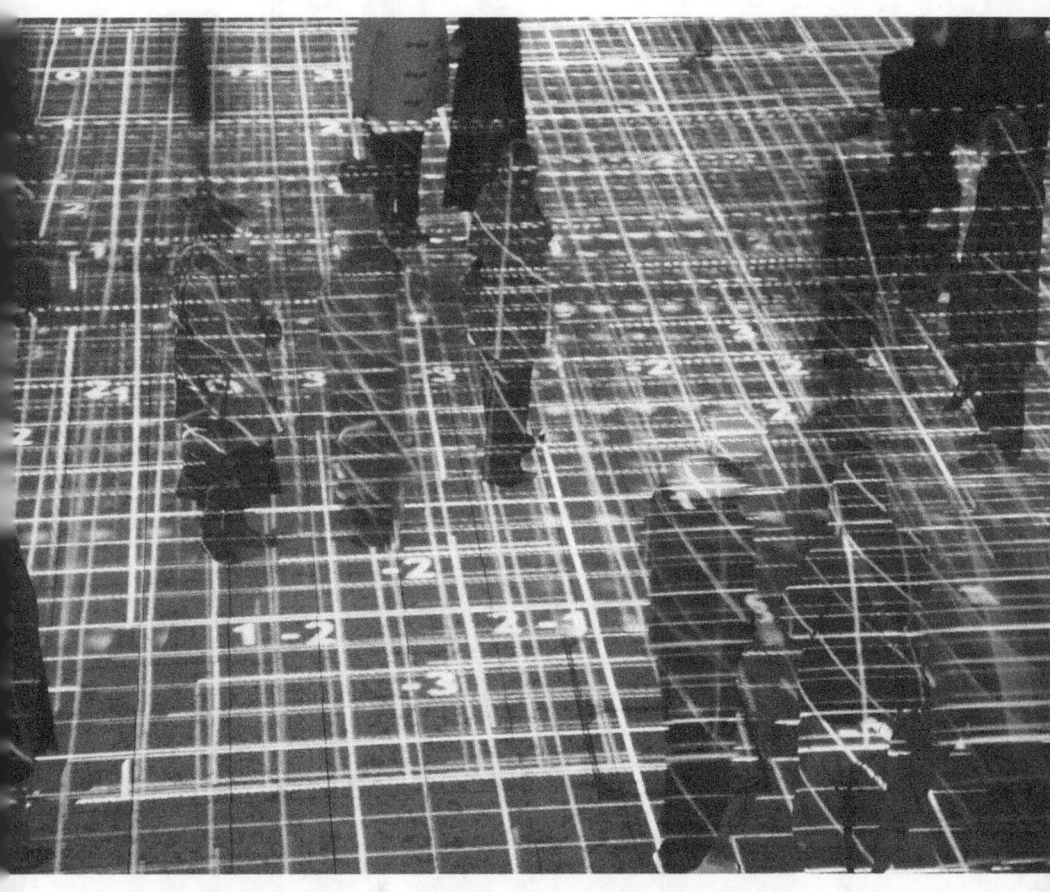

FIGURE 5.8. Rafael Lozano-Hemmer, *Under Scan*, Lincoln, U.K., 2005. Photograph by Antimodular Research.

viewers can also watch the system back, surveying the means of their own surveillance. While opening up these kinds of moments and sites of interaction, Lozano-Hemmer also reveals the ways in which participants interact not only with each other but also with the system that enables their connection in the first place. As people cross back and forth over the invisibly embedded videos, in or out of line with the tracking grid, starting and stopping at differing instances and speeds, their momentary gatherings and accidental meeting points depend on multiple recognitions across various spaces over five different cities (Figure 5.9).

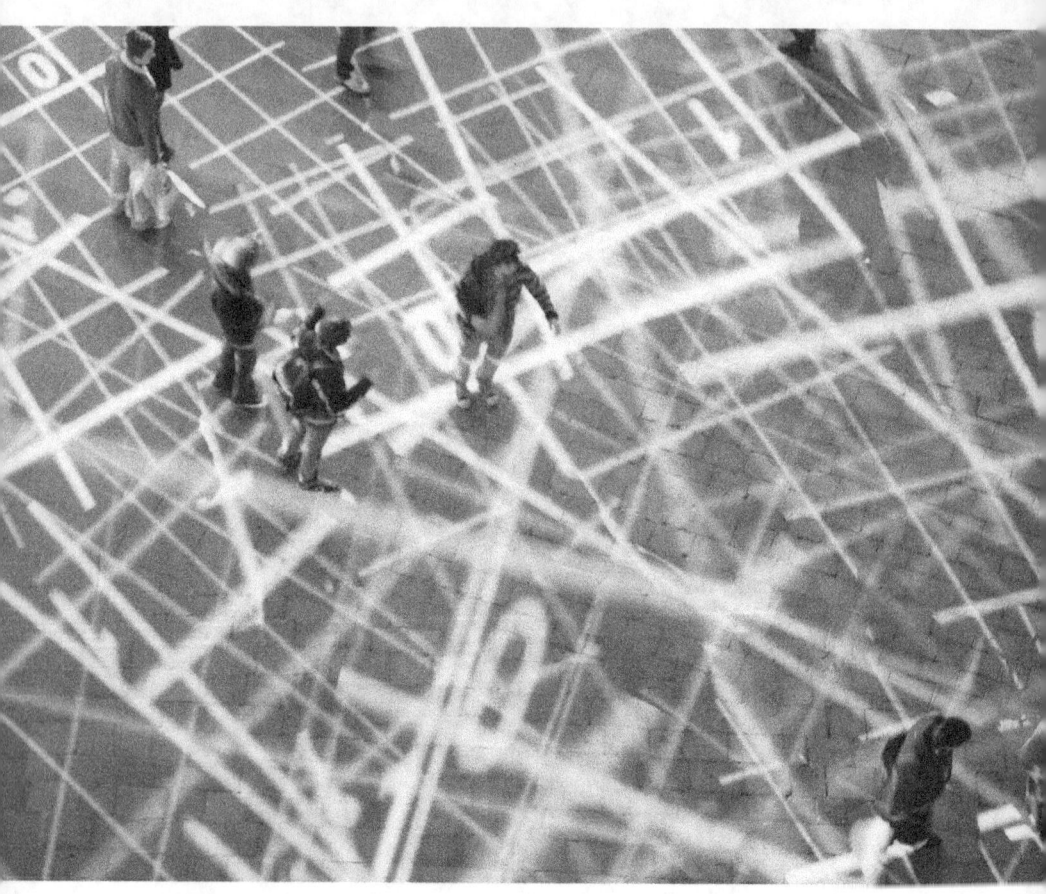

FIGURE 5.9. Rafael Lozano-Hemmer, *Under Scan*, Leicester, U.K., 2006. Photograph by Antimodular Research.

Accessibility, to spaces and to each other, can therefore be potentially revised through relational dependencies that occur in this mixed reality of real and virtual space, as one participant proposes an on-the-ground spatial experience for another or, as in the case of *Vectorial Elevation,* interacts online with the spatial configurations of past participants and creates newly possible ones. Such dependencies mutually constitute individual agency and collective organization. This mutuality is however contingent on accident, miscommunication, delay, and asymmetry as a pedestrian unexpectedly comes upon an embedded video, as another changes her path to intersect with that viewer and video in one of many unplanned gatherings, as the tracking system misfires when someone else moves off course and that video remains unseen, or as it lays a projection down in front of another person who was not tracked but somehow fell into its line. A relational project like *Under Scan* therefore offers a visualization of how this mutual constitution occurs, as the image production of individual bodies is rendered simultaneous to the accidentally shared, unevenly distributed, multiple pathways of others as tracked with and against the larger grid pattern.

For new media theorist Mark Hansen, Lozano-Hemmer's projects "demonstrate that embodiment today can only be conceived *as collective individuation*, as an individuation that requires a certain disembodiment of embodied individuals."[49] Such a disembodiment occurs through digital technologies and networked information that nonetheless make possible the interactions that afford heterogeneously collective embodiment. In other words, disembodiment through technology in the form of information is, for Hansen, a historically necessary dimension of embodiment. Such is the foundational argument of Hansen's book *Bodies in Code,* the definition of its title, and an argument that also expounds on Galloway and Thacker's suggestion that humans are at least partially constituted through nonhuman means. *Technicity,* to use Hansen's word, and not necessarily or only networked technicity, has always been implicit in processes of embodiment.[50] When embodied agents engage with the technologies that trigger their experience of their own bodies, those of others, and the environment in which these experiences occur, Hansen argues that these interactions "establish feedback loops in which embodiment and information mutually catalyze one another's ongoing evolution, rendering it a co-evolution that perfectly expresses the contemporary stage of the technogenesis of the human."[51] Activated through Lozano-Hemmer's portrait projections, this coevolution is based on constant realignments between body and technology, and between alternately disembodied and embodied individuals and collectives.

Hansen makes his argument by focusing on an earlier Lozano-Hemmer relational architecture project, *Body Movies* of 2001, in which prerecorded, unmoving images of bodies in all scales and sizes were invisibly projected onto the sides of large public buildings, beginning initially in Rotterdam. Viewers were able to make these images appear by matching up the shadows of their own bodies with the projections, both of which were rendered in scales ranging from human to superhuman. I have focused on Lozano-Hemmer's later work *Under Scan,* however, because it retains the human scale of both video participant and on-the-ground viewer; as Lozano-Hemmer admits, the video portraits have their own sense of agency, and so the interactions are more "bi-directional."[52] *Under Scan* also centralizes movement, as the passages of people through the square are interrupted and caught by the emerging activities of the video images. In addition, the more recent project visually publicizes the technological network of computerized tracking devices that predicts the unfolding of both planned and unplanned encounters.

These variations between the two works further qualify the processes of embodiment and collectivity as initially proposed by Hansen and, for my purposes, bring to the fore moments and sites of networked dependencies between bodies. In *Under Scan,* invisible individuals who appear very much like their potential viewers but who are disembodied through video and seemingly buried in the ground are then partially and unevenly reembodied within the accidental pathways and temporary communal gatherings of others. This process of social cohesion and individual recognition is not necessarily democratic, as the tracking devices randomly cue up video sequences while passersby, either singularly or in momentary groupings, literally have to step on another body to make its image appear under their shadows. The network of passages and pauses, appearances and disappearances can be contrasted with the regular grid and calculations of the surveillance system that validates, controls, and determines certain sites of interaction and reembodiment. Yet small systemic misfires, coincidental derailings, and variable *détournements* can also afford the possibility of other connections and social engagements as well.

Under Scan therefore actualizes the continuous realignments and replacements inherent in processes of embodiment and situation as directed by planned and unplanned collective forces that may be technologically, and thus socially and politically, heterogeneous. Collective participation, which is purposively asymmetrical and necessarily accidental, is made possible by constantly changing dependencies among bodies, spatial environment, and technology. By uncovering the means by which we are linked together, these replaceable networks of interdependence continuously determine and refigure the ways in which we are conditioned by, at the mercy of, in control of, rest with, trust, and turn to each other. If, as I have been arguing across all these chapters, the process of replacing home punctuates pathways of departure and return, and cycles of use and reuse, with acts and structures of embodied lingering, then we must recognize and situate these tenuous dependencies—dependencies that form between those bodies held coincidentally, but also meaningfully, in place and that approach the experience of being and belonging at home.

For his part, Lozano-Hemmer has suggested that being in place could very well identify a feeling of knowing "that you belong nowhere and that you belong to many places at the same time."[53] To restate a version of this sentiment that has traced its way throughout this book: we may not stand still for very long, but we can continuously move into and out of place; we can resituate and replace our experience of belonging at home in a variety of sites. Resituation by way of replacement is a key process that defines our present mode of momentarily grounding ourselves in space and with others. As a model of being and possibly belonging at home, replacing activates how we come to situate our bodies in relation to one another, and in relation to our dwelling places over time.

We linger in spaces, and then we choose or are forced to move on. But in order to linger somewhere, to be at home for however long, we must incompletely, partially, or virtually replace the ways in which we were just situated, ways that depend on our coming-together over all kinds of distances. If we can attach a politics to these acts of replacing, then we are able to redo these moments of connection—to reuse and remake the sites and structures around us by engaging again with the material residues of past acts undertaken by others, onto and by means of other things. Perhaps then we may acknowledge not only that what we do has a specific and sustained impact on the balance of things and beings around us but also that our impact is never final, that we have the ability to replace our actions, to act again with different outcomes in revisited places and with renewed engagements, to come together and apart again, and to pose that possibility for others to take on either with or after us. We replace home when we are able to rematerialize these lines of connection between past and present sites, structures and dwellers—for ourselves, but also most carefully and consequentially for others.

ALMOST HOME

That we move through an ever-expanding world cannot be avoided, as we travel by choice either physically or virtually, as we are pushed by environmental catastrophe, or as we are urged under political pressure. Yet that we still care about specific spatial situations, that we need to be materially housed, and that we want to belong cannot be ignored. By finding a place for these desires, artists and architects can continue to reimagine and then materially replace the specific interdependencies between a body and a built site, and between the bodies held and housed there. And in disclosing these findings with others, each of us can continue to engage in the ongoing replacement of home, however accidentally, contingently, or momentarily.

This book has charted a pathway that begins by acknowledging idealized narratives of individually situated dwelling and that moves toward a program for socially engaged spatial situation, in which temporary, visible, cohesive, and public moments of being in place are continuously redetermined. By considering a return to the hut, the reuse and reowning of spatial sites, the reintegration of structures within existing spatial frameworks and social systems, and finally by making publically visible the displacement of certain social bodies and the networks of dependency required to resituate us all over time, I have contemplated the viability of home, as both a material structure and an experience of belonging. Throughout such a trajectory, I have proposed a system of replacing that reinstates embodied interactions in specific sites by way of constantly renewable structural analogies, substitutions, and surrogacies. In the end, against a backdrop of unrelenting flows, forces, and upheavals, perhaps the best I can say is that replacing home is founded on a recognition of the ways each of us already makes do with our given spatial and social environments and is enacted when we figure out how to sustain and expand those particular materials and methods over time.

I want to end with an example that speaks to the rationale and faith embedded in such a claim. On one of his first nights spent in New York while trying to fall asleep in his new apartment, the artist Do Ho Suh found himself longing for the familiar surroundings and settings he had left in Seoul. Then he remembered the Korean expression "You walk the house." Denoting the commonplace portability of traditional domestic Korean architecture, this phrase marks both the material foundation and inspiration of Suh's 1999 installation, *Seoul Home/L.A. Home/New York Home/Baltimore Home/London Home/Seattle Home*. The work is a life-size, precisely measured, transportable fabric replica of his family home, easy to pack up and carry, whose ever-expanding title incorporates each new site of its temporary situation and exhibition (Figure E.1).

Traveling back to Korea to visit his parents, Suh began by making detailed notes of both the exterior design and interior spaces of their home, taking care to pause over the little marks and indentations he had made along the walls and floor as a child. While his family home is made up of five contemporary and traditional Korean structures, Suh focused on the section that his father had built out of red-pine timbers collected over the years from a dismantled nineteenth-century building formerly located on the grounds of King Sunjo's palace. Itself already a replica, the Suh's version took its inspiration from the domestic structure that the Yi dynasty king had built in 1828 so that he could experience the ordinary living spaces of his civilian subjects.

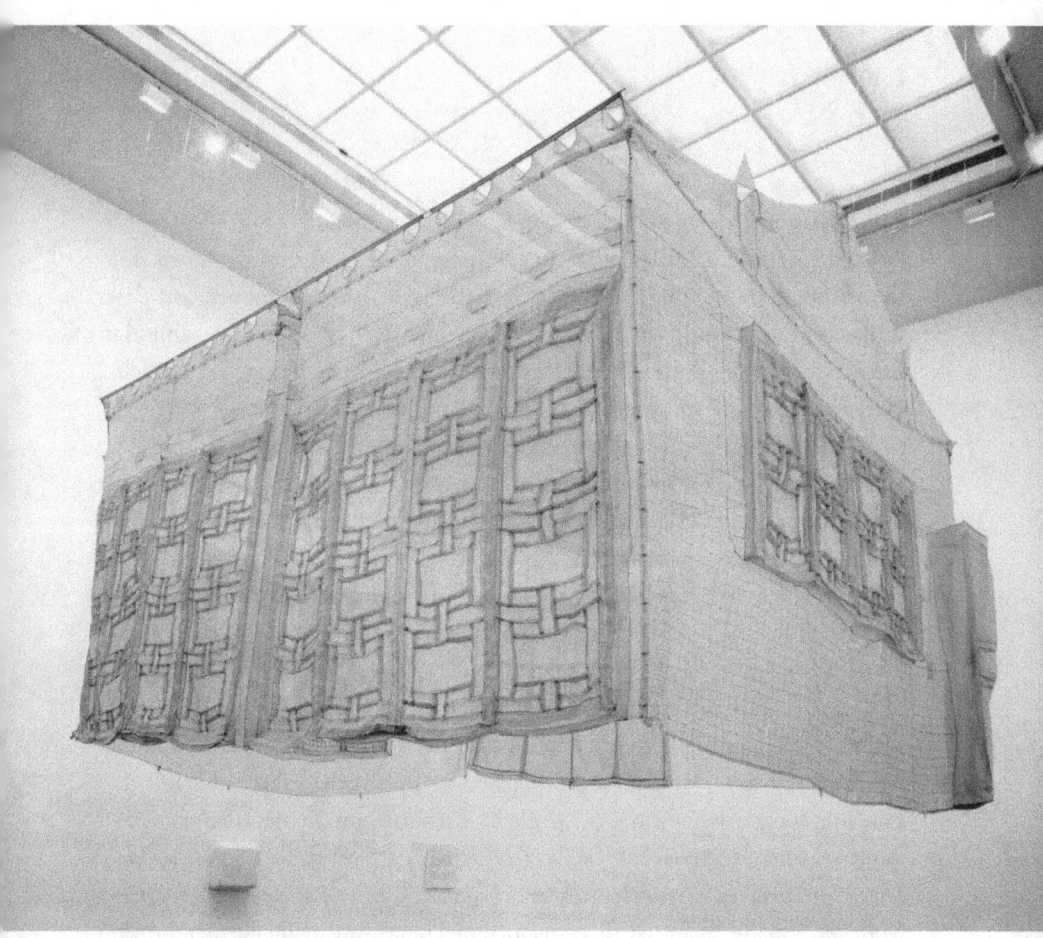

FIGURE E.1. Do Ho Suh, *Seoul Home/L.A. Home/New York Home/Baltimore Home/London Home/Seattle Home/L.A. Home,* 1999. Silk; 149 x 240 x 240 inches (378.5 x 609.6 x 609.6 cm). Collection of the Museum of Contemporary Art, Los Angeles. Purchased with funds provided by an anonymous donor and a gift of the artist. Courtesy of the artist and Lehmann Maupin Gallery, New York.

Walking his family's dismantled, reconstructed, and reimagined home toward yet another site, Do Ho Suh returned to New York with his detailed measurements and childhood memories, and a newly honed skill for traditional Korean dressmaking. Aided by his mother, who helped him find master patternmakers and seamstresses, Suh had learned to sew and create shapes, lines, and volumes with fabric. Back in his studio, Suh crafted his handmade replica out of diaphanous celadon-green silk. Porous and semitransparent to light, the folds and drapes of fabric are meant to be hung and stretched from the ceiling, transforming the designs into three-dimensional rooms, corridors, walls, windows, angles, molding, and paneling. In one of its first exhibition sites at the Korean Cultural Center in Los Angeles, *Seoul Home* was suspended over a large spiral staircase that serves as the entry to the gallery. Viewers climbed up, moving through the interior of the home, looking up from inside, until they reached the landing where they exited through the front door to see the structure from the outside. Enveloped in and then drawn around the fabric replica, viewers became implicated in the private spaces and the personal affective resonances of Suh's longing for home—a longing that materializes into a public call for the possibility of specifically situated dwelling within ongoing nomadic passages.

Do Ho Suh's *Seoul Home* is a construction of place, but as a replication it is also a one-time rematerialization of a former structure that can be expanded to encompass a mode of being in place. In fact, in 2000, Do Ho Suh complemented his *Seoul Home* with his equally detailed *348 West 22nd St., Apt. A, New York, NY 10011 at Rodin Gallery, Seoul/Tokyo Opera House Art Gallery/Serpentine Gallery, London/Biennale of Sydney/Seattle Art Museum,* a made-to-measure, transportable, blue-gray nylon fabric rendition of his apartment in New York City (Figure E.2). This replica of his current living space is sturdy, heavy, and always displayed touching the ground, unlike his *Seoul Home* that, longed for, floats suspended. Together, Suh's *Seoul Home* and *348 West 22nd St.* introduce a particular kind of movement implicit in processes of replaceable spatial situation—that of departure and return, of spatial passages that arc forward and back across both specific sites and times. For Suh, home is inclusive of both his Seoul and New York residences, and his particular passages back and forth between the two sites. Home also incorporates his ongoing experiences within, and specific moments of contact with, the two structures as projected back in memory, carried out over time, and opened up to a new public in each of their various exhibitions (Figure E.3).

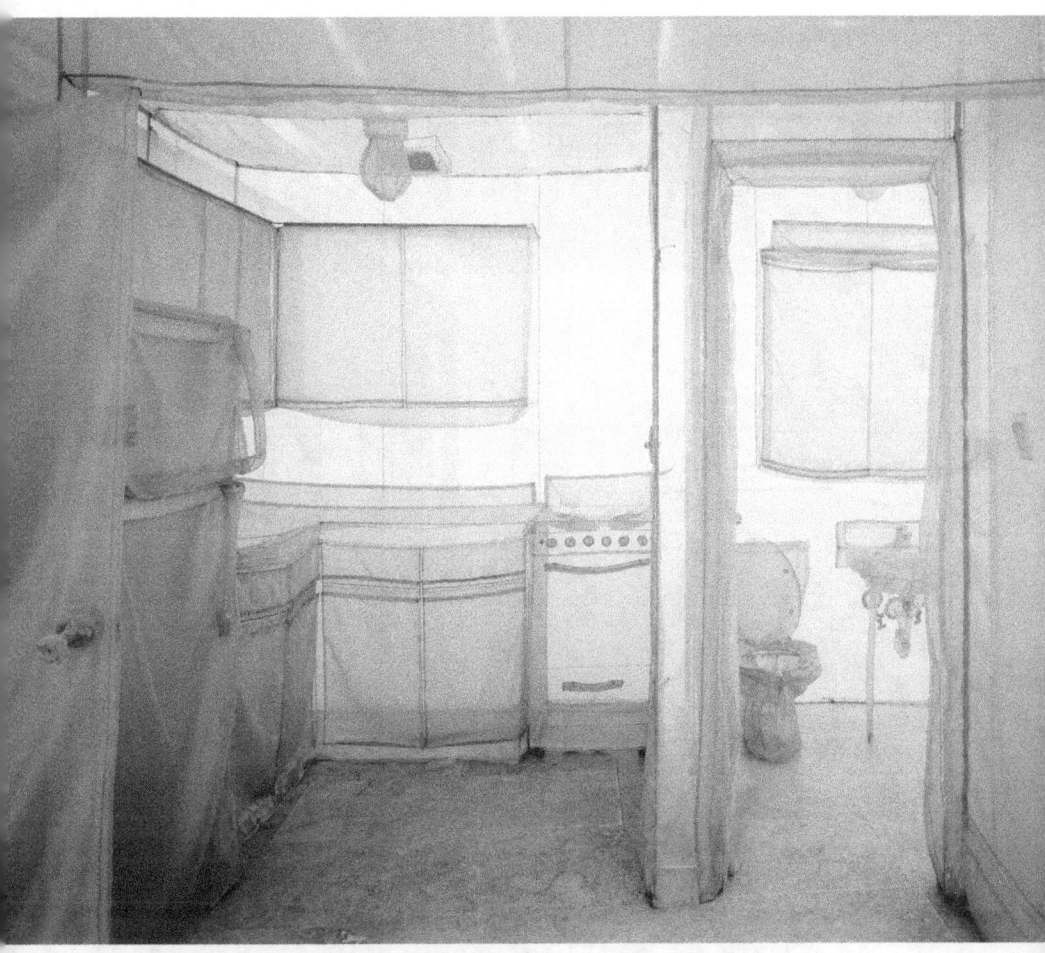

FIGURE E.2. Do Ho Suh, *348 West 22nd St., Apt. A, New York, NY 10011,* 2000. Translucent nylon; 96.46 x 169.29 x 271.65 inches (245 x 430 x 690 cm). Edition of 3. Courtesy of the artist and Lehmann Maupin Gallery, New York.

I evoke Suh's homes here at the end not in order to provide closure or conclusion but quite the opposite. These structures actualize the very issues that initially provoked me to write this book, by suggesting that the entwinement of contemporary art and architecture over issues of home may offer a responsive challenge to the present definition and experience of place. The replications of Suh's homes, the interactions between them, and between the bodies caught within their making and unfolding, also ask more deeply of

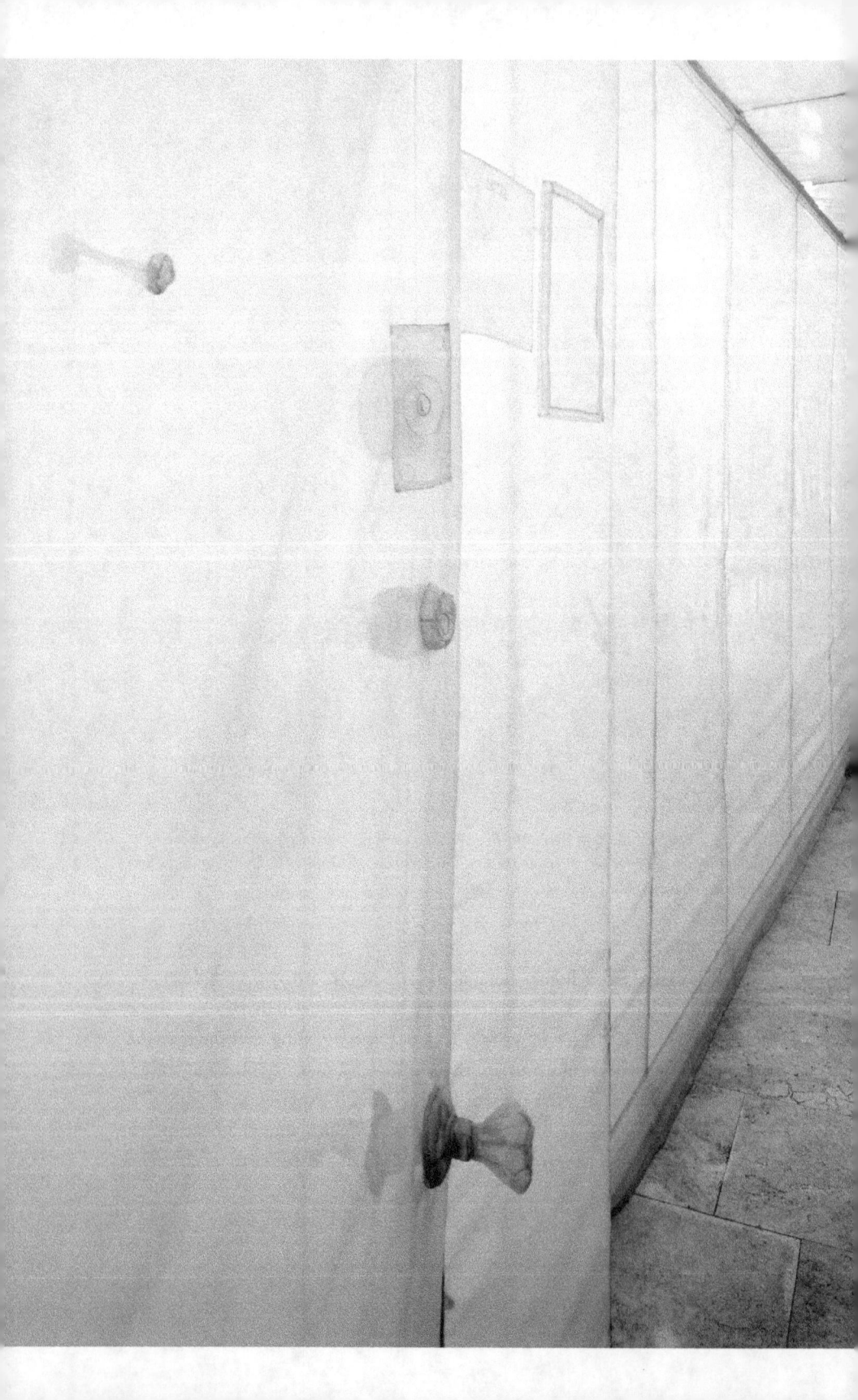

us, what does it mean to be and belong in one place and with another? If we give into a persistent yearning for structures and moments of connection, if we acknowledge the formations and infrastructures necessary for embodied contact, and if we care for the possibility of social and spatial cohesion, then we must keep on asking this question, in new and particular circumstances, with regard to different and specific individuals, social bodies, and built environments. To continue replacing home is to remain unsure whether or not we have answered this call.

FIGURE E.3. Do Ho Suh, *348 West 22nd St., Apt. A, New York, NY 10011*, 2000. Courtesy of the artist and Lehmann Maupin Gallery, New York.

Acknowledgments

The groundwork for this book was laid when I moved from London back to California and found myself in the midst of many exciting voices, practices, colleagues, and faculty in the performance studies department at the University of California, Berkeley. I am indebted to my advisors for guiding and supporting the breadth of my early ideas and for coaxing them toward this present formation. Shannon Jackson showed me that boundless thinking within and across disciplinary boundaries was possible. From Kaja Silverman I learned to care about, and to be careful with, asking the big questions that move us all. Whitney Davis, encouraging and inspiring me at every step, opened up a larger landscape from which my questions could become a book—indeed, a career.

These days, I am fortunate to have found a new home in an unbelievably supportive art history department at the University of Wisconsin, Milwaukee. I thank Kenneth Bendiner, Jeffrey Hayes, Andrea Stone, Ying Wang, Derek Counts, Nancy Hubbard, Tanya Tiffany, Richard Leson, and Elena Gorfinkel for taking in this performance scholar in the guise of an art and architectural historian and for providing an intellectually free, personally rewarding, and friendly working environment. I'm grateful to Jill Baum, who day in and day out saves my life in all kinds of ways. I also thank the generous colleagues who welcomed me as affiliated faculty in the graduate program in media, cinema, and digital studies, especially my friends Patrice Petro, Andrew Martin, Gilberto Blasini, Tasha Oren, Peter Paik, Lane Hall, and Anne Frances Wysocki, and in the Ph.D. program in Buildings, Landscapes, Cultures across both University of Wisconsin campuses in Milwaukee and Madison, in particular my friend Arijit Sen. I am emboldened by my conversations with all of you and grateful for your advice on my work and so much more.

For believing in this project from the beginning, thanks go to Pieter Martin and Richard Morrison at the University of Minnesota Press. Final revisions to my manuscript would not have been possible without a fellowship from the University of Wisconsin, Milwaukee's Center for Twenty-first Century Studies. I thank the other 2009–10 fellows (David Allen, Erica Bornstein, Bruce Charlesworth, Nan Kim, Jason Puskar, Manu Sobti, Deborah Wilk, Robert Wolensky) for engaging so provokingly with my writing, as well as the center's interim director, Mary Wiesner-Hanks, and staff (John Blum, Kate Kramer, Maria Liesegang) for their assistance. During that year, I taught a passionate group of graduate students in the Masters in Liberal Studies program; their thoughtful investments in issues of dwelling enlivened me, and this book, every week. I wish the best in future endeavors to Matthew Anderson, Andrea Avery, Judy Berdan, Katie Egan, Nick Gaddy, Kitty Gaenslen, Diane George, Mairin Hartt, Harry Kohal, Chris Kulhman, Karl Lerud, Ashley Morgan, Aisha Motlani, and Todd Rongstad.

Finally, for those others who commented on this project at different moments along the way, for those who walk with me across all kinds of places, and for those who inspire me to leap ever onward while also granting me home, I am thankful: John, Loretta, Tessa, and Kimberly Johung, Francis Chan, Aiden Johung Chan, Paul and Lydia Chung, David Chung, Tom and Linda Espy, Jessica Guarino, Ashley Minihan, Richard

Wittman, Leslie Elwell, Meredith Hoy, Nathan Lefebvre, Kelly Rafferty, Alfie Turnshek-Goins, Jonathan Combs-Schilling, Morgan Schick, Tami Williams, Charles Springfield, Jessica Kaminski, Tina Poppy, Theaster Gates, Yevgeniya Kaganovich, Nathaniel Stern, Elena Gorfinkel, Marcelino Stuhmer, Lisa Hecht, and Erica Levin (whose gift got me started).

INTRODUCTION

1. De Certeau, *Practice of Everyday Life*, 130.

2. Summers, *Real Spaces*, 15–60.

3. Deleuze and Guattari, *A Thousand Plateaus*, 371.

4. Ibid., 380.

5. Ibid., 381.

6. For example, Christopher Miller has pointed out that Deleuze and Guattari failed to cite non-Western, non-European sources and were often factually wrong when they did, even as they took inspiration from the figure of the non-Western nomad. As nonrepresentational and nonanthropological, Deleuze and Guattari's concept is for Miller primarily "an intellectual nomadism and a nomadism for intellectuals," which denies the material realities of those for whom a real physical spatial deterritorialization applies. Miller warns that such a fantastic and abstract celebration of non-Western nomadic experience runs the risk of glorifying cultural primitivism. See Miller, "The Postidentitarian Predicament," 10.

7. Spivak, "Can the Subaltern Speak?" 24–28.

8. Kaplan, "Deterritorializations," 191.

9. Kaplan, *Questions of Travel*, 89.

10. Braidotti, *Nomadic Subjects*, 36.

11. Gedalof, "Identity in Transit," 342.

12. Ibid., 343.

13. Kaplan, *Questions of Travel*, 163.

14. Bogue, "Apology for Nomadology," 169.

15. Noyes, "Nomadism, Nomadology, Postcolonialism," 160.

16. Ibid., 164.

17. Said, *Culture and Imperialism*, 332.

18. See Carlson, *Performance*; McKenzie, *Perform or Else*; Jackson, *Professing Performance*.

19. Diamond, *Performance and Cultural Politics*, 1.

20. Ibid.

21. Phelan, *Unmarked*, 146.

22. Kaye, *Site-Specific Art*.

23. Fried, "Art and Objecthood," in *Art and Objecthood*.

24. Meyer, "The Functional Site."

25. Kwon, *One Place after Another*, 29.

26. Ibid., 157.

27. Ibid., 156; Deleuze and Guattari, *A Thousand Plateaus*, 380.

28. Bourriaud, *Relational Aesthetics*; Laroen, "Social Aesthetics."

29. Foster, "Chat Rooms," 194.

30. Rancière, "Problems and Transformations," 90.

31. Foster, "Chat Rooms," 193.

32. Raven, *Art in the Public Interest*.

33. Lacy, *Mapping the Terrain*.

34. Kester, *Conversation Pieces*.

35. Mitchell, *Art and the Public Sphere*, 39.

36. Jackson, "What Is the 'Social' in Social Practice?" 144.

37. Leatherbarrow, "Architecture's Unscripted Performance," 7.

38. For example, in attending to Greek sacred architecture in *The Earth, the Temple, and the Gods*, Scully refutes a common critical opinion held from the eighteenth century onward, in which Greek temples were viewed as static shapes. Instead, he argues that the temples actually embodied the presence of a deity through their relationship to the sacred landscape on which they were built. Embedded in their spe-

cifically chosen sites, these sacred built forms, in turn, influenced the way in which the human worshipper understood his relationship to the deity worshipped there. In his later book, *Pueblo: Mountain, Village, Dance*, which verbally and visually depicts Pueblo architecture in New Mexico and Arizona from the Classic period of 1100–1300, Scully turns his attention even more overtly to the role of human action in relating the natural landscape to the man-made structure. While Greek temples sought either to balance or confront the sacred landscape with the specific worshipper's conception of the deity, Pueblo architecture embodied a deeply ritualized, socially unified embedment within the landscape. Such a connection was performed by the human dwellers, since the primary function of this architecture was to frame a large, communal plaza in which various ritual dances could be enacted and from which they would be watched.

39. Cairns, *Drifting*, 42.

40. Diamond, *Performance and Cultural Politics*, 2.

41. Phelan, *Unmarked*, 146.

42. Roach, *Cities of the Dead*, 2.

43. Gaston Bachelard writes, "Through dreams, the various dwelling places in our lives co-penetrate and retain the treasures of former days." See Bachelard, *Poetics of Space*, 5.

44. Laugier, *An Essay on Architecture*.

1. RETURNING TO THE HUT

1. Graham, "Two-Way Mirror Cylinder Inside Two-Way Mirror Cube," 44.

2. Laugier, *Essay on Architecture*, 11.

3. Ibid., 12.

4. Harries, *Ethical Function of Architecture*, 99.

5. Laugier, *Essay*, 13–14.

6. Harries, *Ethical Function*, 115.

7. Wittman, "The Hut and the Altar," 235.

8. Rykwert, *On Adam's House in Paradise*, 190.

9. Vitruvius, *Ten Books on Architecture*, 34.

10. Rykwert, *On Adam's House*, 182.

11. Ibid.

12. Bachelard, *Poetics of Space,* 31.

13. Ibid., 33.

14. Rykwert, *On Adam's House,* 191.

15. Ibid.

16. Graham, "Two-Way Mirror Power," 174.

17. Graham, "Two-Way Mirror Cylinder Inside Cube and Video Salon," 165; Graham, "Feedback," 7.

18. Le Corbusier, *Towards a New Architecture,* 69.

19. Aiming to connect nineteenth-century industrial developments with modern architecture throughout the first few decades of the twentieth century, Le Corbusier outlined several points of contact between modern materials and modern architectural design, many of which are apparent in Graham's structure. First, the reinforced support column could rise through the interior space of the building, taking on a major portion of the structural load so as to leave both exterior and interior walls with much less weight to support. This led to the functional independence of the outer reinforced-concrete structural skeleton. Exterior walls, no longer carrying the bulk of load-bearing support, could then be opened up with transparent walls of glass while inner partitions were able to model vast horizontal spaces. Finally, the use of concrete roof slabs offered usable rooftop terraces, spatially integrating a structure's vertical dimensions with its open-plan interior space

20. Graham, "Two-Way Mirror Cylinder Inside Cube and Video Salon," 166.

21. Graham, "Essay on Video, Architecture, and Television," 59.

22. Functionalism came into use in the mid-1930s with the publication of Italian architectural historian Alberto Sartoris's book *Gli elementi dell'architettura funzionale,* the title of which was influenced by French architect Le Corbusier's proposal to replace Sartoris's originally planned emphasis on "rational" architectural elements with a word change to *functional.* See Banham, *Theory and Design in the First Machine Age,* 320.

23. Graham, "Essay on Video, Architecture, and Television," 59.

24. Ibid.

25. Preziosi, *Rethinking Art History,* 153.

26. Ibid., 129.

27. Hodder, *The Domestication of Europe,* 39.

28. Ibid., 41.

29. Summers, *Real Spaces,* 15–60.

30. Ibid., 61–114.

31. W. Davis, "World without End: Review of David Summers, *Real Spaces: World Art History and the Rise of Western Modernism,*" 7.

32. Ibid., 70.

33. Ibid.

34. Graham, "Feedback," 8.

35. Heidegger, "Building, Dwelling, Thinking," 359.

36. Ibid., 360.

37. Ibid., 363.

38. Harries, *Ethical Function,* 154. For an account of Heidegger's relationship to his own hut in Todtnauberg, see Sharr, *Heidegger's Hut.*

39. Rakatansky, "Why Architecture Is Neither Here nor There," 104.

40. Harries, *Ethical Function,* 213.

41. Ibid., 367.

2. REUSABLE SITES

1. See Carlinsky, "Sliver Buyers Have a Field Day at City Sales," 1, 12.

2. Kastner, Najafi, and Richard, *Odd Lots,* 43.

3. *Gordon Matta-Clark,* video, directed by Jaime Davidovich.

4. Davidovich, quoted in Kastner et al., *Odd Lots,* 45.

5. Sussler, quoted in Kastner et al., *Odd Lots,* 47.

6. Lee, *Object to Be Destroyed,* 103.

7. Ibid., 112.

8. Hegel, *Phenomenology of Spirit,* 158.

9. Matta-Clark, "Interview with Lisa Bear," 164.

10. Wall, "Gordon Matta-Clark's Building Dissections," 181.

11. Ibid., 184.

12. Ibid., 185.

13. Graham, "Gordon Matta-Clark," 197.

14. Graham, "A History of Conceptual Art," 20.

15. Matta-Clark himself also turned his attention to subterranean Paris, taking photographs and video of underground cellars and catacombs for his 1977 series of

photomontages, *Sous-Sols de Paris*, and its accompanying film, *Substrait Paris*. Both theorist and artist noted that Paris was built over a system of caverns and catacombs on which the modern transportation system of the Métro and its connection to the overground railway system was later founded.

16. Benjamin, *Arcades Project*, 417.

17. Matta-Clark, Letter to Carol Goodden, 154–55.

18. Matta-Clark, "Interview with Lisa Bear," 164.

19. Lee, *Object to Be Destroyed*, 105.

20. "Anarchitecture," *Flash Art*.

21. In Wall, "Gordon Matta-Clark's Building Dissections," 185.

22. Collage, specifically photographic collage, was a form that Matta-Clark himself used to document his more famous building cuts. Writing about Matta-Clark's photographic and film documentation, Christian Kravagna isolates a collage style that the artist often used, in which the compiled images "take the viewpoint of a person moving around inside the building, in an evident attempt to convey something of the particular atmosphere or drama of moving through a sculpturally transformed building." Kravagna, "'It's Nothing Worth Documenting," 139.

23. Crawford, "Mythology," 53.

24. Ibid., 52.

25. Ibid., 54.

26. Ibid., 57.

27. Kastner et al., *Odd Lots*, 5.

28. Cited in ibid., 73.

29. Lee, *Object to Be Destroyed*, 104.

30. Cited in Kastner et al., *Odd Lots*, 74.

31. Ibid., 75.

32. Alÿs, "Next Slide Please."

33. Goldfarb, "Coordinate Relocation Program Test."

34. Dion, "The Gordon Matta-Clark Subterranean Museum."

35. Mirra, "Ithaca."

36. Blasco, "Queens Street View."

37. Matta-Clark, "Gordon Matta-Clark: Building Dissections—Interview with Donald Wall," 43.

38. Oppenheimer, "Renovation."

3. IN AND OUT OF PLACE

1. Quoted in Vischer, "Questions Addressed to Andrea Zittel," 17.

2. Zittel, cited in Morsiani and Smith, "These Things I Know for Sure," 14.

3. The term *plug-in* can be traced to Archigram member Peter Cook's 1964 proposal for a "plug-in city." See Sadler, *Archigram,* 197. See also Davies, *The Prefabricated Home.*

4. Le Corbusier, *The Modular,* 60.

5. Ibid., 185.

6. Le Corbusier applied his modular measurement system to such diverse projects as his *Unité Habitation* in Marseilles, his own architecture office, as well as to the organization of an architectural exhibition and a layout of architectural illustrations included in a journal publication.

7. Wright, *When Democracy Builds,* 6.

8. Ibid., 20.

9. Morsiani, "Emanicipated Usage," 24.

10. Zittel, cited in Morsiani and Smith, "These Things I Know for Sure," 201.

11. Kurokawa, *Metabolism in Architecture,* 32.

12. Kurokawa's 1972 *Nagakin Capsule Tower* is his most recognized example. To create the high-rise structure, steel boxes modified from shipping containers were prefabricated in Osaka, transported to Tokyo, lifted into place, and attached to two concrete cores. Each capsule was earmarked for specialized functions associated with living, cooking, sleeping, and bathroom spaces and were linked by access doors. The tower's apartments were bought and leased by workers living in the suburbs who did not want to commute into the city every day, by people who wanted a central location in the Nagakin entertainment district, and by families who needed extra living space in addition to their homes.

13. Kurokawa, *Metabolism,* 17.

14. Expanding on his concept of metabolism, Kurokawa has since embarked on a philosophy of symbiosis that seeks to spatially frame coexistent and often contradictory or opposing forces within a single built structure. See Kurokawa, "Philosophy of Symbiosis."

15. Quoted in Tolla and Lignano, "Ada Tolla and Giuseppe Lignano Speak with Christopher Scoates," 102.

16. Davies, *The Prefabricated Home*, 169.

17. Lot-ek, *Mobile Dwelling Unit*, 62–63.

18. Quoted in Tolla and Lignano, "Ada Tolla and Giuseppe Lignano Speak with Christopher Scoates," 105

19. McQuaid, *Shigeru Ban*, 14.

20. Ban's 1985 design for an exhibition on the architect and designer Emilio Ambasz used paper tubing to frame the display panels and to divide up the gallery space. For a 1986 exhibition on Finnish architect Alvar Aalto, Ban also turned to paper tubing to simulate Aalto's own use of undulating wood panels and posts.

21. Ban, *Shigeru Ban*, ix.

22. Rakatansky, "Why Architecture Is Neither Here nor There," 112.

23. McQuaid, *Shigeru Ban*, 28–33.

24. Ban's *Paper Church* was finally disassembled in June 2005, and all the materials were sent to a city in Taiwan. Reconstruction of a *Paper Dome* in Taiwan occurred in 2008. See www.shigerubanarchitects.com.

4. VISIBLY SKINNED

1. Quinn, *Techno Fashion*, 120.

2. Ibid.

3. Quoted in "Interview with Andrew Bolton," 138.

4. See Sadler, *Archigram*, 93.

5. Quoted in ibid., 113.

6. Pinto, "Collective Intelligence," 34.

7. Ibid.

8. Quoted in "Interview with Andrew Bolton," 141.

9. Individual, self-sufficient, mobile second skins continue to be designed, for example, by C. P. Company. In spring/summer 2000, the Italian-based sportswear company introduced a Transformables range of outerwear. Designed by Moreno Ferrari, its main pieces were individual, portable, wearable membranes that included an orange parka made from waterproof polyurethane that could be transformed into a lightweight sleeping bag as the wearer unfurled a shoulder bag and zipped it around his body. Another piece, a long-hooded, poncho-shaped coat, unfolded to become a "metropolitan igloo tent" made out of aluminum rods and wind- and rain-proof

translucent, rubberized nylon mesh. C. P. Company's self-imagined client is "the dynamic, urban, educated" nomad who is granted the agency of transformation and the luxury of choosing the kind of mobile lifestyle that is impossible for many others. See www.cpcompany.com.

10. Kwon, "The Sitings of Public Art."

11. Deutsche, *Evictions: Art and Spatial Politics*, 66.

12. Fraser, *Justice Interruptus*, 93.

13. Deutsche, *Evictions*, xxiv.

14. In *Evictions*, Deutsche offers insightful analyses of two projects by the artist Krzysztof Wodiczko. In *Homeless Projection*, conceived of in response to civic plans for Union Square's redevelopment, Wodiczko temporarily took over the public space of the park and projected images of transient bodies onto the newly refurbished surfaces of four neoclassical monuments. Forcing viewers to perceive the sculptures in relation to the condition of increased homelessness affected by the city's plan, Wodiczko called attention to the constitutive relationship between the two. In another project that coincided with Mayor Ed Koch's decision to have all mentally unstable homeless people hospitalized, Wodiczko challenged the city's solution to push the homeless problem out of sight by creating a *Homeless Vehicle Project* that would increase the visibility of the homeless while simultaneously presenting them as active residents whose means of subsistence plays a legitimate role in the wider urban social framework. The cage-like structure could serve as a mobile sleeping unit and a means of collecting items to be recycled—both functions refusing to hide the homeless problem out of sight, and thereby enacting the project's critical symbolism.

15. Deutsche, *Evictions*, 89–92.

16. Mitchell, "The Violence of Public Art," 39.

17. "Interview with Paul Virilio," 118.

18. Chalayan, *Hussein Chalayan*, 49.

19. Although the event never officially took place on a grand scale, the invitation remained open, and it is possible, though not documented, that several meetings could have indeed occurred.

20. Augé, *Non-Places: Introduction to an Anthropology of Supermodernity*, 78.

21. Chalayan, *Hussein Chalayan*, 49.

22. Evans, "No Man's Land," 12.

23. Quoted in Quinn, *Techno Fashion*, 67.

24. Bolton, *The Supermodern Wardrobe*, 77–80.

25. Arendt, *The Human Condition*, 50.

26. Ibid., 53.

27. Vale, *From the Puritans to the Projects*, 3.

28. Quoted in Pinto, "Collective Intelligence," 57.

29. Deleuze and Guattari, *A Thousand Plateaus*, 25.

30. "Interview with Paul Virilio," 123.

31. Ibid.

32. Ibid., 119.

33. Although not in the purview of this chapter, the advent of telecommunication technologies offers the actualization of a digitally networked body that is capable of realizing virtual connections with other technologically enhanced bodies and their immediate spatial environment. A new branch of fashion design—intelligent clothing—provides the platform for such connections by giving wearers access to information about themselves and their surroundings, as well as by allowing them to supervise and act on such information by way of invisibly embedded data collecting and transmitting systems. For example, in 1996, Starlab, a private, multidisciplinary research lab founded by Walter De Brouwer and based in Brussels, began investigating the capacity of digitally responsive clothing to enable users to link their bodies with their activities and their environments. In 1999, Starlab established the i-Wear consortium by bringing together companies, such as Adidas, France Telecom, Levi Strauss Europe, and Samsonite, who were interested in financially backing and sharing expertise to further the development of intelligent clothing and networked bodies. See Bolton, *Supermodern Wardrobe*.

34. Kwon, *One Place after Another*, 154–55.

35. Kester, *Conversation Pieces*, 163.

36. Nancy, *The Inoperative Community*, xli, xl.

5. NETWORKED DEPENDENCIES

1. Quoted in video documentation of the project in Mexico, www.lozano-hemmer.com/eproyecto.html.

2. Lozano-Hemmer and Lovink, "Interview with Geert Lovink."

3. Ibid.

4. Ibid.

5. Ibid.

6. Ibid.

7. Lozano-Hemmer and Lozada, "Interview with Priamo Lozada."

8. Lozano-Hemmer and Barrios, "Conversation."

9. Lozano-Hemmer, Adriaansens, and Brouwer, "Alien Relationships from Public Space."

10. Bourriaud, *Relational Aesthetics*, 45.

11. Rafael Lozano-Hemmer says that the term *relational* is "already dated, partly because of the popularization of the term 'relational aesthetics' by Nicolas Bourriaud, which by the way has little to do with my work and was published a number of years after I used the term." See Lozano-Hemmer and Barrios, "Conversation."

12. Maturana and Varela write: "An autopoetic machine is a machine organized (defined as a unity) as a network of processes of production (transformation and destruction) of components which: (i) through their interactions and transformations continuously regenerate and realize the network of processes (relations) that produced them; and (ii) constitute it (the machine) as a concrete unity in space in which they (the components) exist by specifying the topological domain of its realization as such a network." Maturana and Varela, *Autopoiesis and Cognition*, 78.

13. Taylor, *The Moment of Complexity*, 84–85.

14. Maturana and Varela are quoted in Taylor, *Moment*, 90.

15. Taylor, *Moment*, 91.

16. Burke and Tierney, "Introduction," in their *Network Practices*, 25.

17. Wigley, "Network Fever," 382.

18. Giedion, *Building in France, Building in Iron, Building in Ferroconcrete*, 101.

19. Ibid., 142.

20. In a series of lectures given at Harvard University between 1938 and 1939 and published in 1941 under the title *Space, Time and Architecture*, Giedion linked this "space-time" principle of modern architecture to cubism's "research into space" and futurism's "research into movement." Giedion, *Space, Time and Architecture*, 434, 443.

21. Giedion, *Building in France*, 189.

22. For Wigley, Louis Kahn's 1951–53 plan for Philadelphia, Konrad Waksman's 1953 airline hangars, and Buckminster Fuller's 1958 geodesic frameworks all demonstrate that modern architecture was gradually becoming more concerned with the

inclusive field through which bodies move, and in which built structures could be positioned and repositioned, than with the structures themselves. Wigley, "The Architectural Brain," 32.

23. Sadler, *Archigram*, 93.

24. Ibid., 197.

25. Quoted in Lang and Menking, *Superstudio: Life without Objects*, 23.

26. Wigley, "Network Fever," 391.

27. Wigley, "Deconstructivist Architecture," 11.

28. Eisenman, *Moving Arrows, Eros and Other Errors*.

29. See Tschumi, *Questions of Space*.

30. Tschumi, *Architecture and Disjunction*, 123.

31. Lozano-Hemmer, "Interview for the Ars Electronica 2001 Catalogue."

32. Galloway and Thacker, *The Exploit*, 15.

33. Burke, "Redefining Network Paradigms," 59. Burke is quoting Thacker from "Protocol Is As Protocol Does," xviii.

34. Galloway and Thacker, *The Exploit*, 13.

35. Contrasting TCP/IP and DNS, Galloway argues that "protocol is based on a *contradiction* between two opposing machines: one machine radically distributes control into autonomous locales, the other machine focuses control into rigidly defined hierarchies. The tension between these two machines—a dialectical tension—creates a hospitable climate for protocological control." Galloway, *Protocol*, 8.

36. Galloway and Thacker, *The Exploit*, 28.

37. See Galloway, *Protocol*.

38. Galloway and Thacker, *The Exploit*, 29.

39. Lozano-Hemmer, "Interview with Geert Lovink."

40. Ibid.

41. From video documentation of the project in Mexico. See www.lozano-hemmer.com/eproyecto.html.

42. Lozano-Hemmer, "Interview with Geert Lovink."

43. Lozano-Hemmer, Adriaansens, Joke Brouwer, "Alien Relationships from Public Space."

44. Ibid.

45. Fraser and Gordon, "A Genealogy of 'Dependency,'" 123.

46. See www.lozano-hemmer.com/video/uscanlincoln.mov.

47. Ibid.

48. Ibid. Formally inspired by art's own history of looking at its viewer in works ranging from Parmigianino's 1524 "Self-Portrait in a Convex Mirror," Diego Velázquez's 1656 "Las Meninas," Leon Golub's 1981 "Interrogation I," and Gary Hill's 1992 videowork "Tall Ships," Lozano-Hemmer's project calls particular attention to the context of surveillance that places the viewer before the artwork.

49. Hansen, *Bodies in Code: Interfaces with Digital Media*, 95.

50. Hansen's aim is to introduce technicity into the core of Maurice Merleau-Ponty's ontology of the flesh. See Merleau-Ponty, *The Visible and the Invisible* and *The Aesthetics Reader*.

51. Hansen, *Bodies in Code*, 95.

52. Quoted in an interview with Nadja Mounajjed, in Lozano-Hemmer, *Under Scan*, 33.

53. Lozano-Hemmer, Adriaansens, and Brouwer, "Alien Relationships."

Alÿs, Francis. "Next Slide Please." In Kastner et al., *Odd Lots*.

"Anarchitecture." *Flash Art* (June 1974).

Arendt, Hannah. *The Human Condition*. Chicago: University of Chicago Press, 1958.

Augé, Marc. *Non-Places: Introduction to an Anthropology of Supermodernity*, trans. John Howe. London: Verso, 1995.

Bachelard, Gaston. *The Poetics of Space: The Classic Look at How We Experience Intimate Places*, trans. Maria Jolas. Boston: Beacon Press, 1994.

Ban, Shigeru. *Shigeru Ban*. New York: Princeton Architectural Press, 2001.

Banham, Reyner. *Theory and Design in the First Machine Age*. 2nd ed. New York: Praeger, 1967.

Benjamin, Walter. *The Arcades Project*. Cambridge, Mass.: Belknap Press of Harvard University Press, 1999.

Bishop, Claire. *Installation Art: A Critical History*. New York: Routledge, 2005.

———, ed. *Participation: Documents of Contemporary Art*. London and Cambridge, Mass.: Whitechapel and MIT Press, 2006.

Blasco, Isidro. "Queens Street View." In Kastner et al., *Odd Lots*.

Bogue, Ronald. "Apology for Nomadology." *Interventions* 6.2 (2004): 169–79.

Bolton, Andrew. *The Supermodern Wardrobe*. London: V & A, 2002.

Bourriaud, Nicolas. *Relational Aesthetics,* trans. Simon Pleasance and Fronza Woods. Paris: Les Presses du reel, 2002.

Braidotti, Rosi. *Nomadic Subjects: Embodiment and Sexual Difference in Contemporary Feminist Theory.* New York: Columbia University Press, 1994.

———. "Nomadism with a Difference: Deleuze's Legacy in a Feminist Perspective." *Man and World* 29 (1996): 305–54.

Burke, Anthony. "Redefining Network Paradigms." In Burke and Tierney, *Network Practices.*

Burke, Anthony, and Therese Tierney, eds. *Network Practices: New Strategies in Architecture and Design.* New York: Princeton Architectural Press, 2007.

Cairns, Stephen, ed. *Drifting: Architecture and Migrancy.* London: Routledge, 2004.

Carlinsky, Dan. "Sliver Buyers Have a Field Day at City Sales." *New York Times,* 14 October 1973, real estate sec.

Carlson, Marvin. *Performance: A Critical Introduction.* London: Routledge, 1996.

Chalayan, Hussein. *Hussein Chalayan.* Rotterdam: Nai Publishers, 2005. Exhibition catalogue.

Chun, Wendy Hui Kyong, and Thomas Keenan, eds. *New Media, Old Media: A History and Theory Reader.* New York: Routledge, 2006.

Crawford, Jane. "Mythology: The Evolution of *Fake Estates,* Part II." In Kastner et al., *Odd Lots.*

Davies, Colin. *The Prefabricated Home.* London: Reaktion Books, 2005.

Davis, Tracy, ed. *The Cambridge Companion to Performance Studies.* Cambridge: Cambridge University Press, 2008.

Davis, Whitney. "World without End: Review of David Summers, *Real Spaces: World Art History and the Rise of Western Modernism.*" Unpublished.

de Certeau, Michel. *The Practice of Everyday Life.* Berkeley: University of California Press, 1984.

Deleuze, Gilles, and Félix Guattari. *A Thousand Plateaus: Capitalism and Schizophrenia,* trans. Brian Massumi. Minneapolis: University of Minnesota Press, 2003.

Deutsche, Rosalyn. *Evictions: Art and Spatial Politics.* Chicago: Graham Foundation for Advanced Studies in the Fine Arts, 1996.

Diamond, Elin. *Performance and Cultural Politics.* London: Routledge, 1996.

Dion, Mark. "The Gordon Matta-Clark Subterranean Museum." In Kastner et al., *Odd Lots.*

Eisenman, Peter. *Moving Arrows, Eros and Other Errors: An Architecture of Absence.* London: Architectural Association, 1986.

Evans, Caroline. "No Man's Land." In Chalayan, *Hussein Chalayan.*

Foster, Hal. "Chat Rooms." In Bishop, *Participation: Documents of Contemporary Art.*

Fraser, Nancy. *Justice Interruptus: Critical Reflections on the "Postsocialist" Condition.* London: Routledge, 1997.

Fraser, Nancy, and Linda Gordon. "A Genealogy of 'Dependency': Tracing a Keyword of the U.S. Welfare State." In Fraser, *Justice Interruptus.*

Fried, Michael. *Art and Objecthood: Essays and Reviews.* Chicago: University of Chicago Press, 1998.

Galloway, Alexander R. *Protocol: How Control Exists after Decentralization.* Cambridge, Mass.: MIT Press, 2004.

Galloway, Alexander R., and Eugene Thacker. *The Exploit: A Theory of Networks.* Minneapolis: University of Minnesota Press, 2007.

Gedalof, Irene. "Identity in Transit: Nomads, Cyborgs and Women." *European Journal of Women's Studies* 7 (2000): 337–54.

Giedion, Sigfried. *Building in France, Building in Iron, Building in Ferroconcrete,* trans. J. Duncan Berry. Santa Monica, Calif.: Getty Center for the History of Art and the Humanities, 1995.

———. *Space, Time and Architecture: The Growth of a New Tradition.* 5th ed. Cambridge, Mass.: Harvard University Press, 1967.

Goldfarb, Maximillian. "Coordinate Relocation Program Test." In Kastner et al., *Odd Lots.*

Gordon Matta-Clark. Video. Directed by Jaime Davidovich. 1975. Shown at the exhibition *Gordon Matta-Clark: You Are the Measure,* Whitney Museum of American Art, February 22 – June 3, 2007.

Graham, Dan. *Dan Graham: Architecture.* London: Camden Arts Centre, 1997.

———. "Essay on Video, Architecture, and Television." In *Two-Way Mirror Power,* ed. Alexander Alberro.

———. "Feedback: An Exchange of Faxes: Dan Graham and Brian Hatton." In *Dan Graham: Architecture.*

———. "Glass Buildings: Corporate Showcases." In *Two-Way Mirror Power,* ed. Alexander Alberro.

———. "Gordon Matta-Clark." In *Rock My Religion.*

———. "A History of Conceptual Art." In *Two-Way Mirror Power*, ed. Alexander Alberro.

———. *Rock My Religion, 1965–1990.* Cambridge, Mass.: MIT Press, 1993.

———. "Two-Way Mirror Cylinder Inside Cube and Video Salon." In *Two-Way Mirror Power*, ed. Alexander Alberro.

———. "Two-Way Mirror Cylinder Inside Two-Way Mirror Cube." In *Continuous Project #8*, ed. Bettina A. W. Funcke. Chatou, France: Consultants and cneai, 2006.

———. "Two-Way Mirror Power." In *Two-Way Mirror Power*, ed. Alexander Alberro.

———. *Two-Way Mirror Power: Selected Writings by Dan Graham on His Art*, ed. Alexander Alberro. Cambridge, Mass.: MIT Press, 1999.

Hansen, Mark B. N. *Bodies in Code: Interfaces with Digital Media.* New York: Routledge, 2006.

Harries, Karsten. *The Ethical Function of Architecture.* Cambridge, Mass.: MIT Press, 1997.

Hegel, Georg Wilhelm Friedrich. *Phenomenology of Spirit*, trans. A. V. Miller. Oxford: Clarendon Press, 1977.

Heidegger, Martin. *Basic Writings.* 1st ed. New York: Harper & Row, 1977.

———. "Building, Dwelling, Thinking." In *Basic Writings.*

Hodder, Ian. *The Domestication of Europe: Structure and Contingency in Neolithic Societies.* Oxford: Blackwell, 1990.

"Interview with Andrew Bolton." In Pinto, Bourriaud, and Damianovic, *Lucy Orta.*

"Interview with Paul Virilio." In Pinto, Bourriaud, and Damianovic, *Lucy Orta.*

Jackson, Shannon. *Professing Performance.* Cambridge: Cambridge University Press, 2004.

———. "What Is the 'Social' in Social Practice?" In Davis, *The Cambridge Companion to Performance Studies.*

Jacob, Mary Jane. *Gordon Matta-Clark: A Retrospective.* Chicago: Museum of Contemporary Art, 1985. Exhibition catalogue.

Johnson, Philip, and Mark Wigley, eds. *Deconstructivist Architecture.* New York: Museum of Modern Art, 1988. Exhibition catalogue.

Kaplan, Caren. "Deterritorializations: The Rewritings of Home and Exile in Western Feminist Discourse." *Cultural Critique* 6 (Spring 1987): 187–98.

———. *Questions of Travel: Postmodern Discourses of Displacement.* Durham, N.C.: Duke University Press, 1996.

Kastner, Jeffrey, Sina Najafi, and Frances Richard, eds. *Odd Lots: Revisiting Gordon Matta-Clark's "Fake Estates."* New York: Cabinet Books, 2005.

Kaye, Nick. *Site-Specific Art: Performance, Place, and Documentation.* London: Routledge, 2000.

Kester, Grant. *Conversation Pieces: Community and Communication in Modern Art.* Berkeley, Calif.: University of California Press, 2004.

Kolarevic, Branko, and Ali M. Malkawi, eds. *Performative Architecture: Beyond Instrumentality.* New York: Spon Press, 2005.

Kravagna, Christian. "'It's Nothing Worth Documenting If It's Not Difficult to Get': On the Documentary Nature of Photography and Film in the Work of Gordon Matta-Clark." In *Gordon Matta-Clark,* ed. Corinne Diserens.

Kurokawa, Kisho. *Metabolism in Architecture.* Boulder, Colo.: Westview Press, 1977.

———. "Philosophy of Symbiosis." www.kisho.co.jp/.

Kwon, Miwon. *One Place after Another: Site-Specific Art and Locational Identity.* Cambridge, Mass.: MIT Press, 2002.

———. "The Sitings of Public Art: Integration versus Intervention." In *One Place after Another.*

Lacy, Suzanne, ed. *Mapping the Terrain: New Genre Public Art.* New York: Bay Press, 1994.

Lang, Peter, and William Menking, eds. *Superstudio: Life without Objects.* Milan: Skira, 2003.

Larsen, Lars Bang. "Social Aesthetics." In Bishop, *Participation: Documents of Contemporary Art.*

Laugier, Marc-Antoine. *An Essay on Architecture,* trans. Wolfgang and Anni Herrmann. Los Angeles: Hennessey & Ingalls, 1977.

Leatherbarrow, David. *Architecture Otherwise Oriented.* Princeton, N.J.: Princeton University Press, 2008.

———. "Architecture's Unscripted Performance." In Kolarevic and Malkawi, *Performative Architecture.*

Le Corbusier. *The Modulor: A Harmonious Measure to the Human Scale, Universally Applicable to Architecture and Mechanics.* Basel, 2000.

———. *Towards a New Architecture,* trans. Frederick Etchells. New York: Praeger, 1970.

Lee, Pamela M. *Object to Be Destroyed: The Work of Gordon Matta-Clark.* Cambridge, Mass.: MIT Press, 2000.

Lot-ek. *LOT-EK: Mobile Dwelling Unit,* ed. Christopher Scoates. New York: Distributed Art Publishers, 2003.

Lozano-Hemmer, Rafael. "Interview for the Ars Electronica 2001 Catalogue." www.lozano-hemmer.com.

———. *Rafael Lozano-Hemmer: Subsculptures: A Conversation between José Luis Barrios and Rafael Lozano-Hemmer,* ed. Jose Luis Barrios and Galerie Guy Bartschi. Geneve: Galerie Guy Bartschi, 2005.

———. *Under Scan.* Nottingham: East Midlands Development Agency, 2007. Exhibition catalogue.

Lozano-Hemmer, Rafael, Alex Adriaansens, and Joke Brouwer. "Alien Relationships from Public Space: A Winding Dialogue with Rafael Lozano-Hemmer." www.lozano-hemmer.com.

Lozano-Hemmer, Rafael, and José Barrios. "Conversation between José Barrios and Rafael Lozano-Hemmer." 20 April 2005. www.lozano-hemmer.com.

Lozano-Hemmer, Rafael, and Geert Lovink. "Interview with Geert Lovink." www.lozano-hemmer.com.

Lozano-Hemmer, Rafael, and Priamo Lozada. "Interview with Priamo Lozada." www.lozano-hemmer.com.

Matta-Clark, Gordon. *Anarchitecture: Works by Gordon Matta-Clark: 17 November 1997 – 18 January 1998, Schindler House, L.A.* West Hollywood, Calif.: The Center, 1997.

———. *Gordon Matta-Clark,* ed. Corinne Diserens. London: Phaidon, 2003.

———. "Gordon Matta-Clark: Building Dissections—Interview with Donald Wall." In *Surface Tension,* ed. Ken Erlich and Brandon LaBelle. New York: Errant Bodies, 2003.

———. "Interview with Lisa Bear—Gordon Matta-Clark: Splitting the Humphrey Street Building." In *Gordon Matta-Clark,* ed. Corinne Diserens.

———. Letter to Carol Goodden. In *Gordon Matta-Clark,* ed. Corinne Diserens.

Maturana, Humberto, and Francisco Varela. *Autopoiesis and Cognition: The Realization of the Living,* ed. Robert S. Cohen and Marx W. Wartofsky. Boston: D. Reidel, 1980.

McKenzie, Jon. *Perform or Else.* London: Routledge, 2001.

McQuaid, Matilda. *Shigeru Ban.* London: Phaidon, 2003.

Merleau-Ponty, Maurice. *The Aesthetics Reader.* Evanston, Ill.: Northwestern University Press, 1994.

———. *The Visible and the Invisible*, trans. Alphonso Lingis. Evanston, Ill.: Northwestern University Press, 1969.

Meyer, James. "The Functional Site; or, The Transformation of Site Specificity." In Suderburg, *Space, Site, Intervention*.

Miller, Christopher L. "The Postidentitarian Predicament in the Footnotes of *A Thousand Plateaus*: Nomadology, Anthropology, and Authority." *Diacritics* 23.3 (1993): 6–35.

Mirra, Helen. "Ithaca." In Kastner et al., *Odd Lots*.

Mitchell, W. J. T., ed. *Art and the Public Sphere*. Chicago: University of Chicago Press, 1992.

———. "The Violence of Public Art: Do the Right Thing." In *Art and the Public Sphere*.

Morsiani, Paola. "Emanicipated Usage: The Work of Andrea Zittel." In *Andrea Zittel: Critical Space*, ed. Morsiani and Smith.

Morsiani, Paola, and Trevor Smith, eds. *Andrea Zittel: Critical Space*. Munich: Prestel Verlag, 2005.

———. "These Things I Know for Sure. . . ." In Morsiani and Smith, *Andrea Zittel: Critical Space*.

Nancy, Jean-Luc. *The Inoperative Community*. Minneapolis: University of Minnesota Press, 1991.

Noyes, John K. "Nomadism, Nomadology, Postcolonialism." *Interventions* 6.2 (2004): 159–68.

Oppenheimer, Sarah. "Renovation." In Kastner et al., *Odd Lots*.

Phelan, Peggy. *Unmarked: The Politics of Performance*. London: Routledge, 1996.

Pinto, Roberto. "Collective Intelligence: The Work of Lucy Orta." In Pinto, Bourriaud, and Damianovic, *Lucy Orta*.

Pinto, Roberto, Nicolas Bourriaud, and Maia Damianovic. *Lucy Orta*. London: Phaidon, 2003.

Preziosi, Donald. *Rethinking Art History: Meditations on a Coy Science*. New Haven, Conn.: Yale University Press, 1989.

Quinn, Bradley. *The Fashion of Architecture*. Oxford: Berg, 2003.

———. *Techno Fashion*. Oxford: Berg, 2002.

Rakatansky, Mark. "Why Architecture Is Neither Here nor There." In Cairns, *Drifting: Architecture and Migrancy*.

Rancière, Jacques. "Problems and Transformations in Critical Art." In Bishop, *Participation*.

Raven, Arlene. *Art in the Public Interest.* New York: Da Capo Press, 1993.

Roach, Joseph. *Cities of the Dead: Circum-Atlantic Performance.* New York: Columbia University Press, 1996.

Rykwert, Joseph. *On Adam's House in Paradise: The Idea of the Primitive Hut in Architectural History.* 2nd ed. Cambridge, Mass.: MIT Press, 1981.

Sadler, Simon. *Archigram: Architecture without Architecture.* Cambridge, Mass.: MIT Press, 2005.

Said, Edward W. *Culture and Imperialism.* New York: Vintage, 1994.

Scully, Vincent Joseph. *The Earth, the Temple, and the Gods: Greek Sacred Architecture.* Rev. ed. New Haven, Conn.: Yale University Press, 1979.

———. *Pueblo: Mountain, Village, Dance.* 2nd ed. Chicago: University of Chicago Press, 1989.

Sharr, Adam. *Heidegger's Hut.* London: MIT Press, 2006.

Spivak, Gayatri. "Can the Subaltern Speak?" In *Marxism and the Interpretation of Culture,* ed. Cary Nelson and Lawrence Grossberg. London: Macmillan, 1988.

Suderburg, Erika, ed. *Space, Site, Intervention: Situating Installation Art.* Minneapolis: University of Minnesota Press, 2000.

Summers, David. *Real Spaces: World Art History and the Rise of Western Modernism.* London, 2003.

Sussman, Elisabeth, ed. *Gordon Matta-Clark: You Are the Measure.* New York: Whitney Museum of American Art, 2007. Exhibition catalogue.

Taylor, Mark C. *The Moment of Complexity: Emerging Network Culture.* Chicago: University of Chicago Press, 2001.

Thacker, Eugene. "Protocol Is As Protocol Does." Foreword to Galloway, *Protocol.*

Tolla, Ada, and Giuseppe Lignano. "Ada Tolla and Giuseppe Lignano Speak with Christopher Scoates." In Lot-ek, *Mobile Dwelling Unit.*

Tschumi, Bernard. *Architecture and Disjunction.* Cambridge, Mass.: MIT Press, 1994.

———. *Questions of Space: Lectures on Architecture.* London: Architectural Association, 1990.

Vale, Lawrence J. *From the Puritans to the Projects: Public Housing and Public Neighborhoods.* Cambridge, Mass.: Harvard University Press, 2000.

Vischer, Theodora. "Questions Addressed to Andrea Zittel." In *Andrea Zittel.*

Vitruvius Pollio, Marcus. *Ten Books on Architecture: The Corsini Incunabulum,* trans. Ingrid D. Rowland. Cambridge: Cambridge University Press, 1999.

Wall, Donald. "Gordon Matta-Clark's Building Dissections." Interview with Matta-Clark. In *Gordon Matta-Clark*, ed. Corinne Diserens.

Wigley, Mark. "The Architectural Brain." In Burke and Tierney, *Network Practices*.

———. "Deconstructivist Architecture." In Johnson and Wigley, *Deconstructivist Architecture*.

———. "Network Fever." In Chun and Keenan, *New Media, Old Media*.

Wittman, Richard. "The Hut and the Altar: Architectural Origins and the Public Sphere in Eighteenth-Century France." *Studies in Eighteenth-Century Culture* 36 (Spring 2007): 235–59.

Wright, Frank Lloyd. *When Democracy Builds*. Chicago: University of Chicago Press, 1945.

Zittel, Andrea. *Andrea Zittel: Living Units*. Exhibition catalogue. Basel: Museum für Gegenwartskunst, 1996.

architectural theory: impulse to return in, 14–15

architecture: as art of representation, 9; central role in spatial experience and world understanding, 14; development of situated communities and, 11–12; expanded concept of, xix; Laugier on hut as original architectural structure, 7–9, 10; performative, xix–xx; possibility of mediating human connections to natural landscape, 9, 11–12, 15, 16–17; repetitive impulse of, 3; theoretical and material intersections with the network, 143–48

Arendt, Hannah, 121–22

"Art and Objecthood" (Fried), xvi

"art-as-public-places" model, 108–11

art institution: viewing experience within, xvi–xvii

art making and situation: Summers's world-historical narrative of, 24–26

A to Z Living Unit (Zittel), 68

A to Z Management and Maintenance Unit: Model 003 (Zittel), 75

Augé, Marc, 113

autonomy: and dependence, modularity's mediation between structural, 88, 96; individual, linked to structured standardization, 74–76; of individual mobility, negotiation between dependence on structures and systems of social formation and, 104; integration and, modular flexibility and, 78–84

autopoiesis, 141–46; autopoetic machine, 187n12; interplay between open and closed autopoetic systems, 142

A–Z Administrative Services, 67–68, 74

A–Z Cellular Compartment Units (Zittel), 82

A–Z Deserted Island (Zittel), 78–79, 80

A–Z Escape Vehicles (Zittel), 78, 79

Bachelard, Gaston, xxii, 13, 179n43

Ban, Shigeru, x, xxv; paper tube construction of, 72–73, 88–95, 184n20, 184n24

Banham, Reyner, 180n22

Bear, Lisa, 38, 43

belonging: cohesiveness offered by Vexed Generation garments and, 119–21; collaboration of multiple bodies in Chalayan's room-as-home and, 121; experience of, replaced over number of reusable and renewable spaces, 54; independence and sense of, 76; modes of, proposed by *Odd Lots* group show, 36, 37; Orta's connective garment-shelters and, 123–28; in place, relational architecture and, 148; reownership and new opening to spatial, 62; replacement as method and system of being and, xv, xxi–xxiii; return to hut as contemporary model for being and, xxiv

Benjamin, Walter, 41–42; materialist philosophy of history, 42

Bhuj, Gujarat (western India): 2002 earthquake in, 94–95
Biennale de Valencia (2002): *Micro Utopias* exhibition at, 97
biological network as model for relationality, 141–46
Blachly, Jimbo, 34, 35, 48–50, 52, 53, 56, 60
Blasco, Isidro, 59
Blast from the Past (Matta-Clark), 46
Bodies in Code (Hansen), 161
body: Le Corbusier's design based on universal human, 76–77; in motion, Wright's organic architecture based on, 77–81; technology and, coevolution based on constant realignments between, 161
body architecture and transformable clothing, xxv–xxvi, 97–129, 184n9; Archigram's retooling of architectural form and function, 105–7; bodily individuation of, 111–12; of Chalayan, x, xxv–xxvi, 100, 102, 104, 112–18, 119, 121, 128; digitally responsive intelligent clothing, 186n33; mediating between deconstructive and reconstructive tendencies, 100; Orta's *Nexus Architecture*, 97–98, 104; Orta's *Refuge Wear*, xxv, 98–100, 101, 104, 105, 107, 111–12, 124; replacing public visibility, 121–29; of Tsumura, 100, 104, 112, 128; of Vexed Generation, xxv, 102, 103, 104, 118–21, 125–26, 128;

visibility and invisibility of, 111–21; visibility and resistance in, 100–102, 105–11
Body Architecture–Collective Wear (Orta), 123, 125
Body Movies (Lozano-Hemmer), 161–62
Bogue, Ronald, xiii
border crossings, xi
Borge, Jorge Luis, 62
Bourriaud, Nicolas, xvii, xviii, 139–41, 187n11
Braidotti, Rosi, xii–xiii
British Criminal Justice Act (1994), 118
Brook-Higgins, Elizabeth, 109
"Building A for Artists" (Oppenheim), 60, 61
"Building, Dwelling, Thinking" (Heidegger), 29
building task, 31–32
Burke, Anthony, 143, 150
Byumba Refugee Camp, Rwanda: *Paper Emergency Shelters* in, 90, 91

Cabinet magazine, 44, 46, 47; initial three commissions to revisit *Fake Estate* plots, 34–35, 48–53; *Odd Lots* artists commissioned by, 35–36, 53–65
Cairns, Stephen, xx
Camden Arts Centre in London, 28
capsules, Kurokawa's, 82–84
Casa Moda, 105
CAVEs (Cave Automatic Virtual Environments), 137

emergency shelters, Ban's paper tube construction for, 72–73, 88–95, 184n20; Bhuj, Gujarat earthquake (2002) and, 94–95; Kobe, Japan, earthquake (1995) and, 90–92, 93; Rwandan refuge crisis (1995–1999) and, 88–91; Turkish earthquake (1999) and, 92–94

empire: Hardt and Negri's concept of, 151

environmental politics: urban expansion and, 55

Enzensberger, Hans Magnus, 150

Escape Vehicles (Zittel), 67, 78

Essai sur l'architecture (Laugier), xxiv, 7–9; frontispiece to, 7, 8

Evans, Caroline, 117

event-based architecture, 146

"event-based experience," Dion's, 56

Evictions (Deutsche), 185n14

Exploit: A Theory of Networks, The (Galloway and Thacker), 149–50

facture, 25

Fake Estates (Matta-Clark), xxiv, 33–36; Anarchitecture and inspiration to purchase gutter-spaces, 43; Benjamin's *Arcades Project* aligned with, 41–42; *Cabinet* magazine revisitation of, 34–36, 48–65; as challenge to real estate market, 38–39; collages assembled by Crawford, 44–47, 54; first showing as exhibitable work, 44, 45; inaccessibility of

some properties, 37, 38–39, 41, 43, 50, 59; initial three artists commissioned to revisit sites, 34–35, 48–53; *Odd Lots* artists' reuse and replacement of, x, 35–36, 53–65; plans for, 33–34, 35; tax slips excluded from, 46; tours offered to properties, 60. *See also Odd Lots* artists; *Odd Lots: Revisiting Gordon Matta-Clark's Fake Estates*

fashion design: intelligent clothing, 186n33; reconstruction and deconstruction in, 100. *See also* body architecture and transformable clothing

feedback: Graham on, 28

feng shui, 56

Ferrari, Moreno, 184n9

Final Home (Tsumura's label), 112

First Gulf War, 98

Fisher, Norman, 44

fixity of unified cityscape: breaks in, 59

Flash Art magazine, 43

Foster, Hal, xviii

Fraser, Nancy, 109–10, 154

freedom: living off the so-called grid, 78; synthesis of limitation and, 76

Fried, Michael, xvi

Fuller, Buckminster, 187n22

functionalism, 18–19, 180n22; Graham's pavilion resituated in critique of universal, 28–29; intersection between functionality and critique, 108–11, 113; Matta-Clark's challenge to modern, 59–60

homecoming, 31

homeless: clothed in Orta's second skins, visibility of, xxv, 107–11; gentrification as response to visibility of, 109, 110; public housing for, 122–29; Wodiczko's projects involving, 185n14

Homeless Projection (Wodiczko), 185n14

Homeless Vehicle Project (Wodiczko), 185n14

homemaking, 31

Homo erectus hut structure, 20–21

housing, public, 122–29

Houston Museum of Art, 78

Hunter, Joe, 118

hut, return to, xxiii–xxiv, 1–32; as architecture's ideal form of situated dwelling, xxiii; as both stable and flexible motif, 14; through conceptual renewal, 4, 5, 6–15, 32; as contemporary model for being and belonging, xxiv; Graham's *Two-Way Mirror Cylinder Inside Cube* evoking, 1–6, 15–19, 23–32; historical continuity created by material resurrection of, 23; as imagined refuge outside of modern urban expansion, 13; Laugier and, 7–10, 11, 15–16; Le Corbusier and, 16–17; material culture of early hut building, 19–23; through material revision, 4–5, 6, 14, 15–23, 32; psychological force of, as visual motif, 13; replacement of spatial stability with spatial permeability and visual disorientation, 5–6, 23–32; in response to changing natural environment, 12; Vitruvius on evolution of human building, 11–12

"Hut and the Altar: Architectural Origins and the Public Sphere in Eighteenth-Century France, The" (Wittman), 9–10

image making and reception: Summers's world-historical narrative of, 24–26

inaccessibility of Matta-Clark's *Fake Estates*, 37, 38–39, 41, 43, 50, 59

independence: sense of belonging and, 76

individuation: bodily, of body architecture and transformable clothing, 111–12; collective, 161

industrial by-products and practices: Lütek's reuse of, 68–71

inequality: tension between newly developed technology and social, 152–53

inoperative community, 127

Institute for Art and Urban Resources, 34

integration and detachment: modular architecture and, 73, 74–84

intelligent clothing, 186n33

International Standards Organization (ISO) shipping container, 85

Internet: online participation in design of *Vectorial Elevation* through, 133–36; as a technology of control, 152–53 invisibility: collective resistance through bodily anonymity, 102–4; experimental garment design offering resistant modes of, 114, 118–21; glass walls and, 19; of modes of work conventionally gendered as feminine, Ukeles's reversal of, 63; visibility and, 111–21

iron: shift in architectural vision with introduction of, 144–45

IVAM Centro Julio Gonzalez (Valencia, Spain): 1992 retrospective of Matta-Clark's work at, 44

i-Wear consortium, 186n33

Jackson, Shannon, xix

"just-past": Graham's evocation of, 41

Kahn, Louis, 187n22

Kant, Immanuel, 141

Kaplan, Caren: on deterritorialization, xii; on the global and the local, xiii

Kastner, Jeffrey, 34, 44, 47

Kaye, Nick, xvi

Kester, Grant, xviii, 127

Kobe, Japan earthquake (1995): paper tube housing for victims of, 90–92, 93

Koch, Ed, 185n14

Korean architecture: portability of traditional domestic, 166–60

Korean Cultural Center (Los Angeles), 168

Kravagna, Christian, 182n22

Kurokawa, Kisho, 81–84; *Nagakin Capsule Tower,* 83, 183n12; philosophy of symbiosis, 183n14; time-community, 83–84, 86

Kwon, Miwon, xvii, 127

Lacy, Suzanne, xviii

Landes, Joan, 109

Larsen, Lars Bang, xvii

Laugier, Marc-Antoine, xxiv, 7–10, 11; on hut as original architectural structure, 7–9, 10; narrative of return and replication, 7–9, 15–16

Leatherbarrow, David, xix

Le Corbusier, 145, 180n22; grid system based on human figure, 76–77; on modular building and measurement system, 76–77, 183n6; on points of contact between modern materials and modern architectural design, 180n19; return to hut and, 16–17

Lee, Pamela, 38, 43, 48

Lepage, Robert, 153

Lepenski Vir: Neolithic settlement of, 21–22

letting-dwell: Heidegger's concept of, 30–31

Library of Poet (Ban), 89

Lignano, Giuseppe, 68–71, 85, 87

limitation and freedom: synthesis of, 76

"Living Pods" (Greene), 146

Living Units series (Zittel), 67, 74–76

locality: rethinking nomadism through, xiii

location: politics of, xiii

Mirra, Helen, 58

Mitchell, W. J. T., xviii–xix, 110

Mobile Dwelling Unit (MDU) by Lot-ek, xxv, 69–71, 85–87

mobility: Ban's paper tube construction and, 72–73, 88–95, 184n20, 184n24; continuous, of Lot-ek's *Mobile Dwelling Unit*, 86–87; garment shelters and forced, 117; mobile determination of architectural space, 145–48; mobile second skins, 184n9; modularity and, 74, 77, 88; Wright's architecture of democracy emphasizing individual, 78, 79–81; Zittel's modular architecture for individual, 78–82, 84. *See also* body architecture and transformable clothing; modular architecture

modern architecture: characteristic attributes of, Graham's pavilion revisiting, 17, 19; concern with inclusive field, 145, 187n22; conflation of material form and function in, 18–19; ideological complexities of, 19; illusion of transparent intimacies between buildings and bodies upheld in, 16; key building materials, 17–19, 180n19; Le Corbusier and, 16–17, 180n19; Matta-Clark's challenge to functionalist, 59–60; revision of primordial hut with material properties of, 4–5, 6, 14, 15–23, 32; "space-time" principle of, 145, 187n20; universal functionalism, Graham's

pavilion resituated in critique of, 28–29

modernity: globalization of Western, spatial experience transformed by, 23–24; primordial hut as dream image releasing dwellers from, 13; relationship to real space, 24–28

modular architecture, xxiv–xxv, 67–96; allowing for both mobility and temporary grounding, 74, 77, 88; Ban's paper tube constructions, 72–73, 88–95, 184n20, 184n24; detachment and integration, 73, 74–84; detachment and reintegration, 84–88; Le Corbusier and, 76–77, 183n6; Lot-ek's reuse and reintegration of shipping container, 68–71, 85–88; Metabolists and, 81–84; Orta's transformation of garments from individual to collective structure, 123–28; reintegration and replacement, 88–96; standardized dimensions linking spatial plan and embodied use, 76, 77; Wright and "organic architecture," 77–81; Zittel and, x, xxv, 67–68, 74, 78–84

Modular Architecture—The Unit x 10 (Orta), 106, 124

Modulor, Le (Le Corbusier), 76

Morsiani, Paola, 78

movement space: Anarchitecture's reuse of, 43

Museum of Contemporary Art, Los Angeles, 78

Museum of Modern Art, New York, 147

mutuality of networked dependencies in Lozano-Hemmer's *Under Scan,* 160–61

Nagakin Capsule Tower (Kurokawa), 83, 183n12

Najafi, Sina, 34, 44, 47

Nancy, Jean-Luc, 127

Natalini, Adolfo, 146–47

natural landscape: architecture and possibility of mediating human connection to, 9, 11–12, 15, 16–17; destruction of, Goldfarb's sound piece focusing on, 55; return to hut in response to changing environment, 12; role of human action in relating man-made structure to, 30, 179n38

Negri, Antonio, 151

Neolithic *domus*: extension with agriculture and defense, 22; first situated, 21–22

network(s): architecture's theoretical and material intersections with, 143–48; of both control and resistance, 150–54; communications, 142; as contemporary culture's core organizational structure, 141, 143, 149–50; defined, 143; dematerialized site as, 145–47; networked computer "protocol," 151, 188n35; social, evolution of human building and, 11–12

networked dependencies, xxvi, 131–64;

networked participation, 148–54; relational networks, xxvi, 136–48; replacing, 154–64

networked participation, xxvi, 148–54; dependency among environment, technology, and accidental community, 153; utopian metaphor vs. material practice of networks, 150–51

New York City: auctioning of tiny property plots (1973), 33–34; functional public art in, 109, 110; Museum of Modern Art, 147

New York Times, 33

Nexus Architecture (Orta), 97–98, 104

Nexus Architecture x 50 Intervention Köln (Orta), 98, 99

Ninth Annual Havana Biennale, 107

nomadism, xi–xiv, xxiv–xxv; Chalayan's response to, 118; chosen and forced dislocation, xvii, xxv; contemporary critical potential, xiv; cultural revisions of, in late 1990s, xii–xiii; Deleuze and Guattari's concept of, xi–xii, 177n6; deterritorialized territory of nomad, xi–xii, xiii, 177n6; modular architecture reintegrated into nomadic systems, 73; narratives, xvii; reusable structures and, xxiii; subject as socially and politically outcast, xiv; subject defined by mobility and technically induced compression of space and time, xiv; Terra Amata camp, 20–21, 22; transformable clothing and, 185n9. *See also* body

Vectorial Elevation and, 136; Lozano-Hemmer "architecture" intervening into, 137, 139, 149, 155; public art and functional redevelopment of, 109, 110–11; reframing, through visibility of specific embodied connections, 112, 113, 114; Wodiczko's projects involving the homeless in, 185n14

public sphere(s): Fraser's new critical theory of, 109–10; Habermas's concept of, 109; multiple, 110; transformation of, return to early building practices and, 10

public visibility: replacing, 121–29

Pueblo architecture: primary function of, 179n38

Pueblo: Mountain, Village, Dance (Scully), 179n38

"Queens Cookies/Sweet Splits" (Ukeles), 63–64

Queens Museum of Art, 35

Quinn, Bradley, 100

Rakatansky, Mark, 30–31, 89

Rancière, Jacques, xviii

Raven, Arlene, xviii

real estate market: Matta-Clark's challenging of, 38–39. *See also Fake Estates*

Reality Properties: Fake Estates, Little Alley Block 2497, Lot 42 (Matta-Clark), 45

real space(s): attributes of, 30; congruity between Heidegger's "original time" and, 27; modern relation to, 24–26; in process of revision, 26; Summers's concept of, 24; transformed by globalization of Western modernity, 23–24

Real Spaces: World Art History and the Rise of Western Modernism (Summers), 23–27

Realty Positions: Fake Estates and Other Architectural Musings (Matta-Clark), 44

reconstruction in fashion design, 100

refugee shelters: Ban's paper tube construction for, 72–73, 88–95, 184n20, 184n24

Refuge Wear (Orta), xxv, 98–100, 101, 104, 124; bodily individuation in, 111–12; fabrics, 105, 107; industrial version of Habitent, 108; skin-like membranes of, 105; textual tattooing of, 107; two or more joined together as *Body Architecture–Collective Wear*, 123, 125

reinforced support column in modern architecture, 180n19

reintegration: detachment and, 84–88; Kurokawa's metabolic system of, 81; replacement and, 88–96; social, 88–95, 107

relational aesthetics, xvii–xviii, 139–41, 187n11

relational architecture, xxvi, 136–48;

default buildings and, 138; defined by Lozano-Hemmer, 137; dissimulation and, 138; networked participation in, xxvi, 148–54; redefined by Lozano-Hemmer, 139; relational aesthetics and, xvii–xviii, 139–41, 187n11; replacing networks of dependency, 154–64; self-organizing biological networks and, 141–46; site-specific art as distinct from, 139; *Under Scan*, xxvi, 155–64; vampire buildings and, 138; virtual architecture vs., 137–38

relationship-specific architecture, 139

renewal: Kurokawa's metabolic system of, 81

renewal, return to hut through conceptual, xxiii, 4, 5, 6–15, 32; Bachelard and, 13; desire for renewal, as perennial and inescapable, 14; Graham's *Two-Way Mirror Cylinder Inside Cube* and, 4, 5, 6; Laugier and, xxiv, 7–10, 11, 15–16; Rykwert and, 11–12, 13–14. *See also* revision, return to hut through material

reownership: new opening to spatial belonging and, 62; reuse and, 44–53

replaceable collectivity, 136

replacement: building task and, 31–32; Graham's model of spatial, 5–6, 23–32; material residues of past use, 63; as method and system of being and belonging, xv, xxi–xxiii; of networks of dependency, 154–64;

ongoing process of replacing home, xv, xxi–xxiii; as partial haunting made materially real, xxii; of public visibility, 121–29; reintegration and, 88–96; resituation by way of, 163–64; reuse and, 53–65; of social formations, Ban's paper tube construction and, 88–95; temporal dimension of spatial, 27; visual dependencies and spatial, 28, 32

replication: return and, Laugier's narrative of, 7–9, 15–16; in Suh's *Seoul Home* and *348 West 22nd St.*, 166–71

resistance: anonymity of Vexed Generation's wearers and, 125–26; collective, through bodily anonymity, 102–4; debate over potential for resistant collective action, 127; need for individually protective, functional shelter in name of, 128; network of control and, 150–54; visibility and, 100–102, 105–11

resituation by way of replacement, 163–64

return: renewal and, xxiii, 4, 5, 6–15, 32; replacement and, 5–6, 23–32; replication and, Laugier's narrative of, 7–9, 15–16; revision and, 4–5, 15–23, 32; revisitation of Matta-Clark's *Fake Estates*, 34–36, 48–65

reusable sites, xxiii, xxiv, 33–65; Lot-ek and reuse of modern industrial by-products and practices, 68–71, 85–88; original *Fake Estates* of

social transaction: siting of space as, 62–63

Sous-Sols de Paris (Matta-Clark), 182n15

South, Jane, 62

space: demarcation through ownership and protection, 38; Heidegger on place-making function of, 29; metaoptical, 25–26; mobile determination of architectural, 145–48; movement, 43; nineteenth-century industrial developments and modern determination and experience of, 144–45; nomad vs. striated, xi; poetic, oneiric concept of, xxii; sites redefined as spaces of social intervention, 39; siting of, as process linking bodies and sites across time, 62; use-value, redetermination over time, 36, 38–39

Space, Time and Architecture (Giedion lecture series), 187n20

space-time experience of environment, Giedion's, 145, 187n20

spatial replacement: Graham's model of, 5–6, 23–32

spatial situation(s), 23–32; concept of, 3–4; connection between visuality and, 24; dwelling and constant movement toward and away from, 30–31; negotiation between social formation and, 12; possibility of real, 23, 26–28. *See also Two-Way Mirror Cylinder Inside Cube* (Graham), returning to hut through

spectatorship in site-specific artwork, xvi

Speer, Albert, 152

Spivak, Gayatri, xii

splitting: Graham on, 28

Splitting (Matta-Clark), 41

standardization: individual autonomy linked to structured, 74–76; ISO shipping container and, 85; prominence of body in, 77. *See also* modular architecture

Starlab (research lab), 186n33

Stettner Construction Company, 62–63

substitution, xxii–xxiii

Substrait Paris (film), 182n15

subterranean museum, Dion's, 55–56

Suh, Do Ho, 166–71

"Suitaloon" membrane (Webb), 105–7

Summers, David, 23–27, 30; concept of space, x; world-historical narrative of image making and reception, 24–26

Sunjo, King, 166

Superstudio, 81, 145–47

"Supersurface" (Superstudio), 146

surrogation, xxii–xxiii

surveillance: tracking mechanism of Lozano-Hemmer's *Under Scan*, 158–61, 162, 189n48; Vexed Generation's response to urban, 118–21

Survival Sac with Water Reserve (Orta), 111

Sussler, Betsy, 37, 46, 58

symbiosis: Kurokawa's philosophy of, 183n14

Ukeles, Mierle Laderman, xxiv, 62, 63–64

Under Scan (Lozano-Hemmer), xxvi, 155–64; activation of, 155–56; in Leicester, U.K., 160; in Lincoln, U.K., 156, 159; mutuality of networked dependencies in, 160–61; in Nottingham, U.K., 157; participants in, 155; reactions to, 156–58, 159; replaceable networks of interdependence in, 162–63; tracking mechanism, 158–61, 162, 189n48; video documentation of, 156

unification: art integrated within newly developed public spaces in name of public, 109, 110–11

Union Square redevelopment: Wodiczko's response to, 185n14

United Nations High Commission for Refugees (UNHCR), 88, 89–90

Unité Habitation (Le Corbusier), 183

University of California at Santa Barbara Art Museum, 87

urban expansion: cycle of disuse and reuse driven by, 56; Goldfarb's sound piece focusing on destruction of natural landscape and, 55; hut as imagined refuge outside modern, 13; impulse to renew usability of site, 40

urban interventions: Orta's "City Interventions" (1993–1996), 107–11; Orta's *Nexus Architecture* as ordered structure for enacting, 98

urban surveillance systems: Vexed Generation's response to, 118–21

use-value: equivalence between universal user and architectural, Oppenheim's challenge to, 60; reownership and vacillation between uselessness and usefulness, 48–53; in site of disuse, replacement of, 55; of space, 36, 38–39

utopia: body architecture and, 97, 110; Lozano-Hemmer's Web-based interfaces as challenge to utopian visions of architecture, 148–49; Superstudio's antiarchitectural, 146–47; utopian metaphor of network vs. its material operations, 150

Vale, Lawrence J., 122

vampire buildings: relational architecture and, 138

Varela, Francisco, 141–42; on autopoetic machine, 187n12

Vectorial Elevation (Lozano-Hemmer), xxvi, 131–36, 160; access to control of digital technologies gained and lost by participants in, 153; as ephemeral intervention, 152; human perspective of monolithic environment rescaled by, 152; influences for, 152; Internet participation in designs for, 133–36; reinstallations of, 136, 140; video of changing designs from aerial perspective, 133

Velázquez, Diego, 189n48

JENNIFER JOHUNG is assistant professor of art history and director of the Art History Gallery at the University of Wisconsin, Milwaukee.